D0674562

KINGFISHER POCKET GUIDES
TREES
OF BRITAIN AND EUROPE

Written by
DAVID SUTTON

KINGFISHER
Kingfisher Publications Plc
New Penderel House
283–288 High Holborn
London WC1V 7HZ
www.kingfisherpub.com

This edition first published by
Kingfisher Publications Plc 2002

10 9 8 7 6 5 4 3 2 1
1TR/1201/WKT/-(MAR)/128KMALG

Text copyright © David Sutton and Kingfisher
Publications Plc 1990
Material in this edition was first published by Kingfisher
Publications Plc in *Field Guide to the Trees of Britain and
Europe* 1990

A CIP catalogue record for this book is available from the
British Library

ISBN 0 7534 0746 9

Senior Editor : Michèle Byam
Assistant Editor : Mandy Cleeve
Design : Smiljka Surla
Cover design : Mike Davis

Colour separations : P+W Graphics, Singapore
Printed in Hong Kong

Contents

Introduction

There is something special about trees. They are plants on a grand scale and have long inspired philosophers. An imposing feature of most landscapes, they define the character of an area, telling you where you are – billowing crowns of elms and sturdy oaks at middle latitudes, or slender spires of cypresses and umbrella-shaped pines in the Mediterranean region. Trees also hold many of nature's records: the tallest, most massive and oldest living things are all trees. They can be objects of great beauty and many are grown for this reason. We plant cherries from the Orient and Indian Flame-tree for flowers, and maples and Black-gum for their brilliant autumn colour. Many trees are grown for their imposing form, such as Cedar-of-Lebanon, with its massive flat plates of foliage; Lombardy Poplar,

which forms narrow columns; and Golden Weeping-willow, with its hanging curtains of foliage.

Some of the choicest fruits of the earth come from trees. Orchards of apple, plum and pear are planted in the cooler areas, whilst oranges, peaches and nectarines are grown in the warmer south. Even in death, trees contribute to the quality of human life. Softwoods, from conifers, and hardwoods, from broad-leaved trees, provide everything from basic materials for construction to the highly decorative, beautifully figured wood of the walnuts. Timber, converted into paper, holds the world's literature.

Using descriptions, facts panels and illustrations, this book provides the means to identify 430 of the native and most widely planted trees of Britain and Europe.

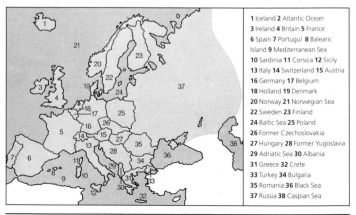

1 Iceland 2 Atlantic Ocean
3 Ireland 4 Britain 5 France
6 Spain 7 Portugul 8 Balearic
Island 9 Mediterranean Sea
10 Sardinia 11 Corsica 12 Sicily
13 Italy 14 Switzerland 15 Austria
16 Germany 17 Belgium
18 Holland 19 Denmark
20 Norway 21 Norwegian Sea
22 Sweden 23 Finland
24 Baltic Sea 25 Poland
26 Former Czechoslovakia
27 Hungary 28 Former Yugoslavia
29 Adriatic Sea 30 Albania
31 Greece 32 Crete
33 Turkey 34 Bulgaria
35 Romania 36 Black Sea
37 Russia 38 Caspian Sea

SCOPE OF THIS BOOK

The area covered by this guide extends from the tree limit in Scandinavia and northern Russia to the islands of the Mediterranean; from the Atlantic coast in the west to the Ural Mountains, Black Sea, Caspian Sea, and Aegean Islands in the east. Emphasis has been placed on those species that are most abundant and visible to the majority of people. Most native species are covered, with the exception of the more restricted and obscure trees. A few of the uncommon species have been included where space permits. The book describes most of the commonly planted trees that have been introduced, including timber trees, fruit trees and amenity trees. The last-named category embraces those grown for shelter, shade or ornament in public places, and street trees, many of which are planted along thousands of miles of roads. The reason for such a broad coverage is that it is often impossible to know whether a tree is native or not without specialist knowledge. Some of the introduced species regularly produce seed and spread, behaving like native trees. Ornamental trees which are also native may be planted far beyond

Chilean Wine Palm is commonly planted along streets in the Mediterranean region.

their natural limits of distribution.

What is a tree?

A general working definition of a tree is a plant with a single, woody stem, which grows to 6 metres or more tall. However, many of the trees that are planted for urban use, in streets, parks and gardens, are typically much shorter, for example Dwarf Cherry. Furthermore, the size of a tree can vary according to the habitat in which it is growing. A native species may be tall at low altitudes but just a few metres high in the mountains. A broader definition has been adopted in this book as there is no precise botanical distinction between trees and shrubs, the latter being typically smaller woody plants with multiple stems. Some large trees, which unquestionably belong here, regularly produce multiple trunks by growing sucker shoots, for example English Elm. Trees that grow in hedgerows, and that at some time have been cut to height, will also sprout extra stems. A few shrubs have been included in the book where they reach tree size, particularly when a common, large shrub represents a group which includes some less common trees.

Although it usually occurs as a shrub, Hazel can sometimes attain tree size.

THE HISTORY OF TREES

Forests and woodland may appear to have been there forever but they are all in a continual, gradual state of change. In the last Ice Age, much of northern Europe was covered by a continuous sheet of ice. As the climate warmed around 10,000 years ago, the ice began to retreat and the bare ground left behind became available for colonization. Light, wind-borne seeds of trees surviving south of the ice soon arrived, with birches, willows, then pines acting as pioneers, and woodlands were gradually established in the north. Trees with heavier seeds arrived much later but as they grew they overshadowed and eventually replaced the pioneer species. During the Ice Age and when the ice began its retreat,

colossal volumes of sea water were frozen solid and the sea-level was about thirty metres lower than it is today. France, Britain and Ireland were connected by land and early colonizing trees easily spread through the area. As the ice melted the sea rose, and some of the forested area disappeared beneath the sea. It also prevented some of the trees with larger seeds, which were spreading from the south, from colonizing many of the islands of northern Europe. Eventually a pattern of fairly continuous tree cover developed, with the northern forests of Europe dominated by conifers, and middle latitudes by broad-leaved oaks, elms and beeches. In the drier south, species with tough leaves resistant to drought formed extensive forests.

The recent history of trees is dominated by humankind. The most profound effects have been in the south, where the longer history of human habitation has resulted in most of the forests being destroyed. Further north, prehistoric people, using stone implements, found it easier to clear for crops upland areas with more open woodland than the rich valleys with their dense forests. With advances in materials and agricultural tools, more and more of the forest fell. Even if land was subsequently no longer farmed, domesticated grazing animals often prevented the trees from becoming re-established. Timber for construction has long been a highly prized commodity and has accelerated land clearance around the more densely populated areas. Though there has been much planting for timber on a forestry scale in recent years, it has often been done with imported species from other temperate regions of the world.

THE IMPORTANCE OF TREES

The economic importance of trees to humankind is immense. Yet it is nothing compared to the role they play in regulating the world's climate and ecosystems – a role which, because of the scale on which we exploit and destroy trees, is increasingly under threat.

A tree takes up water and mineral salts from the soil, moving them up from the roots to the leaves, where energy-rich sugars are produced using sunlight and carbon dioxide. These simple sugars are the building blocks for materials which are incorporated into the tree as it grows during a life-span of hundreds or perhaps even thousands of years. In an act that takes but a few minutes, it is difficult to see the long-term consequences of cutting down a single tree, but deforestation on the scale that has happened in the past and continues to happen around the globe is another matter.

A single tree can take up 1000–2000 litres of water from the ground a year, releasing most from the leaves as water vapour. Carried by the wind, this water vapour will later fall somewhere else as rain. On a forest scale, this capacity to move massive amounts of water has a profound effect on the local water-table and regional climate. Forested ground acts as a gigantic sponge, holding rainfall and releasing it gradually. Without trees, most of the water immediately runs off the land after rain and results in flooding alternating with drought. If the slope is steep or the rainfall heavy, the soil is eroded away to where it silts up rivers, reservoirs and estuaries. Without returning water to the atmosphere, the winds are drier and less rainfall is received somewhere else.

As well as affecting the local habitat, uncontrolled deforestation could have grave consequences for the world as a whole. As trees are destroyed and much material is burned or left to decompose, the carbon dioxide combined for centuries in the tree is released. This is one of the gases that at excess levels causes the Greenhouse Effect that threatens to change the world climate in a profound manner, raise sea-levels, and possibly cause species extinction on a vast scale.

It is important to conserve remaining natural forest, or manage it very carefully as a renewable resource, and re-establish tree cover in many places where it has been lost. Increased planting of native hardwoods in Europe would take longer to yield financial rewards than exotic softwoods, but would take the pressure off the tropics where massive deforestation must rank as one of the greatest crimes against the environment ever committed by humanity.

HOW TO IDENTIFY TREES

When first learning to identify trees, it is important to resolve the general look of a tree into individual characteristics, which can then be checked against the illustrations, key and descriptions. The most useful features for identification are summarized in the following section, with an explanation of the terms used in the book.

Type of tree

A basic distinction to make is between cone-bearing trees (conifers) and flowering trees, which bear typical flowers or specialized flowers, such as catkins. Each type of tree may keep its leaves throughout the year (evergreen), or may lose all its leaves for part of the year (deciduous), either during a cold or a dry season.

Trunk

Unlike most wild flowers, a tree's stem keeps growing from one year to the next.

Stiffening materials are laid down and it becomes a woody trunk, almost invariably increasing in size around its periphery each year. By definition, a tree has a single trunk, but some, such as Coast Redwood, can produce multiple trunks from shoots called suckers that grow around the base of the original trunk. The heavy lower branches of Western Red-cedar become bowed down to the ground, rooting and forming extra trunks in many old trees. Trunks of some species have broad flanges (buttresses) near the base, offering additional support to the tree.

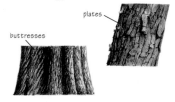

plates

buttresses

Bark

The outer protective layer of the trunk is the bark, which accommodates increases in girth of the trunk in various ways. Older layers of bark commonly split, with new bark laid down internally, resulting in the vertical fissures of Sweet Chestnut or the small, square plates of Evergreen Oak. Cork Oak has a bark which proliferates rapidly to form a thick, soft layer; the fibrous bark of Wellingtonia is also thick and soft. Smooth barks, such as that of London Plane, often peel off in layers.

Crown and branching

The branches, twigs and foliage together, termed the crown, may have a distinctive shape which helps identify a tree. The shape is largely formed by the major branches, which may be spreading, angled upwards or weeping. A very regular pattern with rings of radiating, successively older branches in many young conifers results in a conical shape. Another distinctive shape is the very narrow crown of Lombardy Poplar, with almost vertical branching. Usually the shape is characteristic for an individual species but some trees can have very narrow or weeping cultivated forms as well as the typical form with widely spreading branches.

Twigs and buds

Twigs offer a number of useful characteristics and are particularly important in deciduous trees, as they provide most of the characters for identifying the tree when it is leafless. On bare twigs, there is often a distinctive pattern of scars left where the leaves have fallen. Some trees have stout and rigid twigs, such as Fig and walnuts; others have slender and pendulous twigs, such as Silver Birch. Spines or thorns narrow identification down to a few species scattered through the book.

At the tip of a twig, and usually at the base of each leaf-stalk or leaf-scar, are buds. Most of these buds, with the exception of flower-buds, are juvenile shoots, with the young leaves covered by scales and the growth more or less arrested. The bud at the tip of the twig is generally largest and very noticeable in most deciduous trees. Horse-chestnut has a broad, sticky bud, while that of beeches is slender and smoothly tapered above and below the middle. That of ashes is smooth and blackish while White Willow has buds covered with pale grey hairs. The position of the side buds reflects the arrangement of the leaves and can be a useful feature.

sticky bud

leaf scar

Leaves

Trees are leafy for most of the year, but flowering and fruiting may be restricted to a few months. It can take many years before flowering commences and some mature trees may not develop any mature flowers or fruit in certain years. Consequently, leaves provide the most useful features for general identification. Note the position and whether the leaves are paired or otherwise arranged on the stem. The basic outline of the blade

Introduction

(expanded part) is important. See if the edge is unbroken, toothed or lobed. If the leaf is divided into leaflets, then they may be paired or radiating. Leaves of deciduous trees are commonly thinner than those of evergreen trees and often change colour dramatically in autumn. Leaf surfaces vary from smooth and glossy through varying degrees of hairiness, particularly on the underside. Needle-like leaves occur in many conifers, whilst others have small, scale-like leaves. Junipers can have both sorts on the same plant. A pair of stipules occurs at the base of the leaf-stalk of many flowering trees; they can be large, or small and falling quickly.

needle-like leaves

lobed leaf

leaflets

Flowers

Petals are usually the showiest part of a flower in most insect-pollinated trees. Look to see if they are equal or unequal and separate or joined together towards the base. Sepals are positioned beneath the petals and are usually green. If the petals and sepals are not readily distinguishable, then the term perianth applies to both. The male (♂) parts of a flower are the stamens, which produce pollen in anthers; the female (♀) parts are the stigma, usually supported by a stalk-like part (style), attaching it to the ovary. Most flowers have both male and female parts and are called hermaphrodite (☿). There may be separate male and female flowers, either on the same tree or different trees. The flowers of some trees are tiny and massed in elongated heads called catkins; such flowers are usually wind-pollinated. Conifers bear the male and female parts on the scales of male and female cones respectively.

Fruits and seeds

Important things to note about fruits are shape, colour, whether they are fleshy or dry and, in the latter case, if they open to release the seeds. Berry-like fruits, such as that of Wild Cherry, often have a hard stone inside enclosing the seed. Many fruits have outer layers which become dry as the fruit ripens. Pods are elongated dry fruits that split open to release the seeds when ripe, and are found in species of the Pea family such as Honey Locust. Dry fruits that do not open are commonly nut-like, and usually contain a single seed. Dry fruits of ashes and maples have a long wing which aids dispersal; the wing of elms and Caucasian Wing-nut encircles the part containing the seed. Conifers mostly have woody cones with seeds carried beneath scales. Individual seeds often have membranous wings. Cones of pines and spruces usually hang downwards, but those of firs, cedars and larches are upright. Pine cones fall intact, in some species after many years on the tree. Cones of firs and Monkey-puzzle break up on the tree. Yews and junipers are unusual conifers in which the cone scales become fleshy and berry-like as they mature.

HOW TO USE THIS BOOK

If you want to identify a tree and have no idea of what it is, refer to the key starting on page 14 – which should limit your search to a specific group of pages. If, on the other hand, you have a rough idea of the identity, then turn to the relevant section of the book (using the colour code explained on page 16) and you will find similar species grouped on adjacent pages. Match the species against the illustrations, the description of the tree is mostly summarized in a fact panel, which contains comparable elements for every species. This layout differs from the practice in most other field guides and floras, where the descriptions are often very brief and inconsistent.

Each page of the guide features a main species and up to three similar trees. These may be cultivars, subspecies, or similar species, and may sometimes be as common as the main species. The elements illustrated for the main species include the general habit and details such as leaves, flowers and fruit. For the similar trees, only one or two distinguishing details are shown.

A text summarizes the general look of the tree or how it looks when part of a forest; it draws attention to important distinguishing features and adds points of interest regarding biology or significance to man.

The colour shows which group of plants each species belongs to. Use it to help you find the different groups as you flick through the book. The colour code is explained on page 16.

Accurate illustrations of the whole tree, plus details of the flowers, fruits or other parts of the plant important for identification.

Labels pick out the best clues to identification.

Up to three similar trees are illustrated on the same page, with details of how they differ from the main tree.

A fact panel provides a detailed summary of the main features of the tree; where it grows and when it flowers and fruits; with details on the crown, trunk, leaves, flowers, fruit and seeds.

Sorbus intermedia **Swedish Whitebeam**

Shallow-lobed leaves felted below with yellowish grey hairs identify Swedish Whitebeam. Red fruits are dotted with a few pale lenticels. It flowers *more intensively than most other whitebeams, and is often used as an ornamental tree.

Status: native to the Baltic region; planted elsewhere; sometimes naturalized.

Labels: deciduous; green above; ripen red; longer than broad; smooth, grey; shallowly lobed; grey, woolly

SWEDISH WHITEBEAM

Type	deciduous tree
Height	up to 15m
Habitat	hills and mountains
Flowering	May
Fruiting	September
TRUNK AND CROWN	
Trunk	short
Bark	grey, smooth with wide, shallow cracks
Crown	dense, broadly domed
Twigs	grey to purplish, very hairy, becoming smooth
Buds	8mm, egg-shaped, green or brown, with grey hairs
LEAVES	
Leaves	alternate, 8–12cm, eliptic, shallowly lobed, the lobes reaching one-third of the way to midrib but more pronounced towards base of leaf, edge sharply toothed, smooth and green above, densely yellow-grey woolly below; stalkless
Stipules	small; soon falling
FLOWERS AND FRUIT	
Flowers	♀, many, in branched clusters in angles of leaves, each 12–20mm across, white, leaf stalk smooth
Petals	5, c6mm, equal; sepals 5
Stamens	many, cream
Stigmas	2, styles joined at base
Ovaries	2, in base of flower, hairy
Fruit	berry-like, 12–15mm, much longer than broad, ripening red, dotted with
Seeds	2

SIMILAR TREES

1 *Sorbus austriaca* has leaves with whitish grey wool below. Those of **2** *Sorbus mougeotii* are also grey-woolly below but less deeply lobed. Both are mountain species.
3 *Sorbus umbellata*, from the Balkan region, has deeply lobed, white-woolly leaves and yellow fruits.

Labels: many spots; few small leaves; yellow; white below

107

Introduction

KEY TO SPECIES

This key provides an illustrated guide to the groups of species and their page numbers. At each stage, read the first numbered statement and see if it describes your tree. If not, then the second statement with the same number includes all other plants at this stage of the key. Move on to the next statement below and repeat the process until you key out to the correct group.

1   **leaves crowded at top of trunk or tips of thick branches**
Agaves 180–181; Palms 182–185.

1   **leaves spread along branches and twigs**
2   **leaves all or mostly scale-like, pressed against stem**
Monkey-puzzles 19; Redwoods 38–39; Cypresses 42–45, 47–49; She-oaks 89; Tamarisks 154–155.

2   **leaves not all scale-like**
3   **leaves all or mostly needle-like, spreading**
4   **needles all spirally arranged or forming 2 parallel rows**
Pines 20–29; Redwoods 39–40; Yews 41.

4   **needles mostly borne in clusters, tufts or whorls of 2 or more**
Pines 30–37; Cypresses 46.

3   **leaves not needle-like**
5   **leaves divided into separate leaflets**
6   **leaflets in 2 rows**
Walnuts 90–92; Roses 104; Peas 124–125, 127–129, 131; Quassias 134; Mahoganies 135; Cashews 136–138; Soapberries 139; Maples 144; Olives 170–171; Honeysuckles 178.

6   **leaflets radiating from leaf stalk**
Peas 130; Citruses 133; Horse-chestnuts 140–141.

5   **leaves not divided into separate leaflets**
7   **leaves in opposite pairs on stem**
Maples 142–143, 145–147; Spindles 149; Boxes 150; Buckthorns 153;

Dogwoods 161;
Pomegranates 167;
Olives 172–173;
Bignonias 176–177;
Honeysuckles 178.

7 **leaves alternating or scattered around stem**
8 **flowers (at least males) in slender catkins**
9 **leaves lobed, spiny or fan-shaped**
Maidenhair-tree 18; Willows 58;
Beeches 70–75.

9 **leaves sometimes toothed but neither lobed nor spiny**

Willows 50–57,
59–61; Birches 62–64; Hazels 65–67;
Beeches 76; Bog-myrtles 77.

8 **flowers single or in clusters but not in slender catkins**
10 **leaves lobed or spiny**
11 **flowers white**
Roses 105, 107,
112–115;
Hollies 148.

11 **flowers red, yellow or green**
Mulberries 85; Witch-hazels 86;
Planes 88; Magnolias 95.

10 **leaves sometimes toothed but neither lobed nor spiny**
12 **evergreen**
13 **crushed leaves strong and**

pleasant-smelling
Laurels 96; Myrtles
162–166.

13 **crushed leaves not strong-smelling**
Pittosporums 93;
Magnolias 94; Roses 108, 121;
Citruses 132; Heathers 174;
Myoporums 175.

12 **deciduous**
14 **leaves heart-shaped**
Mulberries 83;
Peas 126;
Limes 156–158;
Davidia 159.

14 **leaves not heart-shaped**
15 **petals white or pink**
Roses 98–103,
106, 109–111,
116–120,
122–123;
Storaxes 169.

15 **petals yellow, greenish, dull red or absent**
16 **leaves with edge toothed**
Beeches 69; Elms 78–82;
Mulberries 84; Witch-hazels 87;
Buckthorns 152–153.

16 **leaves with edge not toothed**
Beeches 68; Mulberries 84;
Oleasters 151;
Buckthorns 153;
Black-gums 160;
Ebonies 168.

Introduction

English language names for native trees have been standardised to the list published by the Botanical Society of the British Isles (Dony, Jury and Perring, 1986). Some plants will have no common name if they only grow in other countries of the area.

Botanical names are more stable and international in usage. Most are those given in the standard European flora (Tutin *et al.* (Editors), 1964–1980) but some are updated according to the British Excursion Flora (Clapham, Tutin & Warburg, 1985). Each Latin name is made up of a genus name (starting with a capital letter) and a species name (starting with a small letter). A third, subspecies (abbreviated as subsp.), name is used to distinguish geographical variation within a species. A multiplication symbol between the first and second names indicates that the plant is a hybrid between two species; if the sign is before the first name then it indicates a hybrid between species of two different genera. Particular selections of cultivated trees are often given horticultural names, indicated in single quotation marks.

Order of trees

The trees in this book are arranged more or less in systematic order. Those that have a similar construction of flowers and fruit are placed together in families. Each group of families is given a colour reference marker. Use this coloured square at the corner of the pages to help you find the different groups of plants as you flick through the book.

Maidenhair-tree and Monkey-puzzles

Pines

Redwoods and Yews

Cypresses

Willows

Birches and Hazels

Beeches and Bog-myrtles

Elms and Mulberries

Witch-hazels, Planes and She-oaks

Walnuts and Pittosporums

Magnolias, Laurels and Phytolaccas

Roses

Peas

Citruses, Quassias and Mahoganies

Cashews, Soapberries, Horse-chestnuts and Maples

Hollies, Spindles, Boxes and Oleasters

Buckthorns, Tamarisks and Limes

Davidia, Black-gums and Dogwoods

Myrtles, Loosestrifes and Pomegranates

Ebonies, Storaxes, Olives and Heathers

Myoporums, Foxgloves, Bignonias and Honeysuckles

Agaves and Palms

KINGFISHER POCKET GUIDES
TREES
OF BRITAIN AND EUROPE

Maidenhair-tree *Ginkgo biloba*

An unmistakable tree, with unique fan-shaped leaves, distinctive irregular crown, and marble-sized, fleshy fruits. This odd species belongs to a group of trees that was important when dinosaurs roamed the earth, but now all but this one species is extinct. Fruits give off a nauseous odour when over-ripe, making the female tree unsuitable for planting in towns of warmer countries. The tree was cultivated for centuries in gardens of Chinese temples and palaces. It is virtually unknown in the wild state.

fan-shaped leaf

stalked fruit

leaves clustered

some paired

Status: introduced from China; planted fairly commonly for ornament, often as a street tree.

Similar trees: none.

paired ♀ flowers

♂ catkins

irregular outline

deciduous

rough

MAIDENHAIR-TREE

Type	conifer, deciduous tree
Height	25–30m
Habitat	street tree, parks
Flowering	March–April
Fruiting	September–October

TRUNK AND CROWN

Trunk	slender, straight or forked
Bark	deeply fissured and ridged
Crown	irregularly cylindrical or sometimes broad
Twigs	of two types: long and straight, with short, stubby side-shoots

LEAVES

Buds	conical, reddish brown
Leaves	spirally arranged, widely spaced on long shoots, clustered on short shoots, 3–12cm, many veins diverging from base, yellowish green, turning bright yellow in autumn

FLOWERS AND FRUIT

Flowers	♂ and ♀ on different plants
♂	cluster of 3–6 yellow catkins, each 60–80mm
♀	1 or 2 on stalk up to 40mm long, pale yellow
Fruit	1–2 on long stalk, 25–30mm
Seeds	1 per fruit, large, nut-like

Amost unusual conifer with broad, spine-tipped leaves, thickly set all around the stems. It is the source of a commercially important timber, but rarely produces wood of sufficient quality in Europe. In its native South America, the seeds are eaten as a delicacy but they often fail to set in Europe.

Status: introduced from Chile and western Argentina; commonly planted in western Europe for ornament.

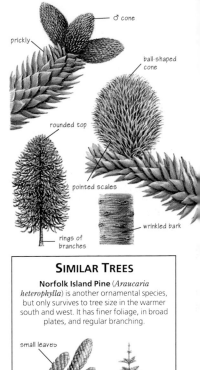

♂ cone

prickly

ball-shaped cone

rounded top

pointed scales

wrinkled bark

rings of branches

MONKEY-PUZZLE

Type	conifer, evergreen tree
Height	25–30m
Habitat	parks, gardens
Flowering	June–July
Fruiting	August–September

TRUNK AND CROWN

Trunk	straight, stout, not forked, sometimes with suckers from roots
Bark	with horizontal ridges, later becoming vertically ridged, blackish grey
Crown	conical; branches in rings at same level
Twigs	concealed by overlapping leaf-bases

LEAVES

Buds	conical, hidden by leaves
Leaves	spirally arranged, 3–4cm, tip spine-tipped, edge unbroken, base broad, dark, glossy green; stalkless

FLOWERS AND FRUIT

Flowers	♂ and ♀ on different plants
♂	cone, c10cm, egg-shaped, brown, clustered at shoot-tip
♀	cone, globular, spiny, on upper side of shoot
Fruit	globular, upright cone, up to 15cm, green with yellowish spines, breaks up on tree when ripe in second or third year
Seeds	up to 4cm, brown, often sterile

SIMILAR TREES

Norfolk Island Pine (*Araucaria heterophylla*) is another ornamental species, but only survives to tree size in the warmer south and west. It has finer foliage, in broad plates, and regular branching.

small leaves

layered branches

Common Silver-fir *Abies alba*

Once commonly planted in north-western Europe, this species is intolerant of exposure or pollution, and is badly damaged by aphids, so other species are now preferred. Older trees have only a cluster of branches left at the top.

Status: native to mountains of central and southern Europe; widely planted for timber and ornament in northern Europe.

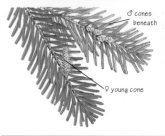

♂ cones beneath

♀ young cone

conical

evergreen

bract shows

cone falls apart

SIMILAR TREES

1 Caucasian Fir (*Abies nordmanniana*) has a denser and broader crown, crowded leaves, and thicker cones with longer bracts. Heavily branched, with a stout trunk,
2 Grecian Fir (*Abies cephalonica*) differs from the latter in the stiff, spiny leaves, and resinous buds.

1

long bracts

crowded

2

prickly

sticky bud

COMMON SILVER-FIR

Type	conifer, evergreen tree
Height	40–55m
Habitat	forests, plantations, parks
Flowering	April
Fruiting	September

TRUNK AND CROWN

Trunk	stout, more or less straight
Bark	dark grey, smooth with resin-blisters, gradually becoming cracked into squarish plates
Crown	narrowly conical; branches in groups at same level
Twigs	greyish brown, shortly hairy

LEAVES

Buds	egg-shaped, reddish brown
Leaves	arising spirally, twisted to either side, parted above twig, 15–25mm, rarely 35mm, needle-like, flattened but thick, tip shallowly notched, dark green with 2 whitish bands below; stalkless

FLOWERS AND FRUIT

Flowers	♂ and ♀ on same tree
	♂ globular, yellow cone, on underside of shoots,
	♀ egg-shaped, greenish cone, on upper side of top branches
Fruit	cylindrical, upright cone, 10–20cm, brown, with woody cone- scales and slender-tipped, downward-pointing, projecting bracts
Seeds	2 per scale, winged

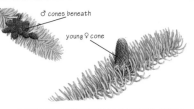

♂ cones beneath

young ♀ cone

A striking tree, with huge, upright cones that have distinctive, downward-pointing bracts. It is commonly planted for its close-grained timber, and plantations thrive even under harsh conditions.

Status: introduced from western North America; widely planted in northern and western Europe for timber or ornament.

evergreen

protruding bracts

conical

falls apart

upright

NOBLE FIR

Type	conifer, evergreen tree
Height	40–50m (taller in America)
Habitat	cultivated mainly in plantations
Flowering	May
Fruiting	October

TRUNK AND CROWN

Trunk	stout, straight, not forked
Bark	pale grey, smooth with resin-blisters, becoming fissured
Crown	narrowly conical or columnar, becoming flat-topped; branches level, forming irregular rings
Twigs	reddish brown, finely hairy, with circular leaf-scars

LEAVES

Buds	resinous only at the tips
Leaves	arising spirally but curved up at sides, parted below, crowded above, 1–3.5cm, needle-like, 4-angled, blunt, greyish green, 2 pale grey bands beneath

FLOWERS AND FRUIT

Flowers	♂ and ♀ flowers on same plant
	♂ globular, crimson cone, c6mm, clustered beneath shoots, becoming yellow with pollen
	♀ cylindrical greenish cone, 40–50mm, scales orange-tipped
Fruit	barrel-shaped, blunt-tipped, upright cone, 15–25cm, with green, downward-pointing bracts protruding beyond purplish brown cone-scales
Seeds	2 per scale, winged

SIMILAR TREES

Two species have very resinous buds and smaller cones, which are bluish until maturity. Native to north-eastern Russia, **1 Siberian Fir** (*Abies sibirica*) has cones with short, hidden bracts. Introduced from Japan, **2 Veitch's Silver-fir** (*Abies veitchii*) has cones with the bracts just projecting.

1

2

bracts hidden

bracts just show

bluish young cones

Grand Fir *Abies grandis*

This large tree is readily distinguished by feather-like shoots with leaves spreading horizontally to either side, and upright, cylindrical cones with hidden bracts. The foliage has a distinct orange-like scent. Remarkably fast growth and tolerance of most soil conditions contribute to the value of this species as a forestry tree.

Status: introduced from western North America; widely planted in northern and central Europe, mainly for timber.

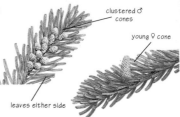

clustered ♂ cones

young ♀ cone

leaves either side

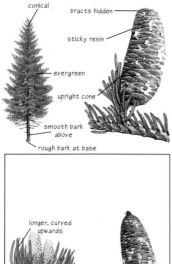

conical

bracts hidden

sticky resin

evergreen

upright cone

smooth bark above

rough bark at base

longer, curved upwards

often larger

GRAND FIR

Type	conifer, evergreen tree
Height	40–60m (over 90m in America)
Habitat	plantations, especially in wetter areas
Flowering	April
Fruiting	October

TRUNK AND CROWN

Trunk	straight, not forked, fairly stout
Bark	brownish grey, smooth with resin-blisters
Crown	narrowly conical or columnar; branches in rings at same level
Twigs	with sparse, short hairs and circular leaf-scars

LEAVES

Buds	c2mm, conical, purplish, becoming covered with resin
Leaves	arising spirally but turning to either side, 2–6cm, needle-like, notched, glossy green above with 2 whitish bands below

FLOWERS AND FRUIT

Flowers	♂ and ♀ on same tree
♂	purplish, cone, c2mm, in cluster below shoot, becomes yellow with pollen
♀	solitary cone, above shoot
Fruit	woody, upright cone, 5–10cm, cylindrical, reddish brown exuding whitish resin; bracts hidden by cone-scales; cone disintegrates on tree leaving thin spike
Seeds	2 per scale, winged

Also known as 'Hedgehog Fir', this species is easily distinguished by stiff, prickly leaves set all around the shoots. Though naturally limited to a few sites in Spain, near Ronda, it is cultivated elsewhere.

Status: native to mountains of southern Spain; frequently planted for ornament or sometimes timber.

red ♂ cones

young ♀ cone

prickly leaves

leaves round shoot

blunt tip

bracts hidden

upright cone

conical

evergreen

SPANISH FIR

Type	conifer, evergreen tree
Height	20–30m
Habitat	north-facing slopes on limestone mountains; also planted elsewhere
Flowering	May
Fruiting	October

TRUNK AND CROWN

Trunk	stout, straight, not forked
Bark	smooth, becoming cracked into squarish plates, dark grey or blackish
Crown	conical, becoming irregular; branches in rings at same level
Twigs	orange-brown, smooth except for circular leaf scars

LEAVES

Buds	3–5mm, egg-shaped, purplish, sticky with resin
Leaves	spreading outwards all round shoot, 10–18mm, needle-like, stiff, spine-tipped, greyish green with 2 greyish bands above and below; stalkless
Stipules	absent

FLOWERS AND FRUIT

Flowers	♂ and ♀ flowers on same plant
	♂ cluster of cones below shoot, each c5mm, globular, red, becoming yellow with pollen
	♀ solitary cone above shoot
Fruit	upright, cylindrical cone, 10–16cm, tip squarish with small bract, ripening brown; bracts hidden by cone-scales
Seeds	2 per cone-scale, winged

SIMILAR TREES

1 Algerian Fir (*Abies numidica*) has longer, broader, more flexible leaves with whitish bands below, and cones with a raised centre to the otherwise squarish tip. **2 Nikko Fir** (*Abies homolepis*) has very pale, grooved shoots with leaves pointing slightly forwards, and violet-blue young cones.

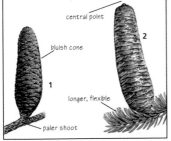

central point

bluish cone

1

2

longer, flexible

paler shoot

Douglas-fir *Pseudotsuga menziesii*

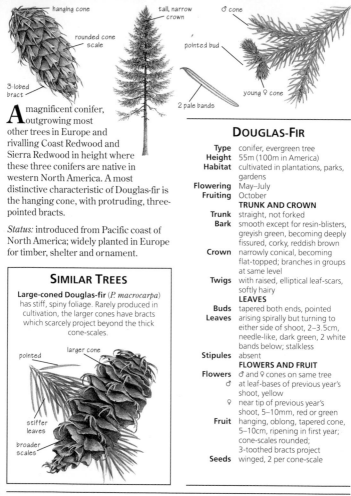

A magnificent conifer, outgrowing most other trees in Europe and rivalling Coast Redwood and Sierra Redwood in height where these three conifers are native in western North America. A most distinctive characteristic of Douglas-fir is the hanging cone, with protruding, three-pointed bracts.

Status: introduced from Pacific coast of North America; widely planted in Europe for timber, shelter and ornament.

SIMILAR TREES

Large-coned Douglas-fir (*P. macrocarpa*) has stiff, spiny foliage. Rarely produced in cultivation, the larger cones have bracts which scarcely project beyond the thick cone-scales.

DOUGLAS-FIR

Type	conifer, evergreen tree
Height	55m (100m in America)
Habitat	cultivated in plantations, parks, gardens
Flowering	May–July
Fruiting	October
	TRUNK AND CROWN
Trunk	straight, not forked
Bark	smooth except for resin-blisters, greyish green, becoming deeply fissured, corky, reddish brown
Crown	narrowly conical, becoming flat-topped; branches in groups at same level
Twigs	with raised, elliptical leaf-scars, softly hairy
	LEAVES
Buds	tapered both ends, pointed
Leaves	arising spirally but turning to either side of shoot, 2–3.5cm, needle-like, dark green, 2 white bands below; stalkless
Stipules	absent
	FLOWERS AND FRUIT
Flowers	♂ and ♀ cones on same tree
♂	at leaf-bases of previous year's shoot, yellow
♀	near tip of previous year's shoot, 5–10mm, red or green
Fruit	hanging, oblong, tapered cone, 5–10cm, ripening in first year; cone-scales rounded; 3-toothed bracts project
Seeds	winged, 2 per cone-scale

Tsuga heterophylla **Western Hemlock-spruce**

An attractive conifer, recognized by the varied length and rather random arrangement of the leaves, set either side of shoots that arch downwards from spreading branches. Western Hemlock-spruce is highly productive as a timber tree. The foliage has a characteristic odour resembling Hemlock.

Status: introduced from western North America; widely cultivated in Europe.

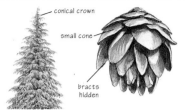

conical crown

small cone

bracts hidden

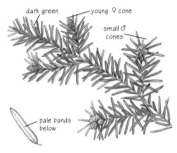

dark green — young ♀ cone

small ♂ cones

pale bands below

WESTERN HEMLOCK-SPRUCE

Type	conifer, evergreen tree
Height	45m (up to 70m in America)
Habitat	cultivated in plantations, parks, gardens
Flowering	April
Fruiting	October
	TRUNK AND BRANCHES
Trunk	straight, unforked
Bark	reddish brown, rough, becoming cracked and fluted
Crown	narrowly conical or cylindrical; branches in groups at same level
Twigs	slender, tip droops, greyish brown, hairy
	LEAVES
Buds	globular, greyish
Leaves	arising spirally, turning to either side of twig, 0.5–2cm, of different lengths, needle-like, flattened, blunt, dark green, 2 white bands below, peg-like base remains after leaf falls
	FLOWERS AND FRUIT
Flowers	♂ and ♀ cones on same plant
♂	clustered at leaf-bases near shoot tip, small, red, turning yellow
♀	solitary at shoot tip, c6mm, purplish pink
Fruit	single egg-shaped cone, 2–2.5cm, hanging, brown, ripening in first year; scales rounded, persisting
Seeds	winged, 2 per cone-scale

SIMILAR TREES

1 Eastern Hemlock-spruce (*T. canadensis*) is smaller, with shorter, tapered leaves, and smaller cones. **2 Mountain Hemlock-spruce** (*T. mertensiana*) has spirally arranged, bluish leaves and larger cones.

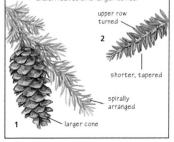

upper row turned

2

shorter, tapered

spirally arranged

larger cone

1

Norway Spruce *Picea abies*

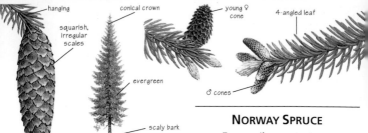

hanging

squarish, irregular scales

conical crown

evergreen

scaly bark

young ♀ cone

♂ cones

4-angled leaf

An important timber tree, though perhaps more familiar as a Christmas tree. Spruces are distinctive in the long, hanging cones with thin scales, and needles borne on short, peg-like projections.

Status: native mainly to northern Europe; planted elsewhere for timber, shelter and ornament.

SIMILAR TREES

Forming intermediates where they grow together, **1 Siberian Spruce** (*picea obovata*) is sometimes regarded as part of the same species as Norway Spruce. It is smaller with a shorter, more pointed cone and short, dense hairs on the twigs. **2 Oriental Spruce** (*Picea orientalis*) is easily distinguished by its very short leaves.

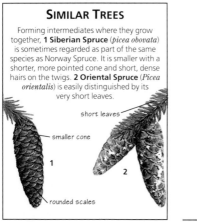

short leaves

smaller cone

rounded scales

1

2

NORWAY SPRUCE

Type	conifer, evergreen tree
Height	30–40m (rarely to 60m)
Habitat	forests, plantations, parks
Flowering	May
Fruiting	September

TRUNK AND CROWN

Trunk	straight, not forked
Bark	reddish brown, rough, scaly, darkens, cracks into plates
Crown	conical or columnar; branches in rings at same level
Twigs	orange brown, grooved, rough with peg-like leaf-bases, usually hairless

LEAVES

Buds	4–7mm, egg-shaped, glossy dark brown
Leaves	arising spirally, turning to either side of shoot and leaving gap below, 10–25mm, needle-like, 4-angled, pointed, dark green with greyish band on each side; peg-like base

FLOWERS AND FRUIT

Flowers	♂ and ♀ flowers on same plant
♂	globular cones, c1cm, near shoot tips, crimson, turning yellow with pollen
♀	solitary cone, dark red, upright, on upper branches
Fruit	cylindrical cone with rounded tip, 12–20cm, hanging, woody, brown; scales thin, diamond-shaped or oval with squarish, irregular tip
Seeds	2 per cone-scale, winged

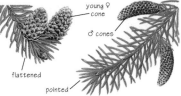

young ♀ cone

♂ cones

flattened

pointed

Native to the Pacific coast of North America, this tall, graceful conifer is now an important timber tree in Europe. It has shallow roots and is often blown over in high winds.

Status: introduced from North America; commonly grown in northern and central Europe for timber or ornament.

conical

hanging

evergreen

scales thin

Irregular tips

SITKA SPRUCE

Type	conifer, evergreen tree
Height	40–55m (up to 80m in America)
Habitat	plantations, parks; often in areas of high rainfall
Flowering	May
Fruiting	October

TRUNK AND CROWN

Trunk	usually straight, not forked
Bark	dark or purplish grey, cracking into irregular, lifting plates
Crown	narrowly conical; lower branches arch downwards
Twigs	pale brown, grooved, rough

LEAVES

Buds	egg-shaped, pale brown, purplish with resin
Leaves	spirally arranged, mostly turning to either side of shoot, the upper close to shoot, 2–3cm, needle-like, flattened, tip sharply pointed, bright green above with 2 narrow, pale bands, 2 bluish white bands below; stalkless

FLOWERS AND FRUIT

Flowers	♂ and ♀ flowers on same plant
♂	blunt, egg-shaped cones, 25–35mm, yellow or purplish
♀	pale red or green cone, 25–50mm, mostly near top of tree
Fruit	solitary, cylindrical, hanging cone, 5–10cm, ripening pale brown; scales thin, papery, crinkled, irregularly toothed
Seeds	2 per scale, winged

SIMILAR TREES

Two species differ in the short, blunt leaves and smaller cones. **1 Hondo Spruce** (*Picea jezoensis var. hondoensis*), from Japan, has a blunt cone with toothed scales. **2 Serbian Spruce** (*Picea omorika*), from Yugoslavia, has hairy twigs and pointed cones with rounded scales. Also with rounded scales, **3 Tiger-tail Spruce** (*Picea polita*) has sharp, four-angled leaves.

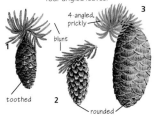

4-angled, prickly

blunt

toothed

rounded

1   2   3

Colorado Spruce *Picea pungens*

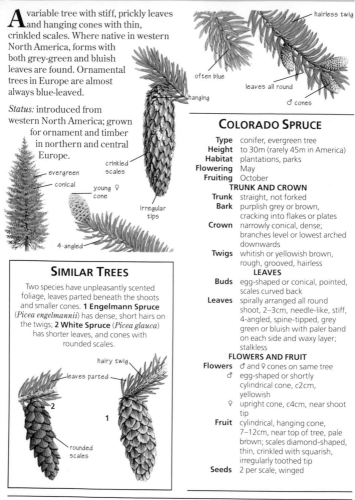

A variable tree with stiff, prickly leaves and hanging cones with thin, crinkled scales. Where native in western North America, forms with both grey-green and bluish leaves are found. Ornamental trees in Europe are almost always blue-leaved.

Status: introduced from western North America; grown for ornament and timber in northern and central Europe.

hairless twig

often blue

leaves all round

♂ cones

hanging

crinkled scales

young ♀ cone

irregular tips

evergreen

conical

4-angled

SIMILAR TREES

Two species have unpleasantly scented foliage, leaves parted beneath the shoots and smaller cones. **1 Engelmann Spruce** (*Picea engelmannii*) has dense, short hairs on the twigs; **2 White Spruce** (*Picea glauca*) has shorter leaves, and cones with rounded scales.

hairy twig

leaves parted

2

1

rounded scales

COLORADO SPRUCE

Type	conifer, evergreen tree
Height	to 30m (rarely 45m in America)
Habitat	plantations, parks
Flowering	May
Fruiting	October

TRUNK AND CROWN

Trunk	straight, not forked
Bark	purplish grey or brown, cracking into flakes or plates
Crown	narrowly conical, dense; branches level or lowest arched downwards
Twigs	whitish or yellowish brown, rough, grooved, hairless

LEAVES

Buds	egg-shaped or conical, pointed, scales curved back
Leaves	spirally arranged all round shoot, 2–3cm, needle-like, stiff, 4-angled, spine-tipped, grey green or bluish with paler band on each side and waxy layer; stalkless

FLOWERS AND FRUIT

Flowers	♂ and ♀ cones on same tree
	♂ egg-shaped or shortly cylindrical cone, c2cm, yellowish
	♀ upright cone, c4cm, near shoot tip
Fruit	cylindrical, hanging cone, 7–12cm, near top of tree, pale brown; scales diamond-shaped, thin, crinkled with squarish, irregularly toothed tip
Seeds	2 per scale, winged

Picea breweriana **Brewer's Weeping-spruce**

A beautiful tree with curtain-like, weeping foliage from upswept branches. An uncommon North American tree of the Siskyou Mountains in California and Oregon, it is not closely related to any other spruce.

Status: introduced from western North America; frequently planted for ornament.

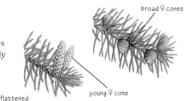

broad ♀ cones

young ♀ cone

flattened

weeping shoots

leaves turn outwards

hanging

rounded scales

evergreen

slender cone

SIMILAR TREES

Morinda Spruce (*Picea smithiana*) has a less dramatic weeping habit and hairless shoots. The buds are smaller and rounded, and the leaves, square in cross-section, are very long and green all round. Relatively broader, the cone has rounded scales which become irregular at the tip as they ripen.

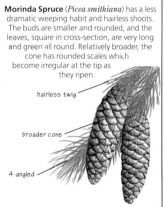

hairless twig

broader cone

4-angled

BREWER'S WEEPING-SPRUCE

Type	conifer, evergreen tree
Height	10–20m (to 35m in America)
Habitat	mainly grown in parks, gardens
Flowering	May
Fruiting	October

TRUNK AND CROWN

Trunk	straight, not forked
Bark	purplish grey, smooth, later with roughly circular flakes
Crown	irregularly conical or columnar; branches level or upswept
Twigs	long, slender, weeping, rough, pinkish brown, finely hairy

LEAVES

Buds	egg-shaped or conical, blunt, with reddish brown hairs
Leaves	arising spirally, curving out all round shoot or sometimes parted below, 2–3.5cm, needle-like, flattened, blunt, dark bluish green with 2 whitish bands below; stalkless

FLOWERS AND FRUIT

Flowers	♂ and ♀ flowers on same tree
♂	egg-shaped cones, 15–30mm, clustered near shoot tip
♀	cylindrical, upright cones, 25–35mm, red or pinkish green, clustered on upper branches
Fruit	narrow, hanging cone, 10–14cm, cylindrical, blunt, purplish, turning brown marked with whitish resin; scales rounded
Seeds	2 per scale, winged

European Larch *Larix decidua*

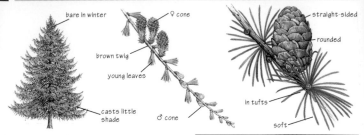

bare in winter
♀ cone
straight-sided
brown twig
rounded
young leaves
in tufts
casts little shade
♂ cone
soft

Leaves of this deciduous conifer turn yellow before falling to reveal knobbly twigs. Soft tufts of emerald-green young leaves in spring accompany pink young female cones and golden male cones.

Status: native to mountains of central Europe; planted elsewhere for timber and ornament.

SIMILAR TREES

1 Japanese Larch (*Larix kaempferi*) differs in the orange twigs, bluish leaves with white bands beneath, yellowish young female cones, and ripe cones with scales curved outwards. Its vigorous hybrid with the former species has intermediate cones. **2 Dahurian Larch** (*Larix gmelinii*) has cones with fewer, scarcely curved, hairless, broad scales.

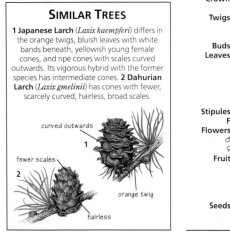

curved outwards
1
fewer scales
2
orange twig
hairless

EUROPEAN LARCH

Type	conifer, deciduous tree
Height	30–50m
Habitat	forest, woodland, plantations
Flowering	March–April
Fruiting	September; ripens first year

TRUNK AND CROWN

Trunk	straight, not forked below
Bark	greyish brown, smooth, becomes reddish and scaly or fissured
Crown	conical, becoming broader; branches irregularly clustered
Twigs	yellowish, hairless; long shoots and short side shoots

LEAVES

Buds	3mm, oval, yellowish brown
Leaves	tuft of 30–40 on short shoots, or spirally arranged on long shoots, 2–4cm, needle-like, thin, soft, pale green, becoming darker and turning yellow in autumn; stalkless
Stipules	absent

FLOWERS AND FRUIT

Flowers	♂ and ♀ cones on same tree
♂	small, drooping cone, yellow
♀	upright cone, pink or red
Fruit	egg-shaped woody cone, 2–3.5cm, with 40–50 scales; cone-scales more or less flat, round-tipped, softly hairy; bracts slightly protruding
Seeds	2 per cone-scale, winged

Massive, spreading branches bearing flat plates of needle-like foliage make this tree easily recognizable at a distance. Bunched needles and barrel-shaped cones carried above the foliage are also distinctive. Mature stands of this tree are a rarity in the wild.

Status: introduced from south-western Asia; frequently planted for ornament.

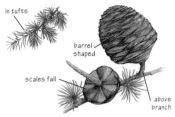

in tufts
barrel-shaped
scales fall
above branch

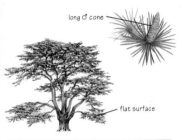

long ♂ cone
flat surface

CEDAR-OF-LEBANON

Type	conifer, evergreen tree
Height	15–40m
Habitat	parks, gardens
Flowering	October–November
Fruiting	ripens in second or third year

TRUNK AND CROWN

Trunk	stout, often forked
Bark	brown or blackish, cracks into fine, scaly ridges
Crown	conical when young, becomes broad, rounded or flat-topped; stout, horizontal branches bear large, flat plates of dense foliage
Twigs	finely hairy, pale brown

LEAVES

Buds	2–3mm, egg-shaped, brown
Leaves	tuft of 10–20 on short shoots, spirally arranged on long shoots, 2–3cm, needle-like, pointed, stiff, dark green, hairless; stalkless
Stipules	absent

FLOWERS AND FRUIT

Flowers	♂ and ♀ cones on same tree
♂	cone 4–5cm, greenish yellow
♀	cone 7–12mm, green or purplish
Fruit	woody cone, 8–15cm, barrel-shaped with squarish or dimpled tip, greyish or pinkish brown, resinous, disintegrates on tree
Seeds	winged, 2 per cone-scale

SIMILAR TREES

1 Atlas Cedar (*Cedrus atlantica*), from North Africa, is commonly planted, usually as the blue-needled variant. It has branches angled upwards and leaves in clusters of 30–45. Himalayan in origin, **2 Deodar** (*Cedrus deodara*) has a pointed crown, longer leaves and drooping young shoots.

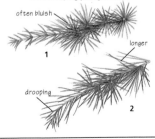

often bluish
longer
1
drooping
2

Scots Pine *Pinus sylvestris*

A widespread conifer from the Atlantic coast of Europe almost to the Pacific coast of Asia. One of several pines with paired needles, it is distinguished by reddish, scaly bark on the upper trunk, relatively short, bluish needles, a small, hanging cone and small buds with scales pressed close together.

Status: native to northern and central Europe; planted elsewhere for timber.

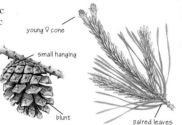

young ♀ cone

small hanging

blunt

paired leaves

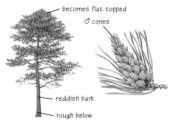

becomes flat-topped

♂ cones

reddish bark

rough below

SCOTS PINE

Type	conifer, evergreen tree
Height	20–40m
Habitat	forests, woods, plantations
Flowering	May–June
Fruiting	ripens in second year

TRUNK AND CROWN

Trunk	straight, not normally forked
Bark	reddish brown, scaling above, blackish brown, fissured below
Crown	conical, becomes broader or flat-topped; branches in groups at same level
Twigs	greenish brown, hairless

LEAVES

Buds	small, pointed, resinous
Leaves	paired on short shoots, 3–7cm, needle-like, twisted, blue-green, hairless; small, scale-like on long shoots
Stipules	absent

FLOWERS AND FRUIT

Flowers	♂ and ♀ cones on same tree	
	♂	globular cone, yellow or sometimes red before pollen is shed
	♀	1–5 cones at tip of shoot, egg-shaped, pinkish purple cones
Fruit		woody cone, 3–7cm, egg-shaped, pointed, hanging, dull, grey-brown; scales with broad, flattened end, raised in centre
Seeds		12–15mm, winged, 2 per scale

SIMILAR TREES

Mountain-pine (*Pinus mugo*) has bright green leaves and a shiny cone projecting at right-angles from the stem. Each scale has a backwardly curved point. Dwarf Mountain-pine is a similar but shorter tree or shrub, with small cones.

greener leaves

small point

Pinus nigra subsp. *laricio* **Corsican Pine**

From its forests in the Mediterranean region, this pine has been introduced to many parts of northern Europe, where it forms extensive plantations. It resembles Scots Pine but has darker bark and longer, more flexible and darker leaves. In colder regions, it is susceptible to disease.

Status: native to the central Mediterranean region; planted for timber, shelter or stabilizing sand.

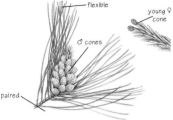

SIMILAR TREES

A dark, heavy-branched tree, **1 Austrian Pine** (*Pinus nigra* subsp. *nigra*) has rigid, straight, spine-tipped leaves, regularly clustered around the stem. **2 Bosnian Pine** (*Pinus leucodermis*) has similar foliage but purple young cones.

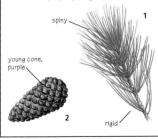

CORSICAN PINE

Type	conifer, evergreen tree
Height	30–50m
Habitat	forests, plantations
Flowering	June
Fruiting	ripens in second year
TRUNK AND CROWN	
Trunk	straight, rarely forked
Bark	grey, scaling above, blackish grey, deeply fissured below
Crown	conical or columnar, rarely becoming broader; branches in groups at same level
Twigs	hairless, yellowish brown
LEAVES	
Buds	conical, pointed, resinous
Leaves	paired on short shoots, 10–18cm, needle-shaped, twisted, flexible, pointed, greyish green, hairless; stalkless
Stipules	absent
FLOWERS AND FRUIT	
Flowers	♂ and ♀ cones on same tree
♂	clustered cones, each 8–13mm, yellow, scales purple-tipped
♀	egg-shaped cone, c5mm, pink
Fruit	woody cone, 6–8cm, egg-shaped, dull, yellowish or greyish brown; scales with broad, flattened end, with horizontal ridge and small central spine
Seeds	2 per scale, winged

Maritime Pine *Pinus pinaster*

A distinctive coastal species with a high, open crown and very long needles. Glossy, woody cones can stay closed on the tree for many years before they open and fall. Resin tapped from the trunk is used in the manufacture of turpentine and for flavouring wines.

Status: native to the western Mediterranean region; planted elsewhere for timber, shelter, sand-binding and resin.

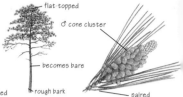

flat-topped

♂ cone cluster

becomes bare

rough bark

paired

stays attached

often pointed

young ♀ cone

slow to open

MARITIME PINE

Type	conifer, evergreen tree
Height	up to 40m
Habitat	hot, dry, coastal areas
Flowering	June
Fruiting	ripens in second year

TRUNK AND CROWN

Trunk	often twisted, becomes bare of branches below
Bark	reddish brown, becomes deeply fissured and ridged
Crown	conical or domed; branches in irregular wide-spaced groups
Twigs	grey or red-brown, hairless

LEAVES

Buds	10–20mm, tapered both ends, reddish brown, not resinous; scales bent back
Leaves	paired on short shoots, 10–25cm, needle-like, twisted, rigid, pointed, glossy grey-green, becoming deeper green, hairless; stalkless
Stipules	absent

FLOWERS AND FRUIT

Flowers	♂ and ♀ cones on same tree
♂	clustered cones, 8–10mm, yellow
♀	groups of 3–5 cones near stem-tip, each 10–12mm, egg-shaped, deep pink
Fruit	woody cones in small clusters, 8–22cm, conical, pointed, glossy brown; scales with horizontal ridges and often a broad, sharp point
Seeds	7–8mm with wing up to 30mm

SIMILAR TREES

1 Aleppo Pine (*Pinus halepensis*) has shorter leaves and smaller cones, with rounded scales and a short stalk, which curves backwards. **2 Calabrian Pine** (*Pinus brutia*) has leaves like the former and a cone like the latter, but with a short, straight stalk.

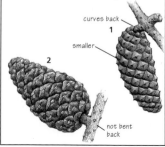

curves back

1

smaller

2

not bent back

Pinus pinea **Stone Pine**

This umbrella-shaped tree forms a distinctive element of the Mediterranean landscape and provides much-valued shade during long, hot summers. Huge woody cones contain seeds differing from those of other pines in having scarcely any wing. They are edible and eagerly sought.

Status: native to Portugal and the Mediterranean region to the Black Sea; often planted as a shade-tree.

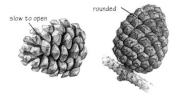

slow to open   rounded

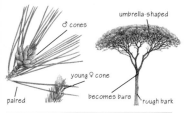

♂ cones   umbrella-shaped

young ♀ cone

paired   becomes bare   rough bark

SIMILAR TREES

Canary Island Pine (*Pinus canariensis*) is planted in the Mediterranean region for its high-quality timber. It differs in the very long leaves, grouped in threes, and seeds with a much larger wing.

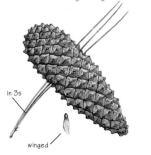

in 3s

winged

STONE PINE

Type	conifer, evergreen tree
Height	20–30m
Habitat	woods on light, sandy soils
Flowering	June
Fruiting	ripens in third year

TRUNK AND CROWN

Trunk	straight, widely forked above
Bark	greyish or reddish brown, fissured forming flat plates
Crown	broad, umbrella-shaped; branches stout, radiating
Twigs	greyish green to orange-brown, often curved, hairless

LEAVES

Buds	5–12mm, oval, reddish brown, not resinous; white-fringed scales curved backwards
Leaves	paired, 10–20cm, needle-like, rather thick, often twisted, pointed, greyish green, hairless; stalkless
Stipules	absent

FLOWERS AND FRUIT

Flowers	♂ and ♀ cones on same tree
♂	cluster of cones, each 10–14mm, egg-shaped, orange-brown
♀	solitary cone 8–12mm, yellowish green
Fruit	woody cone, 8–14cm, globular or slightly elongated, blunt, glossy brown; scale-tips rounded, with radiating folds
Seeds	15–20mm, nut-like with hard coat and narrow, papery wing

Shore Pine *Pinus contorta*

Not the most attractive of pines, this tough species survives to produce useful timber even in windswept places with very poor, waterlogged soils. It has short, paired leaves in bunches, and twisted buds. Cones remain on the tree and in nature ripen late, often after a forest fire.

Status: introduced from the Pacific coast of North America; widely planted in central and northern Europe for timber.

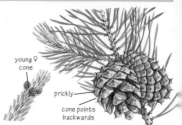

young ♀ cone

prickly

cone points backwards

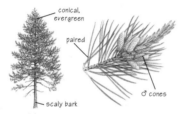

conical, evergreen

paired

♂ cones

scaly bark

SIMILAR TREES

Two other American timber trees differ in having longer leaves in threes and larger cones. **1 Monterey Pine** (*Pinus radiata*) has very asymmetrical cones. **2 Western Yellow-pine** (*Pinus ponderosa*) has symmetrical cones with strong prickles.

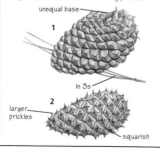

unequal base

1

in 3s

larger prickles

2

squarish

SHORE PINE

Type	conifer, evergreen tree
Height	10–30m
Habitat	plantations, often poor soils
Flowering	April–May
Fruiting	ripens in 2 or more years
TRUNK AND CROWN	
Trunk	straight, not forked
Bark	dark brown, scaly, becoming deeply fissured
Crown	slender, conical or columnar, eventually becoming domed; branches short, often twisted
Twigs	greenish brown, becoming orange-brown, hairless, shiny
LEAVES	
Buds	cylindrical, often twisted, brown, resinous
Leaves	paired, bunched, pointing towards branch tip, 4–7cm, needle-like, twisted, pointing, dark green, hairless; stalkless
Stipules	absent
FLOWERS AND FRUIT	
Flowers	♂ and ♀ on same tree
♂	tiny cones crowded together at base of new shoot, yellow
♀	2–4 cones near tip of shoot, c6mm, dark red, conical
Fruit	woody cone, pointing backwards on shoot, 2.5–7.5cm, conical, elongated, glossy yellowish brown; scale-tips angular with slender, fragile prickle
Seeds	4–5mm, wing c8mm

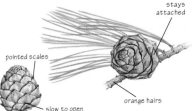

A rolla Pine is characterized by needles in groups of five and short cones with thin, pointed, rather than square-ended, scales. Cones ripen and fall after three years, the seeds released only as the cones are broken open by animals or eventually rot.

Status: native to the mountains of southern and central Europe; planted further north for timber and ornament.

stays attached

pointed scales

orange hairs

slow to open

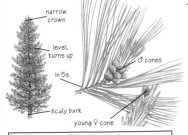

narrow crown

level, turns up

♂ cones

in 5s

scaly bark

young ♀ cone

AROLLA PINE

Type	conifer, evergreen tree
Height	10–30m
Habitat	dry slopes up to 3000m
Flowering	May
Fruiting	ripens in third year

TRUNK AND CROWN

Trunk	straight, sometimes forked
Bark	reddish grey, smooth with resin-blisters, becoming shallowly fissured, scaly
Crown	columnar to broadly conical; branches in groups at same level, tips turn upwards
Twigs	with brownish orange hairs

LEAVES

Buds	egg-shaped, pointed, pale brown; scales white-edged
Leaves	in fives, 5–9cm, needle-like, pointed, hairless, dark green with bluish inner face; stalkless
Stipules	absent

FLOWERS AND FRUIT

Flowers	♂ and ♀ on same tree
♂	cluster of cones, egg-shaped, yellow or purplish
♀	cone at stem-tip, c10mm, egg-shaped, dark red
Fruit	woody cone, 5–8cm, broadly egg-shaped, purple-tinged when young, becoming reddish brown; scales thin, broad, pointed
Seeds	2 per scale, 12–14mm, usually wingless, shed after cones fall

SIMILAR TREES

1 Weymouth Pine (*Pinus strobus*) and other five-needled pines have elongated, hanging, sticky cones and winged seeds. Two species differ in the hairless shoots. **2 Bhutan Pine** (*Pinus wallichiana*) has straight cones, **3 Macedonian Pine** (*Pinus peuce*) has shorter, curved cones.

sticky

long

hairless

shorter

1

2

3

Wellingtonia *Sequoiadendron giganteum*

A massive tree, though no plants in Europe come close to the true giants of western North America. They are very long-lived and may survive for around 3400 years, during which time they can reach over 90m with a buttressed trunk 7m or more across. Thick, fibrous, reddish bark acts as an insulating layer against forest fire and contributes to the longevity of the trees.

Status: introduced from the Sierra Nevada of California; frequently planted for ornament.

narrowly conical

evergreen

young ♀ cone

♂ cone

spirally arranged

hanging

blunt scales

spongy bark

woody

WELLINGTONIA

Type	conifer, evergreen tree
Height	to 50m (85m in North America)
Habitat	parks, ornamental woodland, large gardens
Flowering	March–April
Fruiting	ripens in second year

TRUNK AND CROWN

Trunk	straight, very broad and fluted at base
Bark	thick, fibrous, soft, reddish brown or darker brown
Crown	narrowly conical; drooping lower branches curve upwards
Twigs	stout, grey-green, covered by bases of scale-leaves

LEAVES

Buds	small, not scaly
Leaves	spirally arranged, 4–12mm, oval to spear-shaped, rather scale-like, flattened above, pointed, hairless; stalkless; blade joins stem
Stipules	absent

FLOWERS AND FRUIT

Flowers	♂ and ♀ on same tree
♂	cone at shoot-tip, pale yellow
♀	usually single cone at stem tip, upright, 8–10mm, green with pinkish spines
Fruit	solitary woody cone, 5–8cm, egg-shaped; 25–40 scales, square-ended, wrinkled, centre sunken with small spine
Seeds	3–7 per scale, winged

SIMILAR TREES

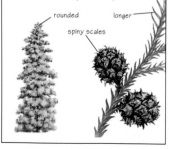

Japanese Red-cedar (*Cryptomeria japonica*) has more slender leaves but differs markedly in the smaller cones; each scale usually has five spines.

rounded

longer

spiny scales

Sequoia sempervirens **Coast Redwood**

In its native environment, this species can claim the record for the tallest living thing on earth, at over 110m. Many Coast Redwoods are around 1000 years old and individuals can reach 2600 years. In the event of lightning damage to the trunk, a tree can re-grow from suckers at the base and may form a grove of trees. This ability extends the life of a plant.

Status: introduced from western North America; widely planted, mainly in western Europe, for ornament or timber.

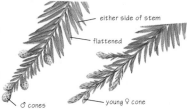

either side of stem
flattened
♂ cones
young ♀ cone

Irregularly conical
evergreen
small, woody
soft bark
blunt scales

COAST REDWOOD

Type	conifer, evergreen tree
Height	to 45m (100m in North America)
Habitat	parks, ornamental woodland
Flowering	February–March
Fruiting	ripens in second year

TRUNK AND CROWN

Trunk	straight, rarely forked, stout, suckers at base
Bark	reddish brown, thick, spongy, sometimes fissured
Crown	columnar; irregular rings of branches, lower bent downwards
Twigs	green, obscured by leaf-bases

LEAVES

Buds	c3mm, pointed, scaly
Leaves	mostly in 2 rows, 6–20mm, narrowly oblong, straight or curved, flattened, pointed, hairless, dark green, 2 white bands below; base of blade joins twig; spirally arranged on leading shoot, scale-like
Stipules	absent

FLOWERS AND FRUIT

Flowers		♂ and ♀ on same tree
	♂	cone at tip of side shoot, 1.5–2mm, whitish yellow
	♀	globular, green cone with bristle-tipped scales
Fruit		woody cone at branch tip, 2–3cm, egg-shaped, hanging, reddish brown; 15–20 scales, square-ended, centre sunken
Seeds		3–5 per scale, winged

SIMILAR TREES

Chinese Fir (*Cunninghamia lanceolata*) has longer, brighter leaves, clustered male cones, and fruiting cones with thin, pointed scales.

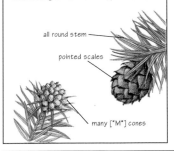

all round stem
pointed scales
many ["M"] cones

Swamp Cypress *Taxodium distichum*

An unusual deciduous conifer with pale, feathery foliage, which in autumn sheds not only leaves but entire leafy shoots. Grown by water it produces curious air-roots, which emerge from the ground as a knobbly mound and enable the roots to function when deprived of oxygen in mud.

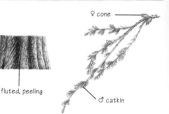

♀ cone

fluted, peeling

♂ catkin

Status: introduced from south-eastern North America; grown for ornament in western and central Europe.

deciduous

spiny

air-roots

SIMILAR TREES

Discovered in China during 1941 but previously known from fossils several million years old, **Dawn Redwood** (*Metasequoia glyptostroboides*) differs in the paired leaves, paired shoots and blunt cone-scales.

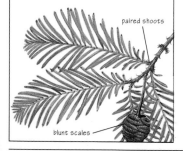

paired shoots

blunt scales

SWAMP CYPRESS

Type	conifer, deciduous tree
Height	20–30m (50m in America)
Habitat	usually planted by water
Flowering	March–April
Fruiting	ripens in first year

TRUNK AND CROWN

Trunk	straight, develops buttresses
Bark	reddish brown, fibrous, peels, vertical or spiral fissures
Crown	conical with rounded top
Twigs	reddish brown, slender long shoots, short side-shoots shed with leaves in autumn

LEAVES

Buds	rounded, small, scaly
Leaves	spirally placed on long shoots, on alternate sides of short shoots, 1–2cm, thin, flat, pointed, pale green, 2 grey bands below, turning reddish brown in autumn; stalkless
Stipules	absent

FLOWERS AND FRUIT

Flowers	♂ and ♀ flowers on same tree, at shoot tip
♂	3–4 hanging catkins, 6–20cm, branched, slender, purplish, becoming yellow with pollen
♀	tiny cone, green
Fruit	woody cone, 2–3cm, globular, ripens purplish brown, stalk 2–4mm; scales spine-tipped
Seeds	2 per scale, irregularly 3-angled, narrowly winged

evergreen

♀ flowers

fleshy, red

♂ flowers

flat, dark

forks low

With distinctive dark foliage and red berries, Yew is a common feature of churchyards, and its strong, supple timber had many uses. Ancient trees occur, more than a thousand years old, with massive, hollow trunks.

Status: native to most of Europe except for the extreme east and north; commonly planted for ornament.

YEW

Type	conifer, evergreen tree or sometimes a shrub
Height	10–25m
Habitat	woods, scrub, mainly on lime-rich soils, planted elswhere
Flowering	February–April
Fruiting	August–September

TRUNK AND CROWN

Trunk	short, forked, sometimes twisted, stout and hollow
Bark	light brown or reddish, thin, scaly and peeling
Crown	conical or domed; branches angled upwards or spreading
Twigs	green, grooved

LEAVES

Buds	minute, egg-shaped, green
Leaves	on 2 sides of most shoots, spiral on upright shoots, 1–3cm, needle-like, flat, pointed, edge curved under, hairless, very dark green above, 2 yellowish green bands below; stalk short

FLOWERS AND FRUIT

Flowers	♂ and ♀ flowers on different trees
♂	cones clustered beneath year-old shoots, 5–6mm, globular, turning yellow with pollen
♀	cone, 1–2mm, green
Fruit	berry-like, 8–12mm, solitary, cup-like, red fleshy layer around woody, nut-like centre
Seeds	solitary, 5–7mm, elongated

SIMILAR TREES

Two species have longer foliage and larger, greenish fruits. **1 California Nutmeg** (*Torreya californica*) has branches in rings, large, conical buds, spine-tipped leaves and an egg-shaped fruit. **2 Plum-fruited Yew** (*Podocarpus andinus*) has softer, brighter blue-green leaves and white-speckled fruit.

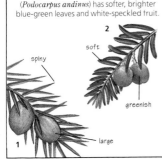

2

soft

spiny

greenish

1

large

Lawson Cypress *Chamaecyparis lawsoniana*

Very commonly planted, this North American species is one of the most popular of all ornamental conifers. The foliage has a distinctive, parsley-like smell. Many cultivated variants exist.

Status: introduced from western North America; planted for ornament, timber and shelter; sometimes naturalized.

evergreen

scale-like, paired

pale below

♂ cone

young ♀ cone

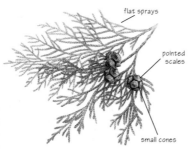

flat sprays

pointed scales

small cones

SIMILAR TREES

Two cultivated species from Japan have brighter leaves, marked with white below and lacking the gland. **1 Hinoki Cypress** (*Chamaecyparis obtusa*) has blunt, often rounded leaves. **2 Sawara Cypress** (*Chamaecyparis pisifera*) has pointed leaves spread apart at the tips; the very slender shoots droop in many plants.

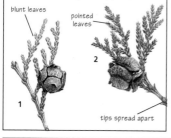

blunt leaves

pointed leaves

1

2

tips spread apart

LAWSON CYPRESS

Type	conifer, evergreen tree
Height	up to 45m
Habitat	plantations, parks, gardens
Flowering	March–April
Fruiting	September–October

TRUNK AND CROWN

Trunk	straight, sometimes forked
Bark	smooth, greyish brown, becomes cracked into vertical plates
Crown	conical; few large branches, sometimes in irregular rings, leading shoot droops
Twigs	forming flat sprays, often hanging at tips

LEAVES

Buds	tiny, hidden by leaves
Leaves	paired, 0.5–2mm, scale-like, diamond-shaped with central, translucent gland, pointed tip curves inwards, hairless, dark green above, paler below; stalkless; occasionally some needle-like leaves
Stipules	absent

FLOWERS AND FRUIT

Flowers	♂ and ♀ on same tree
♂	cone 2–5mm, at shoot-tip, blackish scales turn red, then yellow with pollen
♀	globular cone, bluish green
Fruit	woody cone, 5–8mm, globular, often bluish, turns yellowish brown; scales in 4 pairs, wrinkled, small central spine
Seeds	usually 2–4 per scale, winged

Cupressocyparis leylandii **Leyland Cypress**

Renowned for rapid growth, this hybrid conifer is popular for hedging and wherever a screen is required quickly. It is a cross between species of two genera, the form differing slightly depending whether Nootka Cypress or Monterey Cypress was the female parent.

Status: of garden origin; very commonly planted for ornament.

scale-leaves

evergreen

globular

raised centre

♂ cone   ♀ cone

sometimes yellow

LEYLAND CYPRESS

Type	conifer, evergreen tree
Height	up to 35m
Habitat	parks, gardens, plantations
Flowering	March
Fruiting	October
TRUNK AND CROWN	
Trunk	straight, sometimes forked
Bark	reddish brown, forming shallow, vertical fissures
Crown	narrowly columnar to broadly conical; branches crowded, angled upwards, retained to base, leading shoot leans
Twigs	slender, with old scale-leaves; forms sprays of foliage
LEAVES	
Buds	tiny, hidden by leaves
Leaves	scale-like, paired in 4 ranks, 0.5–2mm, all similar, closely pressed together, pointed, hairless, dark green or grey-green above, yellowish green below; stalkless
Stipules	absent
FLOWERS AND FRUIT	
Flowers	♂ and ♀flowers on same plant
♂	cone 3–5mm, greenish, turning yellow with pollen
♀	small, green, globular cone
Fruit	woody cone, rarely produced by some trees, 2–3cm, globular, brown; few paired scales, each with blunt central spine
Seeds	rarely produced, 2–6 per scale

SIMILAR TREES

Both parent species are commonly planted.
1 Nootka Cypress (*Chamaecyparis nootkatenis*) has dull green foliage, which is rough and oily smelling; small cones ripen in two years. Tolerant of salt-laden winds,
2 Monterey Cypress (*Cupressus macrocarpa*) becomes a large tree with flattish plates of foliage and large, lumpy cones.

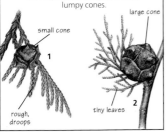

small cone

large cone

1

2

rough, droops

tiny leaves

Italian Cypress *Cupressus sempervirens*

An unmistakable feature of many Italian landscapes, this narrowly columnar conifer is widely planted for its distinctive habit. The wild form is rarely planted as its broad, irregularly conical outline is far less striking.

Status: native to south-eastern Europe; much planted for ornament or timber in southern Europe, often naturalized.

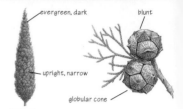

evergreen, dark
blunt
upright, narrow
globular cone

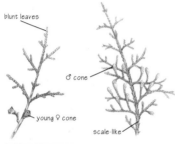

blunt leaves
♂ cone
young ♀ cone
scale-like

ITALIAN CYPRESS

Type	conifer, evergreen tree
Height	15–30m
Habitat	planted mostly near houses
Flowering	March
Fruiting	ripens in second year

TRUNK AND CROWN

Trunk	straight, often forked above
Bark	grey-brown, shallow fissures and twisted, scaly ridges
Crown	narrowly columnar with upright branches or sometimes conical
Twigs	slightly 4-angled, curved upwards near tip, reddish brown

LEAVES

Buds	tiny, hidden by leaves
Leaves	scale-like, paired in 4 ranks, pressed together, 0.5–1mm, diamond-shaped, blunt, dull, dark green, hairless; stalkless; needle-like leaves rarely on leading shoots
Stipules	absent

FLOWERS AND FRUIT

Flowers	♂ and ♀ cones on same tree, each at tip of small shoot
♂	elliptical cone, 4–8mm, green, turning yellow with pollen
♀	oblong cone, 3–4mm
Fruit	solitary cone, 2.5–4cm, shortly oblong or globular, reddish brown to yellowish grey; 4–7 pairs of wavy-edged scales, each with broad point
Seeds	8–20 per cone scale, flattened, narrowly winged

SIMILAR TREES

Two species with broad crowns have smaller cones of 6–8 scales. **1 Mexican Cypress** (*Cupressus lusitanica*) has dull green, scarcely scented foliage, spreading leaf-tips and bluish young cones.
2 Smooth Cypress (*Cupressus glabra*) has smooth, scaling bark and blue-grey, scented, resin-flecked leaves.

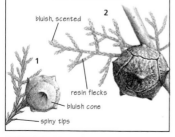

bluish, scented
2
1
resin flecks
bluish cone
spiny tips

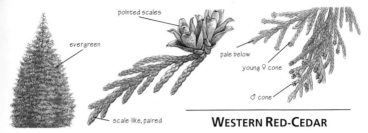

pointed scales

evergreen

pale below

young ♀ cone

♂ cone

scale-like, paired

WESTERN RED-CEDAR

Type	conifer, evergreen tree
Height	up to 40m (50m in America)
Habitat	plantations, parks, gardens
Flowering	March
Fruiting	October of first year
TRUNK AND CROWN	
Trunk	straight or forked above, fluted below; lower branches may root forming new trunks
Bark	reddish brown, soft, thick with lifting strips
Crown	conical or irregular; lower branches curve down, leading shoot upright
Twigs	reddish brown shoots form flattened sprays of foliage
LEAVES	
Buds	tiny, hidden by leaves
Leaves	scale-like, paired in 4 ranks, side pair larger, 1.5–3mm, oval, blunt, with tiny gland, glossy deep green above, paler below with whitish streaks, hairless; stalkless
Stipules	absent
FLOWERS AND FRUIT	
Flowers	♂ and ♀ cones on same tree
♂	cone 1–2mm, dark red, becomes pale yellow with pollen
♀	cone 2–5mm, yellowish green
Fruit	woody cone, 1–1.5cm, elliptical, upright, green, turns brown; 5–6 pairs of spine-tipped scales
Seeds	2–3 per scale, winged

Old, well-grown trees make magnificent specimens, with huge lower branches curved down to the ground, eventually rooting to become new trunks. Glossy, dark green foliage has a distinctive, fruity scent, and small, elongated cones have spine-tipped scales.

Status: introduced from western North America; commonly planted for timber, ornament and hedging.

SIMILAR TREES

1 White-cedar (*Thuja occidentalis*) has leaves with a conspicuous gland, lacking whitish marks below, and blunt cone-scales.
2 Chinese White-cedar (*Thuja orientalis*) has uniformly green, scentless leaves, and cones with fewer pairs of scales, each with a strong, curved spine.

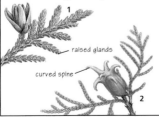

raised glands

curved spine

2

Juniper *Juniperus communis*

Squat and spiny, Juniper is a common shrub scattered on chalk downland, but also forms an understorey to pine woodland, growing to tree size. Highly variable wild plants include low-growing shrubs on sea cliffs, and narrow columns on hills inland.

Status: native to north-western Europe, Asia and North America; planted for ornament.

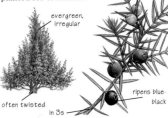

evergreen, irregular

often twisted

berry-like

ripens blue-black

In 3s

♂ cone

♀ cone

1 pale band

SIMILAR TREES

Two Mediterranean species differ in having longer leaves with two pale bands.
1 Syrian Juniper (*Juniperus drupacea*) has much larger blue-black fruits. More widespread, **2 Prickly Juniper** (*Juniperus oxycedrus*) has fruits ripening through yellow to dull red or purple.

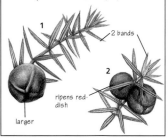

1

2

2 bands

ripens reddish

larger

JUNIPER

Type	conifer, evergreen shrub or sometimes a tree
Height	2–5m, rarely 15m
Habitat	grassland, scrub, woods; lime-rich soils or shallow peat
Flowering	April–June
Fruiting	after 2–3 years

TRUNK AND CROWN

Trunk	short, often twisted or bent
Bark	reddish brown, peels in strips
Crown	very variable, usually irregularly conical, sometimes low-growing or columnar
Twigs	greenish or reddish brown, hairless, the lower twigs often retain dead leaves

LEAVES

Buds	small, hidden by spiny leaves
Leaves	clusters of 3 around stem, 5–20mm, needle-like, sharply pointed, hairless, with broad, white band above, grey-green below; base jointed
Stipules	absent

FLOWERS AND FRUIT

Flowers	♂ and ♀ on different trees, solitary at leaf-base
	♂ cone 6–8mm, yellow
	♀ cone 2–3mm, greenish
Fruit	berry-like cone, 6–9mm, globular, solitary at leaf-base, turning black with bluish waxy layer
Seeds	3, separate, not winged

The tallest of the commonly grown junipers, this slow-growing tree can form a remarkably narrow column. Its foliage has a pleasant aromatic scent.

Status: introduced from eastern North America; much grown for ornament and for timber in central and southern Europe.

young ♀ cone — bluish — egg-shaped

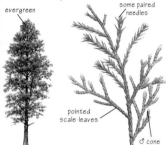

evergreen — some paired needles — pointed scale-leaves — ♂ cone

PENCIL CEDAR

Type	conifer, evergreen tree
Height	15–30m
Habitat	parks, gardens, plantations
Flowering	March–April
Fruiting	September of first year

TRUNK AND CROWN

Trunk	straight, becomes buttressed
Bark	reddish brown, peels in long, narrow strips
Crown	conical or columnar; branches diverge narrowly
Twigs	very slender

LEAVES

Buds	tiny, concealed by leaves
Leaves	juvenile leaves needle-like, paired, 5–6mm, pointed, often at shoot-tip; adult leaves scale-like, paired in 4 ranks, 0.5–1.5mm, pointed tips spread apart, dark green or bluish green, hairless; stalkless
Stipules	absent

FLOWERS AND FRUIT

Flowers	♂ and ♀ on different trees	
	♂	rounded, yellow cone, 4–5mm, at shoot tip
	♀	green cone, 2–3mm, at base of leaf
Fruit		solitary, berry-like, 4–6mm, egg-shaped, ripens brownish violet with bluish waxy layer, short-stalked
Seeds		1 or 2, separate

SIMILAR TREES

Two species have unpleasant-smelling foliage and globular fruits. **1 Chinese Juniper** (*Juniperus chinensis*) has pale-edged scale-leaves and larger fruits, showing scale outlines. Apparently forming hybrids with the latter, **2 Savin** (*Juniperus sabina*) is a native shrub with blunt leaves, pressed together, and small fruits.

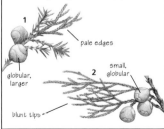

1 — pale edges — globular, larger — small, globular — 2 — blunt tips

Phoenicean Juniper *Juniperus phoenicea*

The curious cord-like foliage of this Mediterranean species consists of widely branched shoots, with minute, pale-edged scale-leaves pressed tightly together. A small tree or sometimes a shrub, it also has a mat-like form that is found by the coast. Amongst the Mediterranean species, it is distinctive in having up to nine seeds in the fruit.

Status: native to southern Europe; rarely cultivated.

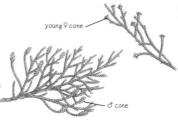

young ♀ cone

♂ cone

tiny scale-leaves

berry-like

ripen red

evergreen

SIMILAR TREES

Native to mountains of southern France and Spain, **Spanish Juniper** (*Juniperus thurifera*) has paired leaves, which lack the pale, minutely toothed edge. Its slightly smaller fruits ripen to blackish purple.

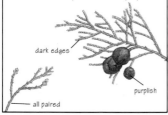

dark edges

purplish

all paired

PHOENICEAN JUNIPER

Type	conifer, evergreen tree or shrub
Height	2–8m
Habitat	dry, rocky places, often coasts
Flowering	March–April
Fruiting	ripens in second year

TRUNK AND CROWN

Trunk	irregular, short
Bark	scaly, reddish brown
Crown	broad, irregular, rarely low-growing; branches spread apart
Twigs	slender, 4-angled, scaly

LEAVES

Buds	tiny, concealed by leaves
Leaves	adult leaves scale-like, paired, in 4 ranks, closely overlapping, 0.7–1mm, oval or diamond-shaped with sunken gland, blunt or slightly pointed, yellowish green with whitish, finely toothed edge; stalkless; juvenile leaves rarely present, needle-like, groups of 3, 5–14mm, pointed, 2 whitish bands on both sides
Stipules	absent

FLOWERS AND FRUIT

Flowers	♂ and ♀ on same tree
	♀ cone 4–5mm, at shoot-tip
	♂ cone 2–3mm, on small shoot, blackish
Fruit	berry-like, 8–14mm, globular or egg-shaped, green with waxy layer, ripens dark red
Seeds	3–9, separate

Juniperus foetidissima **Stinking Juniper**

So-called because of the strong, disagreeable odour given off by the foliage when lightly bruised, Stinking Juniper is largely restricted to mountains of the Balkan Peninsula and Crimea. A scale-leaved species with irregularly branched, four-angled twigs, it is identified by uniformly coloured leaves with pointed tips spread apart.

Status: native to south-eastern Europe; rarely cultivated elsewhere.

♂ cone

tips spread apart

blackish fruit

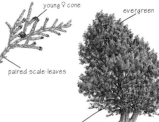

young ♀ cone

evergreen

paired scale-leaves

strong smelling

STINKING JUNIPER

Type	conifer, evergreen tree
Height	up to 17m
Habitat	mountains, rocky places
Flowering	March–April
Fruiting	ripens in second year

TRUNK AND CROWN

Trunk	straight or sometimes forked
Bark	reddish brown, becoming grey and bleached, scaly
Crown	narrowly conical, becoming broad and irregular
Twigs	c1mm thick, 4-angled, scaly, branching irregularly

LEAVES

Buds	tiny, concealed by leaves
Leaves	adult leaves scale-like, paired, in 4 ranks, overlapping, 1.5–2mm, oval or angular, mostly without gland, pointed, tips spread apart, uniformly dull, grey-green, not pale edged, hairless; stalkless; juvenile leaves paired, rarely present
Stipules	absent

FLOWERS AND FRUIT

Flowers	♂ and ♀ on same tree or sometimes different trees
♂	cone 4–5mm, at shoot-tip
♀	cone 2–3mm, on small shoot
Fruit	solitary berry-like cone, 7–12mm, globular, waxy when young, ripening dark reddish brown to almost black
Seeds	usually 1 or 2, separate

SIMILAR TREES

Often confused with Stinking Juniper, **Greek Juniper** (*Juniperus excelsa*) is a taller tree with slender, rounded twigs; smaller, less pointed scale-leaves, pressed together; and fruits with 4–6 seeds.

tips close together

rounded twigs

49

White Willow *Salix alba*

Tall and graceful, this species is commonly found by water. It is readily identified by its leaves, which are silvery and silky, and slender with a very finely toothed edge. Near habitation many are pollarded; cut at head height they produce a regular supply of small timber.

Status: native, common to most of Europe, but rarer in the extreme south; widely planted for ornament and stabilizing river banks.

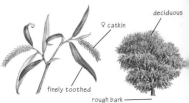

deciduous
♀ catkin
finely toothed
rough bark

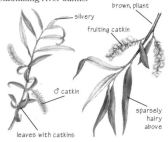

silvery
fruiting catkin
brown, pliant
♂ catkin
sparsely hairy above
leaves with catkins

SIMILAR TREES

Two subspecies are often cultivated.
1 Cricket-bat Willow (*Salix alba* subsp. *coerulea*) has purplish twigs and dull, bluish leaves becoming almost hairless. **2 Golden Willow** (*Salix alba* subsp. *vitellina*) has orange or yellow twigs.

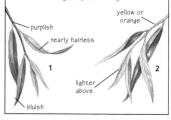

purplish
nearly hairless
yellow or orange
1
2
lighter above
bluish

WHITE WILLOW

Type	deciduous tree
Height	10–25m
Habitat	rivers, damp or wet soils
Flowering	April–May
Fruiting	July

TRUNK AND CROWN

Trunk	mostly upright, often pollarded
Bark	thick ridges, dark grey-brown
Crown	young narrow; old broad; branches angled upwards
Twigs	silkily hairy, becoming smooth, pliant, greenish brown

LEAVES

Buds	egg-shaped, pointed, hairy
Leaves	on alternate side of shoot, 6–10cm, narrowly spear-shaped or elliptical, with pointed tip, small, equal teeth and tapered base, silkily hairy above becoming almost hairless, with greyish, matted hairs below; stalk 5–8mm, hairy
Stipules	very slender, soon falling

FLOWERS AND FRUIT

Flowers	♂ and ♀ catkins on separate trees, opening with leaves
♂	cylindrical catkin, 4–6cm, of tiny flowers, almost upright
Stamens	2 per ♂ flower, separate, yellow
♀	catkin 3–4cm
Stigmas	2, forked, on short style
Ovaries	1 per ♀ flower; stalkless
Fruit	catkin of small capsules, each c4mm, releasing seeds
Seeds	with tuft of cottony hairs

S imilar to White Willow, this large tree
is distinguished by glossy, unevenly
toothed leaves. If twisted, brittle twigs
crack at the base. In water, Crack Willow
produces fine, red, coral-like rootlets.

Status: native or
planted, common in
much of Europe.

deciduous

♀ catkin

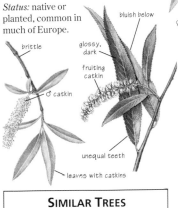

bluish below

brittle

glossy,
dark

fruiting
catkin

♂ catkin

unequal teeth

leaves with catkins

CRACK WILLOW

Type	deciduous tree
Height	10–18m
Habitat	deep, moist soils, by rivers
Flowering	April–May
Fruiting	June–July

TRUNK AND CROWN

Trunk	stout, often pollarded
Bark	thick ridges, dull grey
Crown	broad, conical or domed; widely branched
Twigs	brittle, becoming smooth, glossy, greenish brown

LEAVES

Buds	conical, yellowish brown
Leaves	9–15cm, narrowly spear-shaped with slender tip, coarse, uneven teeth, wedge-shaped base, sparse hairs that soon fall, glossy, dark green above, bluish below; stalk 5–15mm
Stipules	3–8mm, slender, soon falling

FLOWERS AND FRUIT

Flowers	♂ and ♀ catkins on separate trees, in clusters on leafy shoots
	♂ catkin 4–6cm, cylindrical; scales 2–3mm, sparsely hairy
Stamens	2, rarely 3 per ♂ flower, separate, yellow
	♀ with larger scales than ♂
Stigmas	2, each 2-lobed; style short
Ovaries	1, hairless
Fruit	catkin of capsules, each 4–5mm, or commonly sterile, some releasing seeds
Seeds	with cottony hairs

SIMILAR TREES

One of the hybrids between White Willow
and Crack Willow, **1 Basford Willow** (*Salix
x rubens*) differs from the former by glossy
leaves and short catkin scales, and the latter
by reddish twigs and slender, fine-toothed
leaves. **2 Bay Willow** (*Salix pentandra*) has
broad, glossy leaves, which are sticky and
fragrant when young, and male flowers with
five or more stamens.

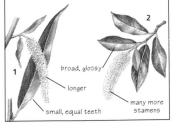

2

broad, glossy

1

longer

small, equal teeth

many more
stamens

Goat Willow *Salix caprea*

More commonly a shrub than a tree, this broad-leaved plant is most distinctive in spring, when leafless shoots are smothered with short, soft catkins. Stripped twigs have distinct raised lines.

Status: native and common to much of Europe.

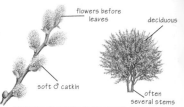

flowers before leaves

deciduous

soft ♂ catkin

often several stems

hairy below

♀ catkin

stout twig

dull green

fruiting catkin

GOAT WILLOW

Type	deciduous shrub or tree
Height	rarely more than 10m
Habitat	hedgerows, woods, scrub
Flowering	March–April
Fruiting	May–June

TRUNK AND CROWN

Trunk	often several
Bark	fissured, greyish brown
Crown	broad, rather open branches mostly angled upwards
Twigs	thick, stiff

LEAVES

Buds	egg-shaped, blunt, glossy
Leaves	5–12cm, oval, elliptical or oblong, with tip shortly pointed, edge often wavy, toothed, base wedge-shaped or rounded, dull green above with sparse hairs, grey-green below with thick, soft hairs; stalk 1–2.5cm, stiff, hairy
Stipules	8–12mm, ear-shaped, toothed

FLOWERS AND FRUIT

Flowers	♂ and ♀ catkins on separate trees, near twig tip, before leaves
	♂ catkins 15–25mm, egg-shaped or shortly cylindrical; scales broadly oval, blackish with silvery grey hairs
Stamens	2 per ♂ flower, yellow
	♀ catkins similar to ♂
Stigmas	2, each often 2-lobed
Ovaries	1, 4–5mm, densely hairy
Fruit	catkins of small capsules, each capsule c10mm
Seeds	with cottony hairs

SIMILAR TREES

1 Grey Willow (*Salix cinerea* subsp. *cinerea*) has dark brown twigs and narrower, more oblong leaves, which are grey-green above and whitish grey with short hairs below. It is common through much of Europe except for the west, where it is replaced by **2 Rusty Willow** (*Salix cinerea* subsp. *oleifolia*). This has rougher leaves, which are glossy and dark green above with reddish hairs below.

whitish hairs

dark, glossy

narrower

reddish hairs

1

2

Salix daphnoides **Violet Willow**

An ornamental species, Violet Willow has dark, reddish twigs overlaid with a bluish, waxy layer, which gradually rubs off. Crimson buds open as large, softly hairy catkins before the narrow leaves appear. It is often grown for winter colour.

Status: native, scattered across northern and central Europe; widely planted for ornament.

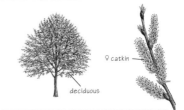

♀ catkin

deciduous

♂ catkins — glossy, dark — unequal teeth — bluish below — softly hairy — red buds — bluish coating — catkins before leaves — fruiting catkin

VIOLET WILLOW

Type	deciduous shrub or tree
Height	6–8m (max 12m)
Habitat	damp places
Flowering	February–March
Fruiting	May–June

TRUNK AND CROWN

Trunk	often several
Bark	rather smooth, greyish brown
Crown	rounded; branches upright or spreading
Twigs	glossy, dark reddish brown with bluish waxy covering

LEAVES

Buds	pointed, flattened, dark red
Leaves	on alternate sides of stem, 7–12cm, oblong or oval, leathery, shortly pointed, edge toothed, base wedge-shaped, slightly woolly but becoming hairless, glossy dark green above, bluish below; stalk 7–20mm, grooved above
Stipules	5–12mm, oval, toothed

FLOWERS AND FRUIT

Flowers	♂ and ♀ catkins on separate trees, before the leaves
♂	catkin 2–4cm, cylindrical, stalkless; scales c2mm, oval, blackish, silkily hairy
Stamens	2, separate; anthers yellow
♀	catkin smaller than ♂
Stigmas	2 per ♀ flower
Ovaries	1 per ♀ flower, hairless
Fruit	catkin of small, narrowly egg-shaped capsules, each c4mm
Seeds	with tuft of cottony hairs

SIMILAR TREES

1 *Salix acutifolia* has more slender twigs, and narrower leaves with a long point and more veins. Almost invariably a shrub, **2 Purple Willow** (*Salix purpurea*) has mostly paired leaves; each male flower has two red stamens fused as one. The hybrid between Violet and Purple Willows (*Salix x calliantha*) makes a small tree.

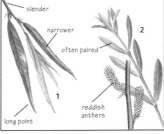

slender — narrower — often paired — long point — reddish anthers

Osier *Salix viminalis*

Commonly lining rivers and streams, this willow forms a large shrub or tree. Plants are cut annually to provide slender shoots, which are stripped of bark for basket-weaving. Male plants are attractive in spring when covered with furry, yellow catkins.

Status: native mainly to central and western Europe; widely planted elsewhere.

♂ catkin

♀ catkin

not toothed

branches turn upwards

fruiting catkin

edge turned under

dull green

deciduous

SIMILAR TREES

1 Hoary Willow (*Salix elaeagnos*) has even narrower leaves with matt white, felted hairs below, curved catkins and a smooth ovary. Though easily distinguished by broader, toothed leaves, the fragrant **2 Almond Willow** (*Salix triandra*) is grown like Osier, as is the hybrid (*S. x mollissima*) between these species.

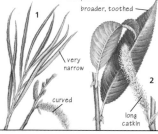

broader, toothed

1

very narrow

curved

2

long catkin

OSIER

Type	deciduous shrub or tree
Height	3–6m, rarely 10m
Habitat	usually near water
Flowering	February–April
Fruiting	May–June

TRUNK AND CROWN

Trunk	sometimes several
Bark	fissured, greyish brown
Crown	usually narrow, top rounded
Twigs	long, pliant, hairy, becoming glossy yellowish brown

LEAVES

Buds	3–7mm, egg-shaped, often blunt, hairy, becoming smooth
Leaves	on alternate sides of stem, 10–18cm, narrow with long tip, edge not toothed but turned under and often wavy, base wedge-shaped, dull green with few hairs above, silky, silvery hairs below
Stipules	5–10mm, slender, soon falling

FLOWERS AND FRUIT

Flowers	[*M*] and ♀ catkins on different plants, before leaves appear
	♂ catkin 15–30mm, egg-shaped or cylindrical; scales *c*2mm, oval, blunt, reddish brown, hairy
Stamens	2 per ♂ flower, yellow
	♀ catkin similar to ♂
Stigmas	2, undivided; style slender
Ovaries	1, densely hairy
Fruit	catkin of small, egg-shaped capsules, each to 6mm, releasing many seeds
Seeds	with tuft of cottony hairs

Salix myrsinifolia **Dark-leaved Willow**

This very variable willow is more often a low, broad shrub than a small tree. It belongs to a group of species mainly of northern regions and occurs in mountains, though not at the highest altitudes. Like other willows, this species is food for larvae of many butterflies and moths.

Status: native to northern and central Europe.

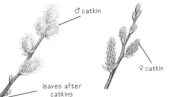

♂ catkin

♀ catkin

leaves after catkins

dull green

unevenly toothed

deciduous

bluish below

fruiting catkin

often several trunks

DARK-LEAVED WILLOW

Type	deciduous shrub or small tree
Height	1–4m
Habitat	by streams, pools, in mountains
Flowering	April–May
Fruiting	July–August
TRUNK AND CROWN	
Trunk	often several, slender
Bark	slightly fissured, dark grey
Crown	broad; rather widely branched
Twigs	slender, usually with whitish hairs, dull brownish green
LEAVES	
Buds	blunt, shortly hairy
Leaves	alternating on stem, 2–6.5cm, oval or elliptical, shortly pointed, unevenly toothed, base wedge-shaped or rounded, sparsely hairy to hairless, dull green above, bluish below; stalk usually less than 1cm
Stipules	rather large, ear-shaped
FLOWERS AND FRUIT	
Flowers	♂ and ♀ catkins on separate trees, produced before leaves
	♂ catkin 15–40mm, cylindrical; scales 1–2.5mm, dark, thinly hairy
Stamens	2 per ♂ flower, separate, yellow
	♀ catkin less compact than ♂
Stigmas	2 mostly forked; style slender
Ovaries	1 per ♀ flower, hairless
Fruit	catkin of small, tapered capsules, each 5–7mm, releasing seeds
Seeds	many, each with long hairs

SIMILAR TREES

Tea-leaved Willow (*Salix phylicifolia*) has glossy brown, usually hairless twigs, tougher leaves, which are glossy green above, smaller stipules, and the ovary is hairy. Catkins are usually produced with the leaves. It forms hybrids (*S. x tetrapla*) with Dark-leaved Willow.

leaves with ♀catkins

tougher, glossy

glossy, hairless

Golden Weeping-willow
Salix x *sepulcralis* nv. *chrysocoma*

A graceful weeping tree, so commonly planted that at times it appears native. It is easily distinguished from other willow species by its pendulous shoots, yellow twigs and bright, yellowish green leaves. For a long time it was treated as a variant of White Willow but it is a hybrid between the golden form of that species and the following Chinese species. Largely sterile, it is propagated by cuttings.

Status: cultivated origin; widely grown for ornament.

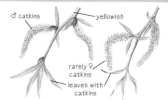

♂ catkins
yellowish
rarely ♀ catkins
leaves with catkins

deciduous
hairless below
rarely fruits
fine teeth
yellowish-green

weeping shoots

GOLDEN WEEPING-WILLOW

Type	deciduous tree
Height	8–22m
Habitat	mainly wet places
Flowering	April
TRUNK AND CROWN	
Trunk	stout, upright
Bark	network of fissures and ridges, pale greyish brown
Crown	broad, domed; branches mostly angled upwards
Twigs	slender, weeping, greenish yellow; sparse hairs soon fall
LEAVES	
Buds	slender, pointed, brown, more or less hairless
Leaves	on alternate sides of stem, 7–12cm, narrowly spear-shaped with slender tip, teeth fine and even, base wedge-shaped, sparsely hairy, becoming hairless, bright, yellowish green above, paler below; stalk up to 8mm
Stipules	small, toothed, soon falling
FLOWERS AND FRUIT	
Flowers	usually ♂ catkins only, with leaves
♂	catkins 3–6cm, slender, cylindrical, pendulous, yellow; scales c2mm, oblong or oval, thinly hairy
Stamens	2 per ♂ flower, separate
♀	sometimes a few ♀ catkins
Stigmas	2, each forked; style short
Ovaries	1, stalkless, hairless
Fruit	usually sterile

SIMILAR TREES

Chinese Weeping-willow (*Salix babylonica*) has brown twigs and short, almost stalkless catkins. Relatively tender and short-lived in western Europe, it is much less planted.

brown

shorter

56

Populus trichocarpa **Western Balsam-poplar**

After a spring shower, the balsamic fragrance of Balsam-poplars pervades the air for many metres around; thick resin exuded by opening buds is the source of this scent. Of rapid growth, this handsome tree soon makes a useful screen or shelter.

Status: introduced from northern North America; widely planted for ornament and timber.

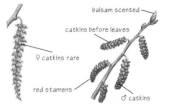

balsam scented

catkins before leaves

♀ catkins rare

red stamens

♂ catkins

toothed

whitish below

deciduous

fruiting catkin

WESTERN BALSAM-POPLAR

Type	deciduous tree
Height	to 35m (60m in North America)
Habitat	roadsides, plantations
Flowering	March–April
Fruiting	May–June

TRUNK AND CROWN

Trunk	upright or angled upwards
Bark	smooth, greenish grey, dark greyish brown below, fissured
Crown	narrow, conical; many main branches, angled upwards
Twigs	angular or rounded, becoming smooth, yellowish grey

LEAVES

Buds	mostly 10–15mm, egg-shaped, pointed, glossy, reddish brown, very sticky, fragrant
Leaves	on alternate sides of stem, 5–15cm (max. 23cm), oval, thick-textured, shortly pointed with shallow, blunt teeth, glossy green above, whitish beneath; stalk 1.5–4cm, stout, grooved above

FLOWERS AND FRUIT

Flowers	♂ and ♀ catkins on separate trees, before leaves
	♂ catkin 5–9cm, red, scales 3–5mm, fringed, sparsely hairy
Stamens	20–60 per ♂ flower
	♀ catkin 6–10cm, green, rarely produced in western Europe
Stigmas	2, broad, irregularly lobed
Ovaries	1, egg-shaped, hairy
Fruit	catkin 15–20cm, of small capsules, each splitting open
Seeds	many, each with tuft of hairs

SIMILAR TREES

Several other poplars have scented buds and are white beneath the leaves. **1 Eastern Balsam-poplar** (*Populus balsamifera*) produces many suckers; their oval leaves have a rounded base, and the stalk is up to 7cm long. **2 Balm-of-Gilead** (*Populus candicans*) has a more slender tip and a heart-shaped base to the leaf.

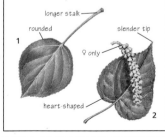

longer stalk

rounded

slender tip

♀ only

1

heart-shaped

2

White Poplar *Populus alba*

Easily recognized by the dark leaves which flash white beneath in the breeze, and the pale grey bark of the upper trunk handsomely marked with blackish diamonds. Leaves of strong, sucker shoots are maple-like and lobed, though other leaves have irregular teeth.

Status: mainly central and eastern Europe; commonly planted in the west for ornament and shelter.

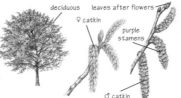

deciduous   leaves after flowers
♀ catkin
purple stamens
♂ catkin

dark above

dense white hairs

pale

diamond-shaped marks

lobed or toothed

SIMILAR TREES

Grey Poplar (*Populus x canescens*) is generally considered to be a hybrid between White Poplar and Aspen, though some regard it as a species. The leaves are grey beneath, becoming hairless, and the edge has blunt, wavy teeth.

mostly ♂

grey below

Irregularly toothed

WHITE POPLAR

Type	deciduous tree
Height	15–25m
Habitat	mainly wet places, sometimes in sandy coastal areas
Flowering	February–March
Fruiting	May–June

TRUNK AND CROWN

Trunk	often leaning; sucker shoots
Bark	pale greyish brown, marked with blackish diamonds, base blackish and coarsely fissured
Crown	irregular, broadest near top
Twigs	densely hairy, gradually becoming smooth and brown

LEAVES

Buds	c5mm, egg-shaped, pointed
Leaves	on alternate sides of stem, 3–9cm, broadly oval, blunt with irregular, blunt lobes, those of sucker shoots often deeply lobed, thinly hairy becoming smooth and dark green above, white with thick hairs below; stalk 5–6cm, rounded, hairy

FLOWERS AND FRUIT

Flowers	♂ and ♀ catkins on separate trees, before leaves
♂	catkin 4–7cm; scales oval, toothed, pale brown
Stamens	5–10 per ♂ flower, purple
♀	catkin 3–5cm
Stigmas	2, each divided into 2 lobes
Ovaries	1, egg-shaped, hairless
Fruit	catkin 8–10cm, of small capsules, each c3mm, shortly stalked, releasing seeds
Seeds	many, with cottony hairs

Populus tremula **Aspen**

luttering ceaselessly in the breeze, leaves of Aspen make a curious clattering sound. It is a remarkably widespread species, from western Europe to Japan and the tree limit of the tundra to the Mediterranean region.

Status: native, most of Europe.

sticky hairless

pinkish ♂ catkins

leaves after flowers

♀ catkin

flutters in wind

wavy teeth

hairless below

mostly rounded

deciduous

cottony seeds

SIMILAR TREES

Two North American species are cultivated.
1 Big-toothed Aspen (*Populus grandidentata*) has leaves with a squarish or wedge-shaped base and large, sharper teeth and greyish hairs on the buds, young twigs, and beneath the young leaves. **2 American Aspen** (*Populus tremuloides*) has finely toothed leaves and yellower bark; its hybrid with Aspen is sometimes grown.

large, pointed teeth

finely toothed

ASPEN

Type	deciduous tree
Height	up to 20m
Habitat	near water, often on mountains
Flowering	February–March
Fruiting	May

TRUNK AND CROWN

Trunk	slender, often several
Bark	smooth, greyish brown above; darker, fissured towards base
Crown	usually broad, much-branched
Twigs	with raised leaf-scars, grey-brown, becoming hairless

LEAVES

Buds	most c5mm, flower-buds larger, egg-shaped, hairless, glossy brown
Leaves	alternately arranged, 1.5–8cm, rarely 15cm, oval to nearly circular, blunt or with irregular, blunt teeth, dark green, paler beneath, turning clear yellow in autumn; stalk 4–7cm, flattened

FLOWERS AND FRUIT

Flowers	♂ and ♀ catkins on separate trees, before leaves
	♂ catkin 5–8cm cylindrical; scales 5–6mm, broad, fringed, dark brown, with white hairs
Stamens	5–12 per ♂ flower, purplish
	♀ catkin like ♂
Stigmas	2, cut into irregular lobes
Ovaries	1, egg-shaped, rough
Fruit	catkin up to 12cm, of small capsules, each c4mm, short-stalked, releasing seeds
Seeds	many, with cottony hairs

Black-poplar *Populus nigra*

Typically broad and rounded, this tree is better known as its narrowly columnar variant, the Lombardy Poplar. Both trees have leaves which are triangular or shaped like an ace-of-spades.

Status: native to central and southern Europe; widely planted for shelter and timber.

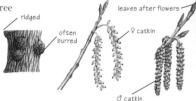

leaves after flowers

ridged

often burred

♀ catkin

♂ catkin

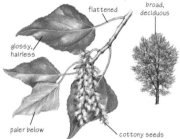

flattened

broad, deciduous

glossy, hairless

paler below

cottony seeds

BLACK-POPLAR

Type	deciduous tree
Height	20–35m
Habitat	damp soils of river valleys; grown by roads, in plantations
Flowering	March–April
Fruiting	May–June

TRUNK AND CROWN

Trunk	often with swellings and burrs
Bark	grey-brown, coarsely fissured
Crown	broad, irregular
Twigs	more or less hairless, rounded, yellowish brown

LEAVES

Buds	to 10mm, egg-shaped, pointed, glossy brown, sticky
Leaves	on alternate sides of stem, 4–10cm, triangular or broadly oval with slender point, edge with small, rounded teeth, base squarish or broadly wedge-shaped, hairless, dark, glossy green above, paler below; stalk 3–7cm, flattened

FLOWERS AND FRUIT

Flowers	♂ and ♀ catkins on separate trees, before leaves
♂	catkin 3–5cm, cylindrical; scales 1–2mm, fringed, green or brownish, soon falling
Stamens	12–30 per ♂ flower, red
♀	catkins more slender than ♂
Stigmas	2 per ♀ flower, each 2-lobed
Ovaries	1, egg-shaped, hairless
Fruit	catkin 9–15cm, of capsules, each 5–6mm, releasing seeds
Seeds	many, each with tuft of cottony hairs

SIMILAR TREES

1 Lombardy Poplar (*Populus nigra* cv. 'Italica') has a very slender crown; typically male, trees with female catkins or a broader crown are probably crosses with Black Poplar.
2 Berlin Poplar (*Populus* x *berolinensis*), a hybrid between Lombardy Poplar and *P. laurifolia*, has angular twigs, and leaves with a whiter underside, a wedge-shaped base and a rounded stalk.

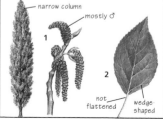

narrow column

mostly ♂

1

2

not flattened

wedge-shaped

Populus x canadensis **Hybrid Black-poplar**

A large, fast-growing hybrid, so commonly planted that it often replaces the native Black Poplar. That and an American species have produced several such hybrids, one of the most widespread being 'Serotina', a male tree illustrated here.

Status: of garden origin; planted for ornament, shelter and pulp-wood.

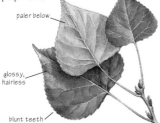

paler below

glossy, hairless

blunt teeth

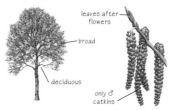

leaves after flowers

broad

deciduous

only ♂ catkins

HYBRID BLACK-POPLAR

Type	deciduous tree
Height	often more than 30m
Habitat	roadsides, parks, plantations
Flowering	March–April
TRUNK AND CROWN	
Trunk	long, unbranched base
Bark	coarsely fissured, without burrs, greyish brown
Crown	broadest above, flattish topped; lower branches heavy, angled upwards, diverging rather narrowly
Twigs	smooth, glossy greenish grey, often angular
LEAVES	
Buds	10–20mm, narrowly egg-shaped, tapered to slender point, glossy greenish brown, sticky
Leaves	on alternate sides of stem, 6–10cm, almost triangular, sharply pointed, with distinct, blunt teeth, base squarish or slightly heart-shaped, sometimes rounded, hairless, bright, glossy green above, paler below, young leaves tinged reddish brown; stalk 4–10cm, flattened sideways
FLOWERS AND FRUIT	
Flowers	♂ catkins, before leaves
♂	catkin 3–6cm, cylindrical; scales 4–5mm, broad, fringed, purplish-tipped
Stamens	20–25 per ♂ flower, anthers crimson
Fruit	not produced

SIMILAR TREES

1 Cottonwood (*P. deltoides*) is the American parent. The leaves have small glands and hairy, sharp teeth; male flowers have up to 60 stamens. Two female hybrids are widely grown. With wider branching and a rounded crown, **2 Maryland Poplar** (*P. x canadensis* cv. 'Marilandica') produces masses of cottony seeds. **3 Railway Poplar** (*P. x canadensis* cv. 'Regenerata') has mostly sterile fruit.

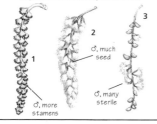

♂, more stamens

♂, much seed

♂, many sterile

Alder *Alnus glutinosa*

A waterside tree, Alder is identified by woody, cone-like, fruiting catkins, which persist for much of the year. Production of new shoots from suckers often results in bushy growth. Alder has the rare ability to turn nitrogen from the air into valuable plant food, thanks to root nodules containing bacteria.

Status: native to most of Europe; sometimes planted.

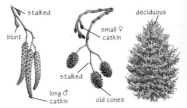

ALDER

Type	deciduous tree
Height	up to 20m (rarely 35m)
Habitat	mainly wet places
Flowering	February–March
Fruiting	October–November

TRUNK AND CROWN

Trunk	often several
Bark	dark brown, fissured
Crown	conical or rounded, open
Twigs	sticky when young, hairless

LEAVES

Buds	5–7mm, blunt; stalked
Leaves	on alternate sides of stem, 4–10cm, elliptical to almost circular, blunt or notched, doubly toothed, 5–8 pairs of veins, hairless where main veins diverge, dark green above and below; stalk 2–3.5cm
Stipules	soon falling

FLOWERS AND FRUIT

Flowers	♂ and ♀, before leaves
	♂ 3–6 catkins in cluster, each 2–6cm, opening yellow; 3 flowers to each bract
Stamens	4 per ♂ flower
	♀ cluster of 3–5 catkins, each 5–7mm, purplish, stalked; 2 tiny flowers to each bract
Stigmas	2 per ♀ flower
Ovaries	1 per ♀ flower
Fruit	cluster of 3–5 woody, cone-like catkins, each 10–30mm, egg-shaped, green, turning brown; stalked; scales 5-lobed
Seeds	nut-like, with narrow wing

SIMILAR TREES

Lacking sticky twigs, **1 Grey Alder** (*Alnus incana*) has grey, smooth bark, pointed leaves that are grey below, and stalkless female catkins. **2 Italian Alder** (*Alnus cordata*) has leaves with shallow, rounded teeth and a solitary female flower or rarely up to 3 in a cluster.

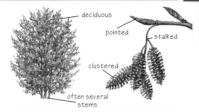

A shrub that only occasionally reaches tree proportions, this is usually much smaller than the more widespread European species. Common in the Alps, Green Alder often forms extensive thickets. It is a variable species and several subspecies are sometimes distinguished by leaf characters.

Status: native in mountains of central and south-eastern Europe; planted elsewhere.

GREEN ALDER

Type	deciduous shrub or tree
Height	1–5m
Habitat	wet places
Flowering	March–April
Fruiting	September–October

TRUNK AND CROWN

Trunk	often several
Bark	rough, brown
Crown	irregular, rounded
Twigs	greenish brown or reddish brown

LEAVES

Buds	12–15mm, conical, pointed, glossy reddish brown; stalkless
Leaves	on alternate sides of stem, sticky when young, 3–9cm, elliptical to almost circular, variably pointed, sharply, doubly toothed, usually with tufts of hairs below; stalk 8–12mm
Stipules	small, soon falling

FLOWERS AND FRUIT

Flowers	♂ and ♀ together, with leaves
♂	small cluster of long catkins, each 5–12cm, yellowish
Perianth	usually 4-lobed
Stamens	4 per ♂ flower
♀	cluster of 3–5 catkins, each 6–10mm, reddish, stalked
Stigmas	1 per ♀ flower
Ovaries	2 per ♀ flower
Fruit	cluster of 3–5 woody, cone-like catkins, each 8–15mm, egg-shaped, stalked, blackish
Seeds	nut-like with papery wing

SIMILAR TREES

Another small Alder, introduced from North America and often naturalized, **Smooth Alder** (*Alnus rugosa*) produces catkins before its leaves and has sticky twigs, with up to 10 fruiting catkins in a head, the upper of which are stalkless.

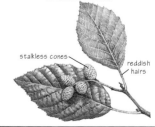

Silver Birch *Betula pendula*

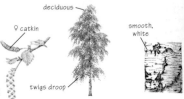

deciduous

♀ catkin

smooth, white

twigs droop

Silver Birch's graceful form is best seen in spring, when the slender, silvery trunk and boughs are barely concealed by a filigree of pale green. A colonizer of treeless wastes, it was important in establishing northern Europe's forests after the last Ice Age.

Status: native to most of Europe; planted for ornament.

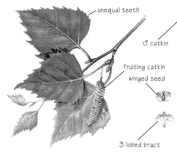

unequal teeth

♂ catkin

fruiting catkin

winged seed

3-lobed bract

SIMILAR TREES

1 Downy Birch (*Betula pubescens*) has hairy, stiffer twigs, leaves with more equal teeth, catkin scales with side-lobes angled forwards, and narrowly winged nutlets.
2 Paper-bark Birch (*Betula papyrifera*) has papery, creamy-white or pink bark, larger leaves with unequal teeth, and catkin scales with narrowly diverging lobes.

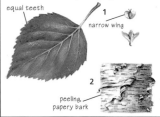

equal teeth

narrow wing

1

2

peeling, papery bark

SILVER BIRCH

Type	deciduous tree
Height	up to 30m
Habitat	light soils, often wasteland
Flowering	April–May
Fruiting	July–August

TRUNK AND CROWN

Trunk	slender, forked above
Bark	smooth, silvery-white, black lenticels above, often peeling, blackish and fissured below
Crown	narrow or broad, light; branches gradually arch down
Twigs	brown, with resin-glands

LEAVES

Buds	long, pointed, not sticky
Leaves	alternating along stem, 2–7cm, triangular, thin, pointed, sharply, doubly toothed, base squarish, yellow in autumn, almost hairless; stalked
Stipules	small, soon falling

FLOWERS AND FRUIT

Flowers	♂ and ♀ flowers on same plant
♂	2–4 catkins at tip of twig, 3–6cm, purplish brown, becoming yellow with pollen
Stamens	2 per ♂ flower
♀	catkin at leaf-base, brownish
Stigmas	2 per ♀ flower
Ovaries	1 per ♀ flower, 2-celled
Fruit	catkin 15–35mm; scales 3-lobed, middle lobe narrow, side lobes curving backwards
Seeds	seed-like nutlet with 2 wings 2–3 times as broad as nutlet

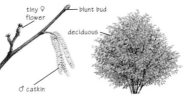

tiny ♀ flower

blunt bud

deciduous

♂ catkin

A t its most striking in late winter when the bright yellow catkins are a welcome sight, Hazel is more often a shrub than a tree. It is frequently coppiced, and the pliant poles and rods were formerly used in building. Large, edible nuts are sought by squirrels, mice, jays and pheasants.

Status: native to most of Europe except the extreme north; planted for hedging, fruit or ornament.

doubly toothed

toothed cup

edible nuts

SIMILAR TREES

Usually a tree, **1 Turkish Hazel** (*Corylus colurna*) has more lobed leaves and the cup beneath the nut has narrower, spiky lobes. **2 Filbert** (*Corylus maxima*) is grown for its larger, edible nuts, which are enclosed by a longer cup.

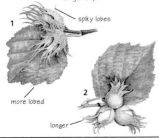

spiky lobes

more lobed

longer

HAZEL

Type	deciduous shrub or tree
Height	2–6m (rarely 8m)
Habitat	woods, hedgerows, scrub
Flowering	January–March
Fruiting	September–October

TRUNK AND CROWN

Trunk	often several
Bark	brown, smooth, slightly peeling
Crown	broad, branches slender
Twigs	dull green or brown, with reddish, gland-tipped hairs

LEAVES

Buds	c4mm, egg-shaped, blunt
Leaves	alternating on stem, 5–12cm, nearly circular, narrowly pointed, doubly toothed, sometimes slightly lobed, base notched, 6–8 pairs of veins, slightly hairy, especially below; stalk 8–15mm, stickily hairy
Stipules	oblong, blunt, soon falling

FLOWERS AND FRUIT

Flowers	♂ and ♀ flowers, before leaves
♂	slender, hanging catkin, 2–8cm, turning yellow with pollen, 1 flower per bract
Stamens	3–5 per ♂ flower
♀	small cluster, bud-like, 4–5mm
Stigmas	2 per ♀ flower, bright red
Ovaries	1 per ♀ flower, 2-celled
Fruit	1–4 rounded, brown, woody-shelled nuts, each 15–20mm, in greenish cup about equalling nut, cut to middle into irregularly toothed lobes

65

Hornbeam *Carpinus betulus*

Agraceful tree, with smooth, grey bark, upswept branches and dark, toothed foliage; it is easily identified by distinctive three-lobed bracts in the fruiting head. In hedges, it responds well to clipping and keeps leaves in winter, much like Beech. Hornbeam is sometimes pollarded or coppiced, and has a hard, fine-grained timber.

Status: native; widespread except in much of northern and western Mediterranean region; planted for timber, shelter or ornament.

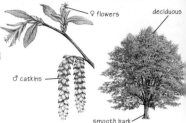

♀ flowers

deciduous

♂ catkins

smooth bark

doubly toothed

3-lobed bract

nut

SIMILAR TREES

Eastern Hornbeam (*Carpinus orientalis*) from south-eastern Europe is a smaller tree with the bract around the nut toothed, not lobed.

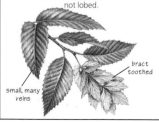

bract toothed

small, many veins

HORNBEAM

Type	deciduous tree
Height	up to 30m
Habitat	woods, hedges; planted in streets and parks
Flowering	March–May
Fruiting	October–November

TRUNK AND CROWN

Trunk	often twisted, fluted below
Bark	greyish brown, smooth, becomes deeply fissured below
Crown	broad, tapered above; branches angled upwards, sinuous
Twigs	slender, hairy, greyish brown

LEAVES

Buds	6–7mm, slender, sharp-pointed, brown, hairy, against twig
Leaves	on alternate sides of stem, 4–10cm, oval, pointed, sharply and doubly toothed, base rounded, hairy beneath on veins, dark green, turning yellow in autumn, c15 pairs of veins; stalk c10mm, reddish
Stipules	small, soon falling

FLOWERS AND FRUIT

Flowers		♂ and ♀ on same tree
	♂	catkin 25–50mm, yellowish, scales red-tipped
	♀	drooping catkin, 20–30mm, 2 flowers per 3-lobed bract, green with pink stigmas
Fruit		nut 6–8mm, 1–2 at base of 3-lobed bract, c35mm long, in cluster 5–15cm long
Seeds		1 per fruit, not released

A small, deciduous tree, with glossy, ribbed leaves. It is easily distinguished from all other native trees by the whitish, hop-like fruits. Hop-hornbeam is occasionally planted for ornament and, in southern Europe, it is used for its hard timber.

Status: native to central and eastern parts of southern Europe; planted elsewhere for ornament.

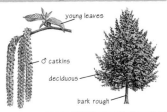

young leaves

♂ catkins

deciduous

bark rough

doubly toothed

hop-like

ribbed

nut inside

SIMILAR TREES

Eastern Hop-hornbeam (*Ostraya virginiana*) is native to eastern North America, but is sometimes cultivated in Europe for ornament. It differs in the larger, less ribbed leaves, which are downy beneath with hairy stalks; the twigs with gland-tipped hairs, and the fruits with longer, hairier stalks.

longer stalk

longer

hairier below

HOP-HORNBEAM

Type	deciduous tree
Height	15–18m
Habitat	woods, hedges, parks
Flowering	April
Fruiting	September–October

TRUNK AND CROWN

Trunk	sometimes several
Bark	brown, scales fall leaving lighter patches, smooth, becoming fissured
Crown	conical, becoming rounded; branches angled upwards
Twigs	reddish brown, hairy

LEAVES

Buds	egg-shaped, pointed, shiny
Leaves	on alternate sides of stem, 5–12cm, oval, pointed, sharply and doubly toothed, base wedge-shaped, hairy, becoming smooth, shiny dark green above, paler below, 12–15 pairs of veins; stalk 3–4mm, softly hairy
Stipules	small, soon falling

FLOWERS AND FRUIT

Flowers		♂ and ♀ on same tree
	♂	catkin 3.5–10cm, hanging, yellow; 1 flower per bract
	♀	♀ catkin 20–30mm, drooping; 2 greenish flowers at bract base
Fruit		nut c5mm, at bract base, in hanging, white or pale brown head, 3–5cm long; elliptical bracts, 15–20mm, hairy, pointed
Seeds		1 per fruit, not released

Beech *Fagus sylvatica*

Sunlight streaming through chinks in the sombre canopy, illuminating massive, smooth, grey trunks and arched boughs, brings a cathedral-like atmosphere to a mature stand of Beech. In the deep shade, spring-flowering bulbs grow in the litter of fallen leaves and fruits.

Status: native mainly to western and central Europe; planted for ornament, shelter and timber.

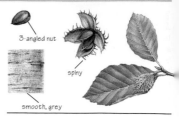

3-angled nut

spiny

smooth, grey

rounded, dense

edge wavy

♀

deciduous

♂

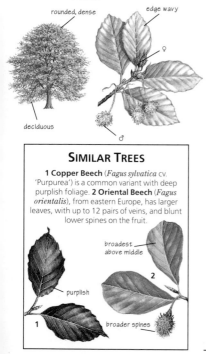

SIMILAR TREES

1 Copper Beech (*Fagus sylvatica* cv. 'Purpurea') is a common variant with deep purplish foliage. **2 Oriental Beech** (*Fagus orientalis*), from eastern Europe, has larger leaves, with up to 12 pairs of veins, and blunt lower spines on the fruit.

broadest above middle

purplish

1

2

broader spines

BEECH

Type	deciduous tree
Height	20–30m (rarely 50m)
Habitat	well-drained soils, especially on chalk hillsides
Flowering	April–May
Fruiting	September–October
TRUNK AND CROWN	
Trunk	stout below, forked above
Bark	smooth, grey
Crown	broad, rounded, dense
Twigs	brownish grey
LEAVES	
Buds	1–2cm, slender, pointed at both ends, reddish brown
Leaves	on alternate sides of stem, 4–9cm, elliptical or oval, pointed, edge not toothed, often wavy, with fine hairs, 5–9 pairs of veins, dark, glossy green, turning orange or brown in autumn; stalk 5–15mm; young plants often with dead leaves over winter
Stipules	brown, papery, soon fall
FLOWERS AND FRUIT	
Flowers	♂ and ♀ on same plant
♂	tiny, many, in tassel-like head on stalk 5–6cm long
Perianth	bell-shaped, with 4–7 lobes
Stamens	8–16 per ♂ flower
♀	usually 2 enclosed by stalked, cup-like structure of 4 bracts
Stigmas	3 per ♀ flower
Ovaries	1 per ♀ flower
Fruit	3-angled nut, 12–18mm, brown, 1 or 2 in spiny, woody casing, which splits into 4

Nothofagus obliqua **Roble Beech**

Introduced from South America, this distant relative of the Beech is becoming popular both for ornament and timber. It is one of the so-called 'Southern Beeches' from the Southern Hemisphere, most of which are evergreen but some are deciduous.

Status: introduced from Chile and Argentina; planted in western Europe, for ornament and timber.

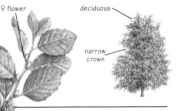

♀ flower

deciduous

narrow crown

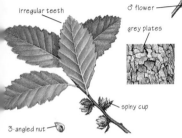

irregular teeth

grey plates

♂ flower

spiny cup

3-angled nut

ROBLE BEECH

Type	deciduous tree
Height	20–30m
Habitat	grown in small plantations, also parks and gardens
Flowering	May
Fruiting	September

TRUNK AND CROWN

Trunk	forked above
Bark	greenish grey, smooth, becoming cracked into small, squarish plates
Crown	rather narrow, open; branches arch outwards
Twigs	slender, with sparse, short hairs

LEAVES

Buds	4–6mm, egg-shaped, blunt, light brown, close to twig
Leaves	on alternate sides of stem, 5–8cm, oval to almost oblong, blunt, sharply and irregularly toothed, base slightly unequal, 7–11 pairs of veins, dark green above, paler below, turning yellow or red in autumn; stalk 4–7mm
Stipules	crinkled, soon falling

FLOWERS AND FRUIT

Flowers	♂ and ♀ flowers on same plant
	♂ solitary, stalked
Stamens	♂ with 30–40
	♀ tiny, pale green, at leaf-base
Stigmas	3 per ♀ flower
Ovaries	1 per ♀ flower
Fruit	nut, 5–10mm, 3 in cup-like, shortly spiny casing which splits into 4

SIMILAR TREES

1 Raoul (*Nothofagus procera*) has stouter shoots with longer, pointed buds, finely toothed leaves with 14–18 pairs of veins, and bark with vertical fissures. **2 Antarctic Beech** (*Nothofagus antarctica*) is a shorter tree with smaller leaves usually having 4 pairs of veins.

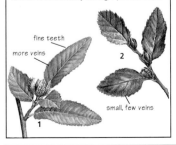

fine teeth

more veins

small, few veins

1

2

Evergreen Oak *Quercus ilex*

Characteristic of the Mediterranean region, this tree has been taken to many other countries where it survives frost and keeps its dense foliage in winter. Usually like a small laurel, it has remarkably variable leaves, which are holly-like on sucker shoots. The tannin-rich bark was used by Ancient Greeks and Romans for tanning leather.

Status: native to the Mediterranean region; much planted elsewhere for ornament and shelter.

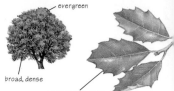

evergreen

broad, dense

some leaves spiny

small plates

thick

greyish-hairy

♂ catkin

scales pressed together

grey below

EVERGREEN OAK

Type	evergreen tree
Height	up to 25m
Habitat	forest, woodland; left in fields for shade; street tree
Flowering	May–June
Fruiting	September–October
TRUNK AND CROWN	
Trunk	stout
Bark	dark grey, cracking into plates
Crown	broad, domed, dense
Twigs	grey-hairy, becoming hairless
LEAVES	
Buds	egg-shaped, hairy
Leaves	2–9cm, variable, oval to oblong, thick, edge unbroken or spiny-toothed on sucker shoots, base tapered or rounded, straight midrib with 7–11 pairs of veins, glossy, dark green above, greyish-hairy below; stalk 6–15mm
Stipules	narrow, hairy, soon falling
FLOWERS AND FRUIT	
Flowers	♂ and ♀ on same tree
♂	drooping catkins, 3–5cm
Perianth	tiny, with 4–7 pointed lobes
Stamens	6–12 per ♂ flower
♀	spike of 1–4 flowers
Stigmas	3–4 per ♀ flower
Ovaries	1 per ♀ flower, 3-celled
Fruit	nut (acorn) ripening in first year, 2–4cm, egg-shaped; cup greyish-hairy, covering less than half of fruit, scales oval, pressed closely together

SIMILAR TREES

1 Cork Oak (*Quercus suber*) has toothed leaves with a wavy midrib and longer scales on the acorn cup. Rarely reaching tree size.
2 Kermes Oak (*Quercus coccifera*) has spiny, hairless leaves and spiny scales on the acorn cup.

very thick bark

spiny

1

2

toothed

pointed scales

longer scales

Quercus cerris **Turkey Oak**

A robust, stately tree with large, lobed leaves, deeply fissured bark, and acorns that are situated on the leafless part of the twig. The timber was once used extensively for panelling walls.

Status: native to central and southern Europe; planted elsewhere for ornament and shelter.

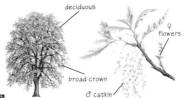
deciduous
♀ flowers
broad crown
♂ catkin

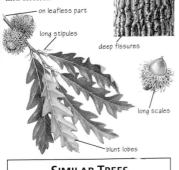
on leafless part
long stipules
deep fissures
long scales
blunt lobes

TURKEY OAK

Type	deciduous tree
Height	20–35m
Habitat	mainly on acid soils
Flowering	May
Fruiting	September–October
TRUNK AND CROWN	
Trunk	stout, forked above
Bark	dark grey, deeply fissured
Crown	broad, domed; branches stout
Twigs	brown, rough, sparsely hairy
LEAVES	
Buds	oval, blunt, shortly hairy
Leaves	alternate along stem, variable, 5–10cm, rarely 18cm, oblong or oval, pointed, 7–9 pairs of unequal, oval, blunt lobes, greyish-hairy becoming dull green, almost hairless but rough above, paler below, minutely hairy; stalk 8–25mm
Stipules	to 25cm, very slender, prominent, remaining attached
FLOWERS AND FRUIT	
Flowers	♂ and ♀ on same tree
♂	catkin, 5–8cm
Perianth	tiny, 4–7 lobes
Stamens	4 per ♂ flower
♀	cluster of up to 5 flowers
Stigmas	4 styles per ♀ flower
Ovaries	1 per ♀ flower, 3-celled
Fruit	nut (acorn), ripens in second year, 2–3.5cm, rarely 5cm, oblong, reddish brown, broad cup covers ½ nut, scales to 1cm, slender, spreading or bent back; stalk to 2cm

SIMILAR TREES

1 Valonia Oak (*Quercus macrolepis*) has smooth leaves with bristle-tipped lobes and a larger acorn cup with long, broad scales.
2 Macedonian Oak (*Quercus trojana*) has glossy, short-stalked leaves and an acorn cup with short, radiating scales. A cultivated hybrid of Turkey Oak and Cork Oak,
3 Lucombe Oak (*Quercus x hispanica*) resembles the former but has mostly evergreen leaves and thicker bark.

wide scales
glossy, evergreen
bristle tip
shorter scales

Pedunculate Oak *Quercus robur*

deciduous

usually broad

fissured

Renowned throughout Europe as a symbol of durability and longevity, this tree can survive for a thousand years. Light brown with silvery, close grain, the hard timber is valuable commercially; formerly it was exploited for architecture and ship-building.

Status: native to much of Europe except for the extreme north and parts of the Mediterranean region; planted for shelter, timber and ornament.

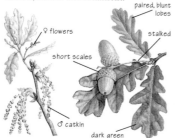

paired, blunt lobes

♀ flowers

stalked

short scales

♂ catkin

dark green

SIMILAR TREES

Native to south-eastern Europe, *Quercus pedunculiflora* differs in having bluish green leaves with yellowish grey hairs below and warty acorn cups with yellowish hairs.

yellowish hairs

greyish hairs

bluish green

PEDUNCULATE OAK

Type	deciduous tree
Height	20–35m, rarely 45m
Habitat	woodland, especially lowland on heavy, fertile soils
Flowering	April–May
Fruiting	September–October

TRUNK AND CROWN

Trunk	stout, often short and burred
Bark	fissured, brownish grey
Crown	usually broad, branches stout, wide-spreading, often sinuous
Twigs	grey-brown, usually hairless

LEAVES

Buds	2–5mm, oval, blunt, hairless
Leaves	alternate along stem, 5–12cm, more or less oblong, blunt, 4–7 pairs of blunt, unequal lobes, base with 2 ear-like lobes, dull green, hairless above, paler and usually hairless below; stalk 1–5mm
Stipules	slender, soon falling

FLOWERS AND FRUIT

Flowers	♂ and ♀ on same tree
♂	clustered catkins, 2–4cm
Perianth	tiny, 4–7 lobes
Stamens	6–8, rarely 12 per ♂ flower
♀	1–5 flowers in stalked head
Stigmas	3 per ♀ flower
Ovaries	1 per ♀ flower, 3-celled
Fruit	nut (acorn) ripens first year, 1.5–4cm, oblong or elliptical, brown; cup 1.5–2cm wide, $^1/_3$–$^1/_2$ covers nut; scales small, oval, flat, closely overlapping, shortly hairy; stalk 2–8cm

A majestic tree but one which tends to be overlooked as it is often confused with Pedunculate Oak, from which it differs by the stalkless acorns. As they are less often attacked by insects, the dark, glossy, distinctly stalked leaves are more ornamental.

Status: native except in the extreme north and the Mediterranean region; planted for timber, shelter and ornament.

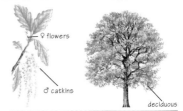

♀ flowers

♂ catkins

deciduous

SESSILE OAK

Type	deciduous tree
Height	20–40m
Habitat	woodland, mainly acid soils
Flowering	April–May
Fruiting	September–October

TRUNK AND CROWN

Trunk	stout, often straight and unbranched below
Bark	brownish grey, fissured
Crown	rather narrowly domed
Twigs	hairless

LEAVES

Buds	5–6mm, many scales, hairy
Leaves	alternate along stem, 7–12.5cm, oval, broadest above, 5–8 pairs of rounded lobes, base tapered, rather glossy, dark green above, finely hairy below with brownish tufts at base of veins; stalk 1.8–2.5cm, grooved
Stipules	soon falling

FLOWERS AND FRUIT

Flowers	♂ and ♀ flowers, with leaves
	♂ clustered, hanging catkins
Perianth	tiny, 4–7 lobes, usually 6
Stamens	6–12 per ♂ flower
	♀ bud-like, within hairy scales
Stigmas	3 per ♀ flower, stalkless
Ovaries	1 per ♀ flower, 3-celled
Fruit	2–6 nuts (acorns), ripening first year, 1.5–3cm, oblong; cup with oval, closely overlapping scales, finely hairy; almost stalkless

fissured

grooved stalk

small scales

blunt lobes

stalkless acorns

finely hairy

SIMILAR TREES

Native to south-eastern Europe, **1** *Quercus dalechampii* has hairless leaves and acorns with a warty, greyish, practically hairless cup. **2 Hungarian Oak** (*Quercus frainetto*) has hairy twigs and leaves with up to ten, deep, wavy-edged lobes.

many wavy lobes

warty hairless

hairless below

short stalk

Downy Oak *Quercus pubescens*

A rather small tree or sturdy shrub, distinguished by grey-green, shallowly lobed leaves, covered with velvety hairs when young. Winter buds and acorn cups are also hairy.

Status: native mainly to southern and western Europe; rarely planted for ornament.

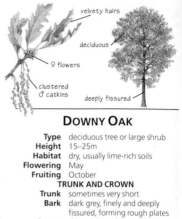
velvety hairs
deciduous
♀ flowers
clustered ♂ catkins
deeply fissured

few lobes
mostly stalkless
blunt, hairy scales
grey-green

DOWNY OAK

Type	deciduous tree or large shrub
Height	15–25m
Habitat	dry, usually lime-rich soils
Flowering	May
Fruiting	October
TRUNK AND CROWN	
Trunk	sometimes very short
Bark	dark grey, finely and deeply fissured, forming rough plates
Crown	domed, branches swollen at junction with trunk
Twigs	brown, densely grey-hairy
LEAVES	
Buds	4–7mm, reddish brown, hairy
Leaves	alternate along stem, 4–13cm, variable, 4–8 pairs of broad, shallow, forward-pointing lobes, base rounded or broadly tapered, grey-green, densely hairy when young, becoming hairless above; stalk 2–15mm
Stipules	soon falling
FLOWERS AND FRUIT	
Flowers	♂ and ♀ flowers, with leaves
♂	clustered catkins
Stamens	6–12 per ♂ flower
Perianth	tiny, with 4–7 lobes
♀	1–3, each within cup of scales
Stigmas	3 per ♀ flower, deep red
Ovaries	1 per ♀ flower, 3-celled
Fruit	nut (acorn), ripens first year, 2–4cm; cup 1–1.5cm wide, $^{1}/_{4}$–$^{1}/_{3}$ covers nut, usually blunt, pressed together, grey-woolly; stalkless or short-stalked

SIMILAR TREES

Two species have longer leaf-stalks and looser scales on the acorn cup. Confined mainly to the eastern half of the Mediterranean region, **1** *Quercus virgiliana* has leaves with broad, often wavy-edged lobes, and the scales of the acorn cup have a slender, upright tip. **2** Pyrenean Oak (*Quercus pyrenaica*) from south-western Europe has narrower, blunt scales on the acorn cup.

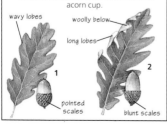
wavy lobes
woolly below
long lobes
pointed scales
blunt scales
1   **2**

Spectacular when a cold snap in autumn turns its leaves fiery shades of orange and scarlet, Red Oak is widely planted for ornament. Like several other introduced North American species, it has relatively large leaves with pointed lobes and teeth.

Status: introduced from eastern North America; commonly planted for ornament, timber and shelter.

deciduous

smooth bark cracks

yellow when young

broad cup, small scales

turns red

lobed

bristle-tip

♂ catkins

RED OAK

Type	deciduous tree
Height	20–35m
Habitat	planted on most soils
Flowering	April–May
Fruiting	October

TRUNK AND CROWN

Trunk	straight below
Bark	silvery grey, smooth above, with brown fissures below
Crown	broad-domed
Twigs	stout, reddish brown, hairless

LEAVES

Buds	5–7mm, oval, reddish brown
Leaves	alternating, 12–25cm, oval or elliptical, variable, cut ½ way into 7–11 pairs of lobes, few bristle-tipped teeth, only few hairs in angles of veins below, yellow, becoming dull green, turning orange, red or brown in autumn; stalk 2.5–3cm

FLOWERS AND FRUIT

Flowers	♂ and ♀ flowers, with leaves
♂	catkins, 5–8cm, yellow
Perianth	tiny, with 4–7 lobes
Stamens	6–12 per ♂ flower
♀	tiny, at leaf-base, red
Stigmas	3–4 per ♀ flower
Ovaries	1 per ♀ flower, 3-celled
Fruit	nut (acorn), ripens second year, 2–3cm, oblong, reddish brown; cup 2–2.5cm wide, covers ⅓ nut, scales oval, pressed closely together, finely hairy; stalk 8–10mm

SIMILAR TREES

Two American species have more deeply divided leaves and short, squat acorns.
1 Scarlet Oak's (*Quercus coccinea*) glossy leaves lack hairs below at the base of the veins. **2 Pin Oak** (*Quercus palustris*) has leaves with tufts of hairs beneath, and a narrow acorn cup.

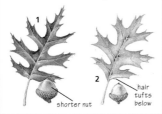

shorter nut

hair tufts below

Sweet Chestnut *Castanea sativa*

A striking attractive tree, with bold, toothed leaves, bunches of long, pale yellow catkins and a stout, deeply fissured trunk, which often has a curious spiral pattern. Long-lived, the trunk may attain a girth of 13m or more, with the crown misshapen from lightning damage or branches shed in high wind. It is grown widely for its edible nuts.

Status: native to southern Europe; widely planted and naturalized elsewhere.

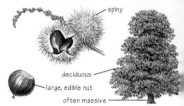

spiny

deciduous

large, edible nut

often massive

♀ flower

♂ catkins

large leaf

many veins

sharp teeth

ridges often spiral

SWEET CHESTNUT

Type	deciduous tree
Height	20–30m
Habitat	well-drained soils, in woods
Flowering	June–July
Fruiting	September–October
TRUNK AND CROWN	
Trunk	often massive and gnarled
Bark	brown, vertically or spirally fissured and ridged
Crown	broad, irregular
Twigs	greenish brown, sometimes grooved, with lenticels
LEAVES	
Buds	4–5mm, egg-shaped
Leaves	on alternate sides of stem, 10–25cm, narrowly oval to oblong, pointed, regularly toothed, teeth point forwards with slender tip, base tapered or rounded, c20 pairs of veins, glossy, dark green above, paler below, turning yellow or brown in autumn; stalk 0.5–3cm
Stipules	papery, soon falling
FLOWERS AND FRUIT	
Flowers	♂ and ♀ on same tree
♂	catkins, 12–30cm, pale yellow
Stamens	10–20 per ♂ flower
♀	2–3 in spiny bracts, in short ♀ catkin or below ♂ catkin
Stigmas	7–9 per ♀ flower
Ovaries	1 per ♀ flower, 6-celled
Fruit	1–3 nuts in husk with branched spines, splits into 2–4; nuts 20–35mm, hemispherical or angular, glossy, reddish brown

SIMILAR TREES

An ornamental species from western North America, **Golden Chestnut** (*Chrysolepis chrysophylla*) is an evergreen with untoothed, leathery leaves, golden beneath, and fruits which mature in 2 years.

not toothed

slow ripening

yellowish below   evergreen

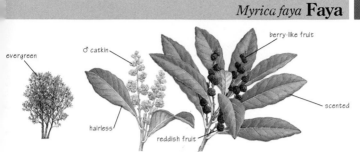

evergreen

♂ catkin

berry-like fruit

hairless

reddish fruit

scented

A strongly aromatic shrub or small tree, related to the shrubby Bog-myrtle (*M. gale*) of north-western Europe. Faya is found mainly in broad-leaved evergreen forests of the western Atlantic islands, remnants of a forest type widespread in the Mediterranean region 30 million years ago.

Status: native to the Azores, Madeira and the Canary Islands; cultivated and naturalized in southern Europe; possibly native to Portugal.

SIMILAR TREES

Bayberry (*Myrica caroliniensis*) is a deciduous shrub, rarely tree-sized, with leaves covered by glossy, yellow glands, unbranched catkins and small, whitish fruits. It is sometimes naturalized.

glossy

waxy

greyish

FAYA

Type	evergreen tree or shrub
Height	2–10m
Habitat	woodland, scrub
Flowering	April–May
Fruiting	September

TRUNK AND CROWN

Trunk	short, forked
Bark	smooth, brown
Crown	rounded, irregular
Twigs	with small, reddish, tack-shaped hairs

LEAVES

Buds	egg-shaped, pointed
Leaves	on alternate sides of stem, 4–12cm, spear-shaped, broadest above middle, edge unbroken, turned under, base wedge-shaped, hairless; stalkless
Stipules	absent

FLOWERS AND FRUIT

Flowers	♂ and ♀ catkins on different plants, among leaves
♂	in branched catkins on growth of current year
♀	usually in unbranched catkins, each flower with 2 or more scales at the base
Perianth	absent
Stamens	2–16 per ♂ flower
Stigmas	2, slender, on short style
Ovaries	1, 1-chambered
Fruit	berry-like, slightly fleshy, reddish to black, with rough, waxy surface

English Elm *Ulmus procera*

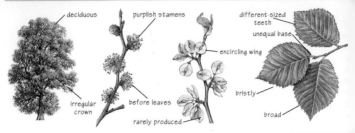

deciduous

purplish stamens

irregular crown

before leaves

rarely produced

encircling wing

different-sized teeth

unequal base

bristly

broad

A prominent tree of the landscape with a billowy crown formed by the domed masses of foliage from each main branch. The roots often produce suckers, so that an old tree is ringed by its younger progeny. In recent years, millions of trees have died from Dutch Elm disease, but young suckers often survive and offer hope for regeneration.

Status: native to western and southern Europe; planted for shelter and timber.

SIMILAR TREES

From central and south-eastern Europe, **European White-elm** (*Ulmus laevis*) has long-stalked flowers and fruit, the latter fringed with hairs. The leaves may have long, soft hairs below.

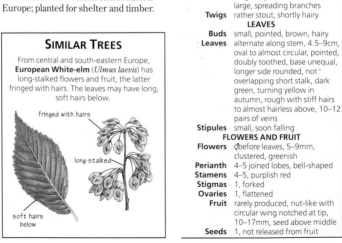

fringed with hairs

long-stalked

soft hairs below

ENGLISH ELM

Type	deciduous tree
Height	20–35m
Habitat	woodland, hedgerows
Flowering	February–March
Fruiting	April–June
TRUNK AND CROWN	
Trunk	straight, forked above, suckers around base
Bark	brown, rough, fissured
Crown	irregularly domed; often few large, spreading branches
Twigs	rather stout, shortly hairy
LEAVES	
Buds	small, pointed, brown, hairy
Leaves	alternate along stem, 4.5–9cm, oval to almost circular, pointed, doubly toothed, base unequal, longer side rounded, not overlapping short stalk, dark green, turning yellow in autumn, rough with stiff hairs to almost hairless above, 10–12 pairs of veins
Stipules	small, soon falling
FLOWERS AND FRUIT	
Flowers	☿before leaves, 5–9mm, clustered, greenish
Perianth	4–5 joined lobes, bell-shaped
Stamens	4–5, purplish red
Stigmas	1, forked
Ovaries	1, flattened
Fruit	rarely produced, nut-like with circular wing notched at tip, 10–17mm, seed above middle
Seeds	1, not released from fruit

Ulmus minor **Small-leaved Elm**

A variable species, especially in Britain, where it is often split into several varieties, subspecies or even species. Small-leaved Elm is common in continental Europe, though its numbers have been decimated by Dutch Elm disease. Smooth, glossy leaves and an elliptical fruit with the seed above the middle distinguish it from other common elms.

Status: native to much of Europe; planted for timber, shelter and ornament.

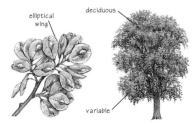

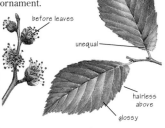

SIMILAR TREES

1 Grey-leaved Elm (*Ulmus canescens*) has young shoots densely covered with white hairs, and leaves downy grey below.
2 Chinese Elm (*Ulmus parvifolia*) is an ornamental species planted for its delicate sprays of much smaller, dark green leaves.

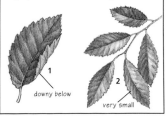

SMALL-LEAVED ELM

Type	deciduous tree
Height	15–30m
Habitat	hedgerows, woodland
Flowering	February–March
Fruiting	May–July

TRUNK AND CROWN

Trunk	straight, suckers around base
Bark	greyish brown, fissured
Crown	variable, domed or conical; few main branches
Twigs	slender, often hanging, pale brown, becoming smooth

LEAVES

Buds	c5mm, egg-shaped, red, downy
Leaves	alternate along twig, 6–8cm, oval, broadest towards slender tip, sharply, doubly toothed, base unequal, shiny dark green, turning yellow in autumn, hairless above, downy tufts below, 7–12 pairs of veins; stalk c5mm, downy
Stipules	small, soon falling

FLOWERS AND FRUIT

Flowers	☿, before leaves, clustered, each 5–8mm, purplish
Perianth	4–5 joined lobes, bell-shaped
Stamens	4–5, purple anthers
Stigmas	1, forked, white
Ovaries	solitary, flattened
Fruit	nut-like with notched, elliptical wing, 7–18mm, seed above middle
Seeds	1, not released from fruit

Labels on images: elliptical wing, deciduous, variable, before leaves, unequal, hairless above, glossy, downy below, very small

Wych Elm *Ulmus glabra*

A handsome, densely-canopied tree, with large, bristly, lop-sided leaves. There is a rounded lobe at the base of each leaf, which usually overlaps the short stalk. Weeping forms are grown, with twisted, pendulous branches. Fruits are enclosed centrally within a broad, oval wing.

Status: native to much of Europe except parts of the Mediterranean region; often planted by fields, in parks or churchyards.

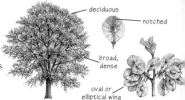

deciduous

notched

broad, dense

oval or elliptical wing

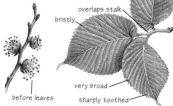

before leaves

overlaps stalk

bristly

very broad

sharply toothed

SIMILAR TREES

Also large-leaved are the hybrids with Small-leaved Elm, distinguished from Wych Elm by their smooth leaves. **1 Dutch Elm** (*Ulmus* x *hollandica* var. *hollandica*) has corky ridges on the crooked shoots. **2 Huntingdon Elm** (*Ulmus* x *hollandica* var. *vegeta*) has straight, scarcely corky shoots.

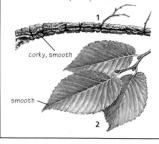

corky, smooth

smooth

WYCH ELM

Type	deciduous tree
Height	25–40m
Habitat	often by water
Flowering	February–March
Fruiting	May–June

TRUNK AND CROWN

Trunk	stout, with burrs and suckers
Bark	grey to brown, smooth becoming cracked and ridged
Crown	rounded, dense; branches angled upwards, twisted, sometimes bent down to ground
Twigs	stout, bristly, become smooth

LEAVES

Buds	stout, with reddish hairs
Leaves	alternate along stem, 8–18cm, broad, almost circular to oval, slender tipped, sharply, doubly toothed, base unequal, longer, rounded side overlaps stalk, bristly, dark green above, paler below, turning deep yellow in autumn, 12–18 pairs of veins; stalk 2–5mm, thick, hairy
Stipules	small, soon falling

FLOWERS AND FRUIT

Flowers	☿, before leaves, clustered, each 7–8mm, purplish red
Perianth	4–5 joined lobes, bell-shaped
Stamens	4–5, anthers purplish red
Stigmas	with 2 styles
Ovaries	1, flattened
Fruit	nut-like, central within oval or elliptical, notched wing, 1.5–2.5cm; stalk 2–3mm
Seeds	1, not released

Zelkova carpinifolia **Caucasian Elm**

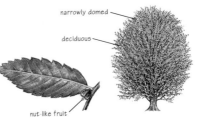

narrowly domed

deciduous

nut-like fruit

An attractive tree with dark green leaves edged by large, rounded teeth. The smooth, scaly bark has rounded, orange patches. Some cultivated trees have many stout, almost upright branches arising near the base, forming a dense crown that is oval in outline.

Status: introduced from the Caucasus; infrequently planted for ornament.

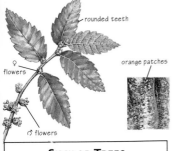

rounded teeth

♀ flowers

orange patches

♂ flowers

SIMILAR TREES

1 Keaki (*Zelkova serrata*) is a Japanese ornamental tree with sharply toothed leaves turning yellow, red or orange. **2 *Zelkova abelicea*** is an uncommon native species from the mountains of Crete, and is sometimes cultivated. It differs in the small leaves with few, rounded teeth, and white, scented flowers.

sharply toothed

few teeth

1

2

CAUCASIAN ELM

Type	deciduous tree
Height	20–35m
Habitat	parks, gardens, rarely hedges
Flowering	April–May
Fruiting	August–September

TRUNK AND CROWN

Trunk	often short, becomes buttressed; suckers at base
Bark	yellowish grey, smooth, scaling leaving orange patches
Crown	narrowly domed; branches angled upwards
Twigs	slender, greyish brown, downy

LEAVES

Buds	small, blunt, reddish, downy
Leaves	alternate along stem, 5–10cm, oval or elliptical, pointed, with rounded teeth, base rounded or squarish, slightly unequal, dark green above, turning orange-brown in autumn, dull or shiny, often with scattered, stiff hairs, veins 6–12 pairs; stalk 1–2mm
Stipules	small, soon falling

FLOWERS AND FRUIT

Flowers	♂ and ♀ flowers on different plants, with leaves
♂	on lower part of twig
♀	solitary at leaf-base
Perianth	5 joined lobes
Stamens	5, yellow, upright
Stigmas	2 on slender styles
Fruit	nut-like, solitary, 4–5mm, rounded, ridged
Seeds	1, not released

Southern Nettle-tree *Celtis australis*

This graceful tree differs from the related elms by the narrow, nettle-like leaves drawn out into a long, slender point. Berry-like fruits are sweet-tasting with an edible nut-like centre, and were important in the diet of Stone Age people.

Status: native to southern Europe; planted elsewhere for ornament and shade.

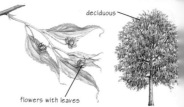
deciduous

flowers with leaves

sharp teeth

smooth

berry-like, ripens blackish

long tip

SOUTHERN NETTLE-TREE

Type	deciduous tree
Height	10–25m
Habitat	woodland, scrub, roadsides
Flowering	May
Fruiting	August

TRUNK AND CROWN

Trunk	straight below, forked above
Bark	grey-brown, smooth with rows of lenticels, some fissured
Crown	domed
Twigs	slender, downy, reddish brown

LEAVES

Buds	small, downy
Leaves	alternate along stem, 4–15cm, narrowly oval, with long, slender, sometimes twisted point, edge often wavy, sharply toothed, base rounded or shallowly notched, dark green, turning yellow in autumn, stiffly hairy above, downy below with white hairs, 3 main veins from base; stalk 1–3.5cm
Stipules	small, soon falling

FLOWERS AND FRUIT

Flowers	♂ and ♂ on same tree, with leaves, 7–10mm, yellowish, long-stalked
Perianth	4–5 separate lobes
Stamens	4–5, yellow
Stigmas	2, on slender styles
Ovaries	1, rounded
Fruit	berry-like, solitary, 9–12mm, globular, smooth, blackish brown, long-stalked
Seeds	pitted, nut-like centre to fruit retains single seed

SIMILAR TREES

1 *Celtis tournefortii* is a native shrub or small tree with oval, bluntly toothed leaves. The fruit has a 4-ridged, nut-like centre.
2 Hackberry (*Celtis occidentalis*), a cultivated species from eastern North America, has rough bark and leaves with fewer, long, whiskered teeth. The orange or purple ripe fruit has a shorter stalk.

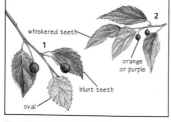
whiskered teeth

orange or purple

blunt teeth

oval

Morus nigra **Black Mulberry**

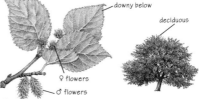

downy below

deciduous

♀ flowers

♂ flowers

Commonly a short, broad, gnarled tree, Black Mulberry has been cultivated for its sweet-and-sour fruit in Europe since Greek and Roman times. The exact origin of this species is unknown since all trees are apparently cultivated or naturalized from cultivation.

Status: introduced, probably from central Asia; widely grown for fruit in southern Europe, often naturalized.

ripen blackish

heart-shaped

toothed

sometimes lobed

BLACK MULBERRY

Type	deciduous tree
Height	3–16m
Habitat	fields, gardens
Flowering	April–May
Fruiting	August–September
TRUNK AND CROWN	
Trunk	short, often leaning
Bark	dark orange-brown, rough, scaling, fissured, with burrs
Crown	low, domed; branches stout, rough, twisted
Twigs	stout, become reddish brown
LEAVES	
Buds	stout, conical, glossy brown
Leaves	alternate along stem, 6–20cm, broadly oval or heart-shaped, sharply pointed, toothed, sometimes deeply lobed, base notched, dark green, roughly hairy above, paler, downy below; stalk 1.5–2.5cm, stout, hairy
Stipules	soon falling
FLOWERS AND FRUIT	
Flowers	♂ and ♀ flowers on same tree, in short spikes
	♂ 2–2.5cm, yellowish green
Stamens	4, yellow
	♀ 1–1.5cm
Perianth	4 lobes, joined at base
Stigmas	2, slender
Ovaries	1 per ♀ flower
Fruit	at leaf-base, 2–2.5cm, many berry-like segments, deep red to blackish purple, almost stalkless, becomes sweet
Seeds	1 per fruit segment

SIMILAR TREES

Introduced from China, **White Mulberry** (*Morus alba*) is the food plant for silk-worms and fuels the silk industry. It differs in the glossy, almost hairless leaves and stalked, white or pale purplish fruit.

pale

glossy

almost hairless

Osage Orange *Maclura pomifera*

This small, thorny tree is most easily distinguished by its orange-sized, yellowish fruit, with milky white, inedible flesh. When trimmed, the plant forms an impenetrable hedge and is used as such in southern Europe.

Status: introduced from North America; planted for ornament and hedges; naturalized in southern Europe.

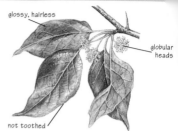

glossy, hairless

globular heads

not toothed

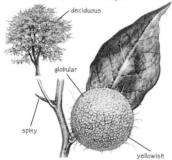

deciduous

globular

spiny

yellowish

OSAGE ORANGE

Type	deciduous tree
Height	up to 14m
Habitat	hedges, street tree, parks
Flowering	June
Fruiting	October–November
TRUNK AND CROWN	
Trunk	often forked, slender
Bark	rough, orange-brown
Crown	irregular, domed; branches twisted
Twigs	spiny, downy becoming hairless
LEAVES	
Buds	small, brown
Leaves	alternate along stem, 5–12cm, oval, pointed, edge unbroken, base wedge-shaped or rounded, glossy dark green, hairless above, paler below; stalk 5–8mm, shortly hairy
Stipules	soon falling
FLOWERS AND FRUIT	
Flowers	♂ and ♀ on different trees
♂	greenish yellow, in broad, stalked heads, 1.5–2.5cm
Stamens	4, yellowish
♀	many in globular head, 2–2.5cm, green
Perianth	4-lobed
Stigmas	2, on slender styles
Ovaries	1 per ♀ flower
Fruit	10–14cm, globular, green, turning yellow or orange, with white, stringy flesh
Seeds	not released

SIMILAR TREES

Paper Mulberry (*Broussonetia papyrifera*) has hairy, toothed leaves, which are sometimes deeply lobed. Male flowers are in hanging catkins; female flowers form globular, woolly heads, which turn into spiky, globular fruits. From eastern Asia, it is naturalized in southern Europe.

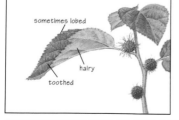

sometimes lobed

hairy

toothed

Much cultivated in the Mediterranean region for its delicious fruit, which is eaten fresh or dried. Though these edible figs are an exception, fruits of most fig species are pollinated by tiny wasps that enter a hole at the fruit tip and lay eggs in specialized flowers.

Status: native to southern Europe; cultivated for fruit, ornament and shade.

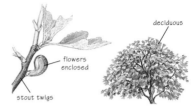

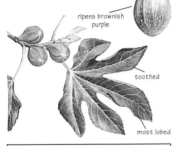

FIG

Type	deciduous tree or shrub
Height	up to 10m
Habitat	fields, orchards, parks, gardens, naturalized by roads
Flowering	September–November
Fruiting	July–October, following year

TRUNK AND CROWN

Trunk	usually short, often forked
Bark	pale grey with darker streaks, smooth or uneven
Crown	domed, wide-spreading; branches twisted
Twigs	stout, with large leaf-scars

LEAVES

Buds	conical, pointed
Leaves	alternate along stem, 7–30cm, most with 3–5 deep, blunt lobes, thick, leathery, irregularly toothed, base notched, glossy dark green, roughly hairy; stalk 5–10cm, stout
Stipules	broad, soon falling leaving circular scar around twig

FLOWERS AND FRUIT

Flowers	♂ and ♀ tiny, inside hollow structure that becomes fruit
Perianth	2–6 tiny segments
Stamens	♂ flowers with 4
Stigmas	♀ flowers with 2, slender
Ovaries	1 per ♀ flower
Fruit	5–8cm, pear-shaped, green to brownish purple, hollow structure containing individual tiny fruits
Seeds	retained within tiny fruits

SIMILAR TREES

Two evergreens with leathery leaves, grown as street trees in the south, have curious roots sprouting from branches. **1 Indian Rubber-tree** (*Ficus elastica*), with oblong leaves, is grown as a pot plant in northern Europe. **2 Banyan Tree** (*Ficus benghalensis*) has broad, wavy-edged leaves.

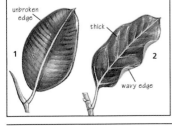

Sweet-gum *Liquidambar styraciflua*

A magnificent tree in autumn, when the whole crown can turn bright shades of red, purple or yellow. Similar to maples, it is easily distinguished by the alternate leaves and globular, spiky fruit. Where it is native in North America, it is the source of scented gum, and the fine-grained timber is used for furniture.

Status: introduced from North America; frequently planted in northern Europe for ornament, especially for autumn colour.

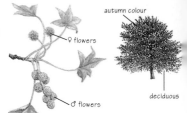

autumn colour

♀ flowers

♂ flowers

deciduous

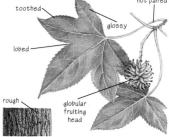

not paired

toothed

glossy

lobed

rough

globular fruiting head

SWEET-GUM

Type	deciduous tree
Height	5–30m (45m in North America)
Habitat	parks, gardens, street tree
Flowering	May
Fruiting	October–November

TRUNK AND CROWN

Trunk	usually short and broad
Bark	pale grey to brown, rough
Crown	conical to broadly domed; branches widely spreading
Twigs	slender, downy becoming hairless

LEAVES

Buds	conical, glossy green
Leaves	alternate along stem, 8–15cm, with 3–7 lobes, pointed, finely toothed, glossy green above, turning red, purple or orange in autumn, reddish hairs in tufts below; stalk 10–15cm, grooved
Stipules	small, soon falling

FLOWERS AND FRUIT

Flowers	♂ and ♀ flowers on different plants
♂	yellow, globular heads clustered into spike, 5–10cm
♀	in globular head, 1–1.5cm, solitary or sometimes paired
Stamens	many in ♂ head
Stigmas	1 per ♀ flower
Ovaries	1 per ♀ flower
Fruit	globular, spiny head, 2–3.5cm, of many slender capsules, each 6–8mm, stalk 4–6cm
Seeds	each capsule with 1 or 2 seeds

SIMILAR TREES

Oriental Sweet-gum (*Liquidambar orientalis*), from south-west Asia, has smaller, more deeply lobed, dull green leaves with coarser, irregular teeth.

dull green

deeper lobes

Irregularly toothed

Hamamelis mollis **Witch-hazel**

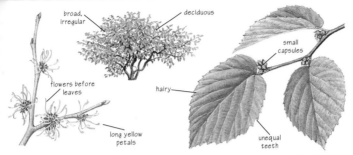

broad, irregular

deciduous

small capsules

flowers before leaves

hairy

long yellow petals

unequal teeth

Flowering in mid-winter, this ornamental species is valued for the colour and scent of its flowers. The commonest of several cultivated species, it is usually a shrub though some species and cultivars form small trees. An extract is used for treating bruises and inflammation.

Status: introduced from China; commonly planted for ornament.

SIMILAR TREES

1 Virginian Witch-hazel (*Hamamelis virginiana*), from North America, flowers in the autumn. **2 Persian Ironwood** (*Parrotia persica*) is a small tree with scarcely toothed leaves, small, purplish flowers and smooth grey bark flaking to reveal pink or yellow patches.

small flowers

scarcely toothed

autumn-flowering

1   2

WITCH-HAZEL

Type	deciduous shrub, rarely reaching tree size
Height	2.5–4m
Habitat	parks, roadsides near towns
Flowering	December–March
Fruiting	August–September

TRUNK AND CROWN

Trunk	often several, forked
Bark	smooth, greyish brown
Crown	broad, irregular; branches angled upwards, twisted
Twigs	slender, pale grey

LEAVES

Buds	conical, pointed
Leaves	alternate along stem, 7–12cm, broadly oval or rounded, long-pointed, doubly toothed, base rounded or wedge-shaped, softly hairy, yellow or orange in autumn; stalk short
Stipules	large, soon falling

FLOWERS AND FRUIT

Flowers	☿, before leaves, few in compact, short-stalked cluster, 3–4cm long, deep yellow
Petals	4, long, narrow; sepals 4, rounded, reddish
Stamens	4, purplish
Ovaries	single
Fruit	oblong capsule, splits lengthwise
Seeds	2, black, shiny

London Plane *Platanus × hybrida*

Tolerant of pollution, this tree is common in towns of southern and western Europe. Of rapid growth, it makes a huge tree with lobed leaves, globular, spiky fruits and scaly bark revealing large patches of creamy white. Of obscure origin, it is considered to be a hybrid between Oriental Plane and American Plane (*P. occidentalis*).

Status: of garden origin; widely planted for ornament, shade and timber.

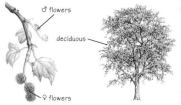

♂ flowers

deciduous

♀ flowers

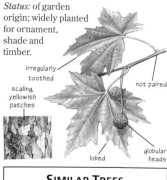

irregularly toothed

scaling, yellowish patches

not paired

lobed

globular heads

SIMILAR TREES

Oriental Plane (*Platanus orientalis*) has more deeply lobed leaves with a narrower base, and fruiting heads in clusters of 3–6. Native to south-eastern Europe, it is also planted elsewhere.

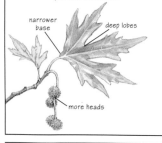

narrower base

deep lobes

more heads

LONDON PLANE

Type	deciduous tree
Height	up to 45m
Habitat	parks, roadsides
Flowering	April–June
Fruiting	February–April

TRUNK AND CROWN

Trunk	long, straight
Bark	grey-brown, scaling leaving whitish yellow patches, becomes fissured at base
Crown	domed; branches often twisted
Twigs	slender, often hanging

LEAVES

Buds	6–8mm, reddish brown
Leaves	alternate along stem, 8–24cm, variably 5-lobed, pointed, irregularly toothed, base squarish or notched, glossy, bright green above, paler below, veins woolly; stalk long, broad-based
Stipules	oval, toothed, usually falling

FLOWERS AND FRUIT

Flowers	♂ and ♀ on same tree, in globular heads
♂	2–6 yellowish heads in cluster 4–8cm long
Perianth	4–6 lobes
Stamens	4–6 per ♂ flower
♀	2–5 reddish heads on stalk
Ovaries	3–6 per ♀ flower, surrounded by long hairs at base
Fruit	usually 2 globular heads on stalk, breaks into segments, each with tuft of hairs
Seeds	1 per segment, not released

Casuarina equisetifolia **Horsetail She-oak**

This puzzling tree looks superficially like some sort of cypress from afar, but it has very slender twigs and scale-like leaves resembling a Horsetail *(Equisetum)*. Originally from New South Wales, it is remarkably resistant to drought and tolerant of salt, making it ideal for stabilizing sand dunes. The hard wood is so dense that it sinks in water.

Status: introduced from Australia; planted in the Mediterranean region for ornament, shelter or stabilizing sand.

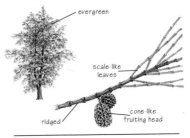

evergreen
scale-like leaves
cone-like fruiting head
ridged

slender twigs

cracks and peel

flowers in spikes

SIMILAR TREES

Drooping She-oak *(Causarina stricta)* has much longer male flower-heads and larger fruiting heads. It is more tolerant of frosts.

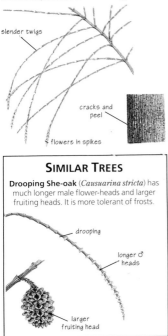

drooping

longer ♂ heads

larger fruiting head

HORSETAIL SHE-OAK

Type	evergreen tree
Height	5–20m
Habitat	well-drained, light soils
Flowering	February–March
Fruiting	September–October

TRUNK AND CROWN

Trunk	upright, forked above
Bark	grey-brown, peels in long strips
Crown	conical or columnar; branches slender, angled upwards
Twigs	very slender, wiry, ridged, drooping

LEAVES

Buds	minute
Leaves	in rings of 6–8 around twigs, scale-like, sharply pointed, edge unbroken, base broad, hairless, grey-green; stalkless
Stipules	absent

FLOWERS AND FRUIT

Flowers	♂ and ♀ on same tree, minute, in heads at shoot tip
♂	in dense spike 1–1.5cm long, brownish, each flower formed by 1 stamen
Stamens	1 per ♂ flower
♀	compact, reddish head, 3–4mm
Stigmas	2, on short style
Ovaries	1 per ♀ flower
Fruit	cone-like head, 1–1.5cm, cylindrical, of tiny, woody scales, fruit nut-like with short wing
Seeds	1 per fruit, not released

Caucasian Wing-nut *Pterocarya fraxinifolia*

An impressive tree with huge leaves composed of paired leaflets. Suckers at the base can grow into new trees, forming a dense, impenetrable clump if left untended. In fruit the tree is easily recognized, as it has long clusters of broadly winged nuts.

Status: introduced from south-western Asia; grown mainly for ornament in Europe.

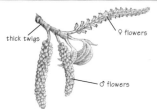

♀ flowers
thick twigs
♂ flowers

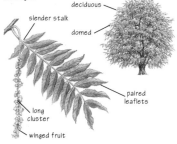

deciduous
slender stalk
domed
paired leaflets
long cluster
winged fruit

SIMILAR TREES

Chinese Wing-nut (*Pterocarya stenoptera*) differs in the hairy shoots and leaves with a flattened wing either side of the central stalk. The hybrid between these two species is also grown, distinguished by its intermediate leaves and great vigour.

winged stalk

CAUCASIAN WING-NUT

Type	deciduous tree
Height	up to 35m
Habitat	woods, parks, often near water
Flowering	April–May
Fruiting	September–October

TRUNK AND CROWN

Trunk	often clumped, with suckers
Bark	grey-brown, fissured, ridged
Crown	domed; branches spreading
Twigs	stout, smooth

LEAVES

Buds	stalked, slender, not scaly
Leaves	alternate along stem, up to 60cm, with 5–15 pairs of oblong, pointed, sharply toothed leaflets, often overlapping, leaflet at tip, glossy green above, paler below, turning bright yellow in autumn; central stalk rounded
Stipules	absent

FLOWERS AND FRUIT

Flowers		♂ and ♀ catkins on same tree, with leaves
	♂	on year-old twigs, 5–12cm, thick, hanging, many yellowish green flowers
Stamens		many
	♀	on new growth, 10–15cm, hanging, many greenish flowers
Stigmas		2 on single style, pink
Ovaries		1 per ♀ flower
Fruit		nut with rounded or oblong wing c2cm wide, in cluster 25–50cm long
Seeds		1 per nut, not released

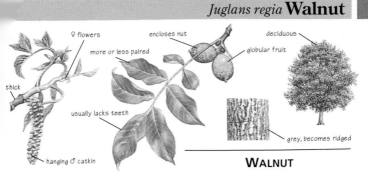

♀ flowers

more or less paired

encloses nut

deciduous

globular fruit

thick

usually lacks teeth

grey, becomes ridged

hanging ♂ catkin

A magnificent tree with a rugged grey trunk and large, scented leaves bearing paired leaflets. The large fruit is best known as a nut after the spongy outer wall has been removed. Immature fruits are also pickled whole. The timber is hard and beautifully marked, especially when cut from burrs.

Status: native to south-eastern Europe; often planted for fruit, timber or ornament, and widely naturalized.

SIMILAR TREES

Black Walnut (*Juglans nigra*) is a North American species grown mainly for timber. It has many sharply toothed leaflets, and shortly hairy fruits containing a ridged, very hard nut.

sharply toothed

more leaflets

WALNUT

Type	deciduous tree
Height	up to 30m
Habitat	woodland, fields, parks
Flowering	May–June
Fruiting	September–October

TRUNK AND CROWN

Trunk	stout, often short
Bark	grey, young smooth, becomes deeply fissured and ridged
Crown	broad, domed; branches spreading, twisted
Twigs	stout, hairless, pith with separate cavities

LEAVES

Buds	c6mm, broad, scaly, blackish
Leaves	alternate along stem, mostly with 3–4 pairs of oval or elliptical leaflets, leaflet at tip, each leaflet 6–15cm, pointed, edge almost unbroken, downy when young, becoming hairless; stalked
Stipules	absent

FLOWERS AND FRUIT

Flowers	♂ and ♀ on same tree
♂	catkins on year-old twigs, 5–15cm, hanging, green
Stamens	♂ flowers with many
♀	few flowers, on new growth
Stigmas	2 on single style
Ovaries	1 per ♀ flower
Fruit	solitary or few, 4–5cm, globular, green, hairless, spongy wall around large, wrinkled nut
Seeds	1 per nut, not released

Bitternut *Carya cordiformis*

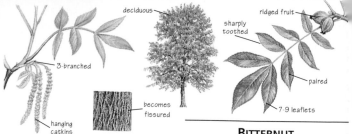

deciduous

3-branched

hanging catkins

becomes fissured

ridged fruit

sharply toothed

paired

7-9 leaflets

A tall, narrowly domed tree with leaves similar to the related Walnut, but the fruit differs in having a thin husk, which splits to release a bitter, inedible nut. In winter it has distinctive bright yellow buds. Bitternut and several related species are grown in North America and Europe for the very tough but flexible timber.

Status: introduced from eastern North America; planted for ornament and timber.

SIMILAR TREES

1 Pignut-tree (*Carya glabra*) has dark buds with more scales, fewer leaflets and a smoothly rounded fruit. **2 Shagbark Hickory** (*Carya orata*) has very scaly bark, larger buds and large leaves with the end leaflet stalked.

hairless

not ridged

stalked

1

5-7 leaflets

2

larger

BITTERNUT

Type	deciduous tree
Height	up to 30m
Habitat	parks, gardens, plantations
Flowering	May–June
Fruiting	October

TRUNK AND CROWN

Trunk	stout, usually straight
Bark	grey-brown, smooth becoming scaly and fissured
Crown	conical to narrowly domed; branches angled upwards
Twigs	rather slender, hairless

LEAVES

Buds	bright yellow, slender, 4–6 scales
Leaves	alternate along stem, 20–30cm, usually with 4 pairs of oval leaflets, each 5–15cm, stalkless leaflet at tip, leaflets pointed, sharply toothed, downy below when young, becoming hairless, golden-yellow in autumn
Stipules	absent

FLOWERS AND FRUIT

Flowers	♂ and ♀ on same tree
♂	3-branched catkins, 5–7.5cm, hanging, green
♀	2–3, tiny, on new growth
Stamens	many
Stigmas	2 on single style
Ovaries	1 per ♀ flower
Fruit	2–4cm, almost globular, 4-ridged, shortly hairy, tough husk enclosing nut
Seeds	1 per nut, not released

Pittosporum undulatum **White Holly**

C ommonly grown as an ornamental
tree or for hedging in southern
Europe, White Holly's tough leaves resist
scorching by the Mediterranean sun, and
its fragrant, white flowers scent the
evening air.

Status: introduced from south-eastern
Australia; widely planted for ornament in
the Mediterranean region and western
Europe, sometimes naturalized.

globular,
ripens orange

white

fragrant

evergreen

unbroken
edge

wavy   glossy

SIMILAR TREES

1 Karo (*Pittosporum crassifolium*) has thick,
blunt leaves and red flowers. **2 Pittosporum**
(*Pittosporum tenuifolium*) has blackish stems,
thin, glossy, crinkled leaves and purplish,
honey-scented flowers. It is commonly used
with cut flowers; variegated cultivars are
also grown for ornament.

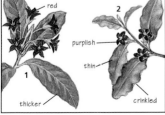

red

purplish

thin

1

thicker

2

crinkled

WHITE HOLLY

Type	evergreen tree or large shrub
Height	up to 20m
Habitat	parks, gardens, street tree
Flowering	May–June
Fruiting	September
TRUNK AND CROWN	
Trunk	usually short, forked
Bark	grey-brown, smooth, becomes fissured
Crown	pyramidal or domed; branches spreading
Twigs	green, rather stout
LEAVES	
Buds	small, inconspicuous
Leaves	alternate along stem, 7–20cm, oval or narrowly oval, sharply pointed, edge unbroken, rather wavy, base wedge-shaped, hairless, dark, glossy green; stalk short
Stipules	absent
FLOWERS AND FRUIT	
Flowers	♂, rather few in broad, branched heads, white, fragrant
Petals	5, equal, oval, pointed; sepals 5, slender
Stamens	5, yellow
Stigmas	1
Fruit	almost globular capsule, 1–1.2cm, ripens orange, hairless, leathery wall splits into 2, releasing seeds
Seeds	many, in sticky substance

Evergreen Magnolia *Magnolia grandiflora*

A spectacular species with large, glossy leaves and huge flowers, the size of dinner plates. White flowers open a few at a time over a long period; later flowers are damaged by frosts and blotched brown. In cooler areas, it is most often grown against a wall.

Status: introduced from south-eastern North America; commonly grown in western Europe for ornament.

evergreen

short

fleshy segments

white

leathery

huge flowers

edge unbroken

hairy

glossy

SIMILAR TREES

A taller tree, flowering in the spring before the leaves, **1 Campbell's Magnolia** (*Magnolia campbellii*) has deep pink flowers that gradually fade. **2 Hybrid Magnolia** (*Magnolia x soulangiana*) is shorter, with smaller flowers, which are white inside and tinged purplish outside.

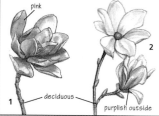

pink

1

deciduous

2

purplish outside

EVERGREEN MAGNOLIA

Type	evergreen tree or shrub
Height	to 10m (30m in North America)
Habitat	parks, large gardens
Flowering	June–October
Fruiting	September–November

TRUNK AND CROWN

Trunk	usually short, forked
Bark	smooth, dark grey
Crown	narrow; branches spread apart
Twigs	stout, with reddish hairs

LEAVES

Buds	8–15mm, conical
Leaves	alternate along stem, 8–16cm, elliptical or oval, broadest above middle, thick, leathery, edge unbroken, sometimes wavy, hairless, glossy deep green above, thickly covered with reddish brown hairs below; stalk 2–2.5cm, stout
Stipules	large, soon falling

FLOWERS AND FRUIT

Flowers	⚥, single at shoot tip, 20–25cm, bowl-shaped, creamy white, scented
Petals	almost equal, separate to base, thick; no distinct sepals
Stamens	many, arranged spirally
Stigmas	1 per ovary
Ovaries	many, in narrow cone
Fruit	4–6cm, conical, composed of separate fleshy segments,
Seeds	each fruit-segment with large seed on slender thread

A spectacular tree when fully grown, with a massive, straight trunk leading up to a tall, narrow crown. Four-lobed leaves are quite unlike those of other trees, and curious, cup-shaped, green and orange flowers bear a faint resemblance to tulips. Only two species of Tulip-tree are known, one in North America and the other in Asia.

Status: introduced from eastern North America; widely planted for ornament and timber.

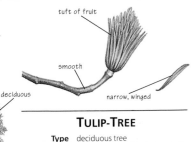

tuft of fruit

smooth

deciduous

narrow, winged

narrow

orange marks

greenish

broad, paired lobes

notched

TULIP-TREE

Type	deciduous tree
Height	to 40m (60m in North America)
Habitat	parks, gardens, plantations
Flowering	June–July
Fruiting	September

TRUNK AND CROWN

Trunk	straight, oldest buttressed
Bark	grey, smooth, becoming ridged
Crown	narrow; most branches angled upwards, lower bent down
Twigs	smooth, green or reddish brown

LEAVES

Buds	5–12mm, oblong, flattened
Leaves	alternate along stem, 7–16cm, broad with 2 or 4 oval or triangular lobes, tip squarish or notched, hairless, glossy green above, paler below, turning yellow or orange in autumn; stalk 5–10cm
Stipules	large, oblong or elliptical, blunt, eventually falling

FLOWERS AND FRUIT

Flowers	☿, at stem-tip, cup-shaped, 6–8cm wide, whitish green, inner marked with orange
Perianth	6 petal-like parts, 4–5cm, equal, separate; 3 smaller, sepal-like parts fold back
Stamens	many, long, spirally arranged
Stigmas	1 per ovary
Ovaries	many in central spike
Fruit	tuft of brown fruits from each flower, each 4–5cm, narrow, flattened with long wing
Seeds	1 per fruit, not released

SIMILAR TREES

Chinese Tulip-tree (*Liriodendron chinense*) has unfolding, coppery leaves with a more deeply divided, narrowly lobed blade and a reddish stalk.

narrower lobes

Sweet Bay *Laurus nobilis*

A small evergreen with tough, leathery leaves emitting a wonderful spicy aroma if lightly crushed. Dried leaves are widely used for flavouring food. Plants in towns are often trimmed to shape.

Status: native to the Mediterranean region; widely cultivated for ornament, shelter, or as a herb; often naturalized.

evergreen

tough leaves

wavy edge

blackish berries

♂ flowers

spicy aroma

♀ flowers

compact head

SWEET BAY

Type	evergreen tree or shrub
Height	2–20m
Habitat	woodland, scrub, parks
Flowering	April–June
Fruiting	September–October
TRUNK AND CROWN	
Trunk	usually short, forked
Bark	grey, smooth or fissured below
Crown	broadly conical; branches angled upwards
Twigs	slender, hairless, green or reddish
LEAVES	
Buds	2–3mm, conical, reddish brown
Leaves	5–10cm, narrowly oval or oblong, tough, pointed, edge wavy, dark green above, dotted with glands, hairless, paler below; stalk 4–6mm, red
Stipules	absent
FLOWERS AND FRUIT	
Flowers	♀ and ♂ on same tree
	♂ in short-stalked, compact head, each 7–10mm, dull whitish yellow
	♀ 2–6 in head, greenish white, with 2–4 sterile stamens
Perianth	4-lobed, petal-like
Stamens	8–12 per ♂ flower
Stigmas	1 on short style
Ovaries	1 per ♀ flower
Fruit	small cluster of almost globular berries, each 8–15mm, black, stalk 3–4mm
Seeds	1 per fruit

SIMILAR TREES

Planted in the Mediterranean region, **Avocado** (*Persea americana*) has larger leaves and elongated clusters of flowers, each of which have 6 lobes to the perianth. The large, edible fruit is pear-shaped and rough-skinned with soft, creamy-textured, yellowish flesh.

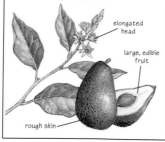

elongated head

large, edible fruit

rough skin

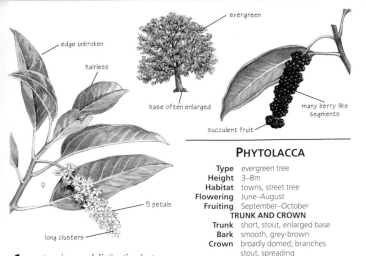

evergreen

edge unbroken

hairless

base often enlarged

many berry-like segments

succulent fruit

♀

5 petals

long clusters

A most curious and distinctive feature on older trees of Phytolacca is that the area where the base of the trunk adjoins the roots becomes greatly enlarged at soil level. It is as though the trunk had melted and flowed across the ground. It may spread for a metre or more from the trunk in each direction and is most noticeable on a bank or where the soil has been washed away. Phytolacca's succulent, berry-like fruits hang in long clusters. Related species occurring in Europe are all herbaceous plants, and are sometimes used for their edible young leaves or berries.

Status: introduced from South America; planted in the Mediterranean region for ornament and shade; naturalized in places.

Similar trees: none.

PHYTOLACCA

Type	evergreen tree
Height	3–8m
Habitat	towns, street tree
Flowering	June–August
Fruiting	September–October

TRUNK AND CROWN

Trunk	short, stout, enlarged base
Bark	smooth, grey-brown
Crown	broadly domed; branches stout, spreading
Twigs	stout, rather succulent, hairless

LEAVES

Buds	small, green
Leaves	alternate along stem, 5–12cm, oval or elliptical, pointed, edge unbroken, base wedge-shaped, bright green, hairless; stalked
Stipules	absent

FLOWERS AND FRUIT

Flowers	♂ and ♀ on different trees, in hanging clusters, mostly at stem-tip
♂	clusters 8–15cm, greenish white, stalk 1–1.5cm
♀	slightly larger than ♂
Perianth	5 petal-like, oblong lobes
Stamens	many per ♂ flower
Stigmas	1 per ovary
Ovaries	7–10 per ♀ flower
Fruit	long clusters of fruits, each with globular berry-like segments, 5–7.5mm, purplish black
Seeds	each fruit segment with single seed

Quince *Cydonia oblonga*

Introduced in ancient times from Asia, the Quince is nowadays widespread in Europe. In northern and western regions it is most often planted as an ornamental shrub. In southerly areas it is grown for its edible fruits, which have a delightful fragrance and are extremely hard.

Status: native to south-western and central Asia; cultivated and naturalized in much of Europe.

deciduous

hard

fragrant

often thorny

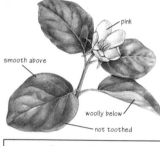

pink

smooth above

woolly below

not toothed

SIMILAR TREES

Two species with similar fruits are widely cultivated shrubs with toothed leaves and red flowers. **1 Flowering Quince** (*Chaenomeles speciosa*) has larger flowers and leaves than **2 Dwarf Quince** (*Chaenomeles japonica*).

toothed

small

red or orange

1

2

QUINCE

Type	deciduous tree or shrub
Height	1.5–7.5m
Habitat	hedges and copses
Flowering	April–May
Fruiting	September

TRUNK AND CROWN

Trunk	slender, usually short
Bark	grey-brown, smooth
Crown	often very broad, spreading
Twigs	woolly, becoming smooth, spiny

LEAVES

Buds	2–3mm, reddish-brown, hairy
Leaves	alternate, 5–10cm, oval, blunt, green and smooth above, greyish and woolly below; stalkless
Stipules	small, usually falling very early

FLOWERS AND FRUIT

Flowers	☿, single in angles of leaves, 3.8–5cm, bowl-shaped, pink, rarely white
Petals	5, broad, blunt or slightly notched at the tip, tapered at base; sepals 5, smaller, very hairy, persistent on fruit, toothed
Stamens	15–25
Stigmas	5, styles woolly towards base
Ovaries	1, in base of flower
Fruit	fleshy but extremely hard, 2.5–3.5cm, rarely 12cm, globular or pear-shaped, ripening yellow, very fragrant
Seeds	many, brown to blackish

Pyrus communis Common Pear

often thorny
white
deciduous

This widespread tree is a hybrid of complex and obscure origin. Wild trees have small, sour fruit; orchard trees, which produce the familiar large, sweet-tasting fruit, belong to var. *culta*. The trees often seen in hedgerows or on field margins may be escapes from cultivation, but sometimes represent the remains of old orchards.

Status: cultivated throughout Europe, except for the far north and far south, often on a large scale.

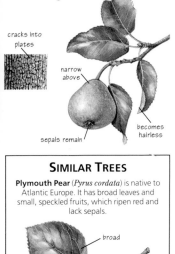

cracks into plates

narrow above

becomes hairless

sepals remain

SIMILAR TREES

Plymouth Pear (*Pyrus cordata*) is native to Atlantic Europe. It has broad leaves and small, speckled fruits, which ripen red and lack sepals.

broad

speckled

no sepals

ripens red

COMMON PEAR

Type	deciduous tree
Height	up to 20m
Habitat	orchards, hedges, often as isolated trees
Flowering	April–May
Fruiting	September–October

TRUNK AND CROWN

Trunk	straight, often suckering
Bark	blackish, forms small plates
Crown	broadly pyramidal; branches angled upwards on young trees, spreading on old trees
Twigs	stout, reddish brown, soon smooth and shiny, often spiny

LEAVES

Buds	5mm, yellowish brown, smooth, egg-shaped, pointed
Leaves	alternate, 5–8cm, oval to elliptical, pointed, finely short-toothed, hairy, becoming smooth; stalkless
Stipules	soon falling

FLOWERS AND FRUIT

Flowers	♂, 5–9 in clusters with leaves, white, stalks up to 1cm
Petals	5, 12–14mm, broadly oval, tapering abruptly at base; sepals 5, 6–8mm, narrow, persistent on fruit
Stamens	20–30, red
Stigmas	5, free, often hairy at base
Ovaries	1, in base of flower
Fruit	fleshy, firm, gritty-textured, 6–16cm, pear-shaped, oblong or almost globular, ripening green or yellowish
Seeds	several, black

99

Wild Pear *Pyrus pyraster*

toothed

white

small

usually thorny

deciduous

becomes hairless

brown, speckled

Often confused with Common Pear, Wild Pear can be distinguished by its more bushy and spiny growth, and by the much smaller, hard and tart fruit.

Status: native throughout much of Europe, absent from some Mediterranean islands and parts of the far north.

SIMILAR TREES

Two species with narrower leaves are **1 Sage-leaved Pear** (*Pyrus salvifolia*), from central Europe; and **2 Almond-leaved Pear** (*Pyrus amygdaliformis*), from France and Spain eastwards. The former has leaves with unbroken edges, and larger fruits. The latter usually has a few teeth towards the leaf-tip.

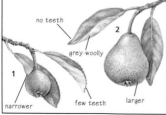

no teeth

grey-woolly

narrower

few teeth

larger

WILD PEAR

Type	deciduous tree
Height	8–20m
Habitat	thickets, open woodland
Flowering	April–May
Fruiting	September–October

TRUNK AND CROWN

Trunk	straight, short
Bark	rough, cracked
Crown	round-headed; branches spreading or angled upwards
Twigs	grey to brown, usually spiny

LEAVES

Buds	small, brown, scales 5–8
Leaves	alternate, 2.5–7cm, elliptical, oval or circular, pointed, base wedge-shaped, rounded or heart-shaped, finely toothed, hairy but soon smooth; stalkless
Stipules	soon falling

FLOWERS AND FRUIT

Flowers	☿, in clusters, white
Petals	5, 10–17mm, elliptical to circular, slightly crinkled, tapered at base; sepals 5, 3–8mm, persistent on fruit
Stamens	20–30, red
Stigmas	5, styles often hairy at base
Ovaries	1, 5-chambered, in base of flower
Fruit	1–3.5cm, fleshy, firm, gritty-textured, globular or top-shaped, ripening yellow, brown or black, with conspicuous lenticels
Seeds	several, black

Pyrus salicifolia **Willow-leaved Pear**

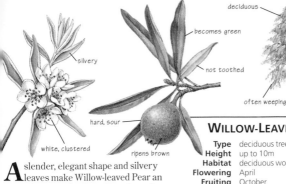

silvery

becomes green

not toothed

deciduous

often weeping

white, clustered

hard, sour

ripens brown

A slender, elegant shape and silvery leaves make Willow-leaved Pear an attractive tree of parks and gardens; the weeping cultivar 'Pendula' is common. The small fruits do not always develop fully, and are unsuitable for eating.

Status: native to Asia from the Caucasus mountains and Iran to Siberia; widely cultivated in Europe.

SIMILAR TREES

Two species have broader leaves, toothed towards the tip. **1** *P. elaeagrifolia*, from south-eastern Europe, has woolly leaves and styles that are hairy up to the middle. **2** *P. nivalis* has leaves that become hairless above, and larger fruits.

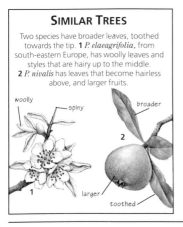

woolly

spiny

broader

1

larger

toothed

2

WILLOW-LEAVED PEAR

Type	deciduous tree
Height	up to 10m
Habitat	deciduous woods
Flowering	April
Fruiting	October
TRUNK AND CROWN	
Trunk	slender, straight
Bark	dark silver-grey, smooth
Crown	domed; main branches horizontal
Twigs	drooping, densely white-woolly
LEAVES	
Buds	4–6mm, pyramidal, brown, downy
Leaves	alternate, 3.5–9cm, narrow, pointed, grey-green and silvery downy on both sides, becoming smooth and glossy green above; stalkless
Stipules	soon falling
FLOWERS AND FRUIT	
Flowers	☿, in tight clusters, white, opening with the emerging leaves, stalks downy
Petals	5, c10mm, rounded or notched at tip, tapering at base; sepals 5, woolly, persistent on fruit
Stamens	15–30, red
Stigmas	2–5, styles woolly at base
Ovaries	1, in base of flower
Fruit	2.5cm, fleshy, firm, gritty-textured, sour, pear-shaped, top-shaped or cylindrical, ripening brown, stalk white, woolly
Seeds	several

Crab-apple *Malus sylvestris*

white tinged pink

deciduous

often thorny

small, sour

becomes hairless

The sour-fruited Crab-apple was once cultivated for fruit. Truly wild trees are spiny and have white flowers. Descendants of domesticated trees which have escaped back into the wild are unarmed and have pink-tinged flowers.

Status: native to most of Europe and western Asia.

SIMILAR TREES

1 *Malus dasyphylla* has woolly young twigs and occurs in the Balkan Peninsula and Danube basin. **2 Cultivated Apple** (*Malus domestica*) is a hybrid with leaves that are hairy below, and large, sweet fruit. It is the most widely grown orchard fruit, with more than one thousand cultivars recorded.

woolly when young

large fruit

hairy below

CRAB-APPLE

Type	deciduous tree
Height	2–10m
Habitat	woods, hedges, in hilly, chalky areas
Flowering	April–June
Fruiting	September–October

TRUNK AND CROWN

Trunk	short, often branching low down
Bark	brown, cracking
Crown	spreading, often dense; branches large and twisted
Twigs	reddish brown, numerous short shoots, sometimes thorny

LEAVES

Buds	4mm, reddish, hairy
Leaves	alternate, 3–11cm, oval, elliptical or nearly circular, pointed, wedge-shaped or rounded at base, finely toothed, hairy but soon becoming smooth; stalkless
Stipules	soon falling

FLOWERS AND FRUIT

Flowers	☿, in few-flowered clusters, 3–4cm, white tinged pale pink
Petals	5, oval, widest above middle, tapered at base; sepals 5, 3–7mm, hairy on inside
Stamens	15–50, yellow
Stigmas	2–5, styles joined and sometimes hairy at base
Ovaries	1, in base of flower
Fruit	fleshy, firm, 2.5–3cm, globular, ripening yellowish green tinged with red, sour
Seeds	several, brown to blackish

Malus x floribunda **Japanese Crab-apple**

long stalk

downy below

pink

deciduous

ripens yellowish

Wreathing the branches in spring, the pink and white flowers of this small tree are produced in great profusion. One of the most popular ornamental species of all time, it probably arose as a garden hybrid in Japan, from where it was introduced to many countries.

Status: exact origin unknown but probably Japan; widely planted in Europe for ornament.

SIMILAR TREES

Two widely grown ornamentals from China are **1 Siberian Crab-apple** (*Malus baccata*), with white flowers and red fruits; and **Purple Crab-apple** (*Malus x purpurea*), a garden hybrid with purplish flowers and fruits.

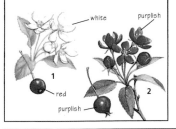

white

purplish

1

red

2

purplish

JAPANESE CRAB-APPLE

Type	deciduous tree
Height	6–9m
Habitat	parks and gardens
Flowering	April–May
Fruiting	October
TRUNK AND CROWN	
Trunk	short, straight, tapering
Bark	grey-brown
Crown	rounded, dense; branches numerous
Twigs	reddish when young, drooping, hairy
LEAVES	
Buds	2–4mm, dark red-brown, pointed
Leaves	alternate, 4–8cm, oblong to oval, pointed, sharply toothed, sometimes lobed, downy beneath but becoming smooth; stalkless
Stipules	small, soon falling
FLOWERS AND FRUIT	
Flowers	⚥, 4–7 in clusters, 2.5–3cm across, deep pink in bud, opening pale pink, fading white, fragrant
Petals	5, 13–15mm, oblong, blunt, base abruptly tapered; sepals 5, short, triangular, hairy within, soon falling
Stamens	15–50, yellow, pink at base
Stigmas	2–5, styles joined at base
Ovaries	1, in base of flower
Fruit	fleshy, firm, 2.5cm, globular, ripening bright yellow
Seeds	several, brown

Rowan *Sorbus aucuparia*

A small, attractive tree, with paired leaflets, broad heads of white flowers followed by red berries and, in colder areas, autumn colour. Berries are eagerly sought by fruit-eating birds and, rich in Vitamin C, the fruit can be made into a jelly. Cv. 'Beissneri' is planted for its orange-pink bark and more intense autumn colour.

Status: native; common in much of Europe; planted for ornament in streets and parks.

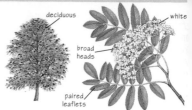

ROWAN

Type	deciduous tree
Height	up to 20m
Habitat	mountainous areas, lowland on light soils
Flowering	May–June
Fruiting	August–September
TRUNK AND CROWN	
Trunk	slender, sometimes forked
Bark	smooth, rarely slightly ridged, greyish brown
Crown	irregularly rounded, open
Branches	angled upwards
Twigs	hairy becoming smooth, purplish brown
LEAVES	
Buds	10–17mm long, narrow, egg-shaped, tip curved, purplish
Leaves	on alternate sides of stem, up to 25 x12cm; 5–9 pairs of oblong leaflets 3–6cm long, pointed, sharp-toothed, hairy, becoming smooth, dark green above, paler below, stalk 2–4mm
Stipules	small, soon falling
FLOWERS AND FRUIT	
Flowers	♀, many, in branched heads, 8–10mm, creamy white
Petals	5, c3.5mm, equal; sepals 5, triangular, hairy
Stamens	many
Stigmas	3–4
Ovaries	3–4, in base of flower
Fruit	many, in broad head, berry-like, almost globular, each 6–9mm, ripening bright red
Seeds	several, not released

SIMILAR TREES

1 Hupeh Rowan (*Sorbus hupehensis*) a Chinese ornamental species differing in the white or purplish fruits. Native in southern Europe and planted elsewhere, **2 Service-tree** (*Sorbus domestica*) is a larger tree with much larger, brownish green fruits.

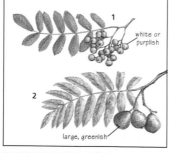

104

Sorbus torminalis **Wild Service-tree**

An unusual relative of the Rowan and Whitebeam, with distinctive, maple-like leaves and brown, speckled fruits resembling those of the Service-tree. Also like some maples, the foliage turns deep red in the autumn. Acid until late in ripening, the fruit eventually becomes sweet enough to eat.

Status: native to most of Europe except parts of the north; occasionally planted for ornament.

bark fissured

purplish in autumn

brown fruit

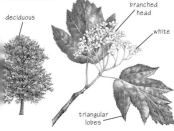

deciduous

branched head

white

triangular lobes

SIMILAR TREES

Two related plants are often regarded as hybrids. **1 Broad-leaved Whitebeam** (*Sorbus latifolia*) has slightly lobed leaves with grey hairs beneath. **2 Bastard Service-tree** (*Sorbus hybrida*), from Scandinavia, has a few pairs of leaflets at the leaf-base and red fruit.

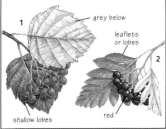

1

grey below

leaflets or lobes

2

shallow lobes

red

WILD SERVICE-TREE

Type	deciduous tree
Height	up to 25m
Habitat	woods, often lime-rich soils
Flowering	May–June
Fruiting	September
TRUNK AND CROWN	
Trunk	slender, sometimes forked
Bark	shallowly fissured, forming squarish scales, greyish brown
Crown	conical to broadly rounded
Branches	spreading
Twigs	woolly, soon becoming smooth
LEAVES	
Buds	4–5mm, globular, green, smooth
Leaves	on alternate sides of stem, 5–9cm, oval with 3–5 pairs of triangular lobes, pointed, sharply toothed, base rounded or heart-shaped, green above and below, turning purplish red in autumn, hairy below, becoming smooth, 4–6 pairs of veins; stalk 15–40mm
Stipules	small, soon falling
FLOWERS AND FRUIT	
Flowers	♂, in loose, heads, 10–15mm, white; stalk hairy
Petals	5, equal, rounded; sepals 5, triangular, hairy
Stamens	many
Stigmas	2
Ovaries	2, in base of flower
Fruit	berry-like, egg-shaped to globular, each 12–18mm, brown, speckled
Seeds	several, not released

Common Whitebeam *Sorbus aria*

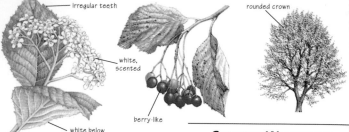

irregular teeth

white, scented

rounded crown

berry-like

white below

S ilvery white as they unfold in spring, the leaves of this tree gradually turn green on the upper surface as their pale hairs are shed; the lower leaf surface remains densely hairy. It is a characteristic tree of chalk downland.

Status: native to most of Europe; several cultivars are commonly planted street trees.

SIMILAR TREES

Two rather shrubby species have more or less globular fruits. **1** Greek Whitebeam (*Sorbus graeca*) has leathery leaves, which are greenish-woolly below and have rounded teeth; fruits have white spots.
2 Rock Whitebeam (*Sorbus rupicola*) has leaves with symmetrical teeth and fruits with many spots.

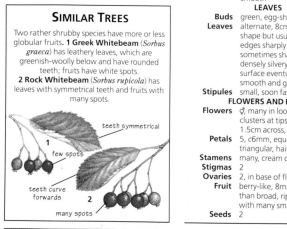

teeth symmetrical

few spots

1

teeth curve forwards

2

many spots

COMMON WHITEBEAM

Type	deciduous tree
Height	up to 15m
Habitat	chalky soils
Flowering	May–June
Fruiting	September
TRUNK AND CROWN	
Trunk	well-defined
Bark	grey, smooth, becoming flaky
Crown	conical in young trees, later broadly domed
Twigs	olive brown, hairy, becoming smooth
LEAVES	
Buds	green, egg-shaped, often hairy
Leaves	alternate, 8cm, variable in shape but usually broadly oval, edges sharply toothed and sometimes shallowly lobed, densely silvery-hairy, the upper surface eventually becoming smooth and green; stalkless
Stipules	small, soon falling
FLOWERS AND FRUIT	
Flowers	⚥, many in loose, branched clusters at tips of shoots, each 1.5cm across, white
Petals	5, c6mm, equal; sepals 5, triangular, hairy
Stamens	many, cream or pink
Stigmas	2
Ovaries	2, in base of flower, hairy
Fruit	berry-like, 8mm, usually longer than broad, ripening scarlet with many small lenticels
Seeds	2

Sorbus intermedia Swedish Whitebeam

deciduous
green above
ripen red
longer than broad

Shallow-lobed leaves felted below with yellowish grey hairs identify Swedish Whitebeam. Red fruits are dotted with a few pale lenticels. It flowers more intensively than most other whitebeams, and is often used as an ornamental tree.

Status: native to the Baltic region; planted elsewhere; sometimes naturalized.

smooth, grey
shallowly lobed
grey, woolly

SWEDISH WHITEBEAM

Type	deciduous tree
Height	up to 15m
Habitat	hills and mountains
Flowering	May
Fruiting	September
TRUNK AND CROWN	
Trunk	short
Bark	grey, smooth with wide, shallow cracks
Crown	dense, broadly domed
Twigs	grey to purplish, very hairy, becoming smooth
LEAVES	
Buds	8mm, egg-shaped, green or brown, with grey hairs
Leaves	alternate, 8–12cm, elliptic, shallowly lobed, the lobes reaching one-third of the way to midrib but more pronounced towards base of leaf, edge sharply toothed, smooth and green above, densely yellow-grey woolly below; stalkless
Stipules	small, soon falling
FLOWERS AND FRUIT	
Flowers	☿, many, in branched clusters in angles of leaves, each 12–20mm across, white, leaf stalk smooth
Petals	5, c6mm, equal; sepals 5
Stamens	many, cream
Stigmas	2, styles joined at base
Ovaries	2, in base of flower, hairy
Fruit	berry-like, 12–15mm, much longer than broad, ripening red, dotted with
Seeds	2

SIMILAR TREES

1 *Sorbus austriaca* has leaves with whitish grey wool below. Those of **2** *Sorbus mougeotii* are also grey-woolly below but less deeply lobed. Both are mountain species. **3** *Sorbus umbellata*, from the Balkan region, has deeply lobed, white-woolly leaves and yellow fruits.

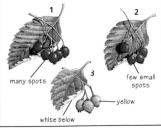

many spots
few small spots
yellow
white below

Loquat *Eriobotrya japonica*

brown hairs

woolly below

white,fragrant

glossy green

branched clusters

clustered

toothed

ripen yellow

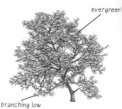

evergreen

branching low

Easily recognized by its leathery, evergreen leaves and the copious reddish, velvety hairs on twigs, leaves and flowers, this small tree is a common sight in Mediterranean areas. It is widely grown for its golden-yellow, sweet fruits, which resemble apricots and are often sold in markets. It may be grown in orchards but is more common as a single tree. The tree sometimes escapes and has established itself in the wild in many areas. Farther north, Loquat is grown mainly as an ornamental.

Status: introduced from China and widely cultivated; often naturalized.

Similar trees: none.

LOQUAT

Type	evergreen tree
Height	up to 10m
Habitat	dry, light soils
Flowering	October–February
Fruiting	April–June

TRUNK AND CROWN

Trunk	very slender, often branching near base
Bark	grey, slightly rough
Crown	irregular but usually narrow
Twigs	velvety-hairy

LEAVES

Buds	c4mm, pointed, very hairy
Leaves	alternate, 12–25cm, elliptical or oval and widest above middle, sharply toothed, leathery, conspicuously veined, dark glossy green above, densely woolly with reddish brown hairs below; stalkless
Stipules	very narrow

FLOWERS AND FRUIT

Flowers	⚥, in branched, pyramidal clusters, c1cm, creamy-white, almost hidden by dense brown hair, fragrant
Petals	5, oval or nearly circular, tip notched, base tapered; sepals 5, persisting on fruit
Stamens	20
Stigmas	2–5, styles joined at base
Ovaries	1, in base of flower
Fruit	fleshy, sweet, 3–6cm, elliptical to pear-shaped, ripening deep yellow
Seeds	1–several, each 1–1.5cm

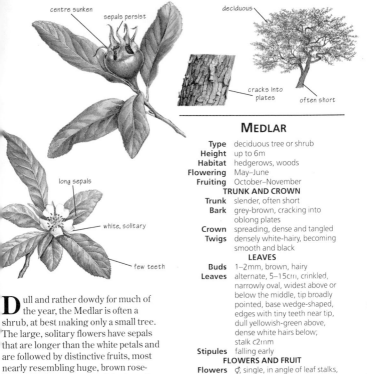

centre sunken

sepals persist

deciduous

cracks into plates

often short

long sepals

white, solitary

few teeth

MEDLAR

Type	deciduous tree or shrub
Height	up to 6m
Habitat	hedgerows, woods
Flowering	May–June
Fruiting	October–November

TRUNK AND CROWN

Trunk	slender, often short
Bark	grey-brown, cracking into oblong plates
Crown	spreading, dense and tangled
Twigs	densely white-hairy, becoming smooth and black

LEAVES

Buds	1–2mm, brown, hairy
Leaves	alternate, 5–15cm, crinkled, narrowly oval, widest above or below the middle, tip broadly pointed, base wedge-shaped, edges with tiny teeth near tip, dull yellowish-green above, dense white hairs below; stalk c2mm
Stipules	falling early

FLOWERS AND FRUIT

Flowers	☿, single, in angle of leaf stalks, 3–6cm, white
Petals	5, 12mm; sepals 5, 1–1.6cm, narrowly triangular, persistent on fruit
Stamens	30–40, red
Stigmas	5, each on a long style
Ovaries	1, in base of flower
Fruit	fleshy but hard, roughly globular, ripening brown and remaining on tree
Seeds	10

Dull and rather dowdy for much of the year, the Medlar is often a shrub, at best making only a small tree. The large, solitary flowers have sepals that are longer than the white petals and are followed by distinctive fruits, most nearly resembling huge, brown rose-hips, with the narrow persistent sepals forming a crown. The fruits are edible, but only after they are 'bletted' – softened by overripening or being frosted.

Status: native to south-eastern Europe but often cultivated as a fruit tree and naturalized in many central and western parts as far north as southern Britain.

Similar trees: none.

109

Juneberry *Amelanchier lamackii*

The contrast of white blossom against coppery young leaves makes this tree a striking sight in spring; leaves also produce rich autumn colours. Of uncertain origin and perhaps a hybrid, it has been established in the wild in Britain for over one hundred years.

Status: possibly native to eastern North America; introduced and naturalized in northern Europe; often planted for ornament.

deciduous
small teeth
often shrubby
purple, juicy
red in autumn

white
purplish when young
narrow petals

JUNEBERRY

Type	deciduous tree or shrub
Height	up to 10m
Habitat	woods and scrub on acid soil
Flowering	April–May
Fruiting	September–October

TRUNK AND CROWN

Trunk	slender, short, often several
Bark	pale grey-brown
Crown	open and spreading
Twigs	shaggy white-hairy, becoming smooth

LEAVES

Buds	7–11mm, reddish, pointed
Leaves	alternate, oval-oblong to elliptical, shortly pointed, base rounded to heart-shaped, edges curled upwards, young leaves coppery red, silky beneath, turning green, rich yellow and red in autumn; stalk hairy, becoming smooth
Stipules	small, soon falling

FLOWERS AND FRUIT

Flowers	☿, 6–12 in loose, often drooping clusters with the leaves, white, flower-tube bell-shaped, stalks 1.5–2.5cm, hairy
Petals	5, 9–14mm, narrow, widest above middle, blunt; sepals 5, 3–5mm, hairy within, persistent on fruit
Stamens	about 20
Stigmas	5, on a single style
Ovaries	1, in base of flower
Fruit	berry-like, ripening purple-black, sweet-tasting
Seeds	4–10

SIMILAR TREES

The only European native is the less showy **Snowy Mespil** (*Amelanchier ovalis*). It has more coarsely toothed leaves, whitish woolly below, and blackish fruit.

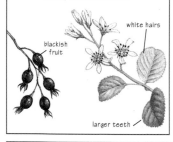

blackish fruit
white hairs
larger teeth

Himalayan Tree-cotoneaster
Cotoneaster frigidus

branched flower-head

dull green

berry-like

white hairs below

deciduous

One of the few cotoneasters to form a tree, this species is deciduous. The berries remain on the tree through the winter, showing conspicuously against the bare boughs. It is widely planted as an ornamental and has become naturalized in hedgerows and woods.

Status: native to the Himalayas; widely cultivated; occasionally naturalized in various parts of Europe.

SIMILAR TREES

1 Waterer's Cotoneaster (*Cotoneaster* x *watereri*) forms a large, evergreen shrub or small tree with narrow leaves. It produces larger clusters of red or orange fruits.
2 *Cotoneaster bullatus* reaches tree size and has broader, corrugated leaves.

semi-evergreen

long, narrow

corrugated

HIMALAYAN TREE-COTONEASTER

Type	deciduous tree
Height	20m
Habitat	parks, gardens, hedges, woods
Flowering	June
Fruiting	September–October

TRUNK AND CROWN

Trunk	short, slender, often several
Bark	grey-brown, smooth
Crown	broad, domed; branches arching
Twigs	greenish, ridged

LEAVES

Buds	small, lacking scales, hairy
Leaves	alternate, 6–16cm, elliptical to oval, widest above the middle, bluntly pointed, base wedge-shaped, dark green above, densely white hairy below; stalkless
Stipules	falling early

FLOWERS AND FRUIT

Flowers	☿, 20–40 in flat, branched clusters, white, fragrant
Petals	5, broadly oval, widest above middle, blunt, tapering at base; sepals 5, persistent on fruit
Stamens	20
Stigmas	2, on free styles
Ovaries	1, 2-chambered, in base of flower
Fruit	berry-like, 5mm, globular, ripening bright red, remaining on tree through winter
Seeds	2, stony

Common Hawthorn *Crataegus monogyna*

When left to grow undisturbed, Common Hawthorn forms a densely-crowned tree. However, if cut or trimmed regularly, it soon makes a dense thorny barrier ideal for enclosing fields and fencing in animals. It is very variable in leaf shape and lobing, and in fruit colour.

Status: native throughout Europe and much of Asia, widely used for hedging.

rough, scaly

dark red

small, deciduous

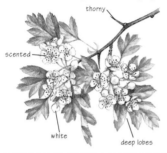

thorny

scented

white

deep lobes

COMMON HAWTHORN

Type	deciduous tree or shrub
Height	18m but often less
Habitat	woods, hedges, especially on chalky soils
Flowering	May–June
Fruiting	September–October
TRUNK AND CROWN	
Trunk	fluted, often branching
Bark	silvery grey, cracking to show orange or pink beneath
Crown	variable, usually dense
Twigs	brown, thorns up to 15mm
LEAVES	
Buds	2mm, rounded
Leaves	alternate, 1.5–4.5cm, oval to diamond-shaped in outline, 3–5 deep lobes, toothed near tips, leathery, dark, shiny green above, paler and dull below; stalk dark pink, grooved
Stipules	small, curved, sometimes toothed
FLOWERS AND FRUIT	
Flowers	♂, 9–18, in loose, branched clusters, 8–15mm, white, rarely pink, sickly sweet-scented, stalks woolly
Petals	5, 4–6mm, oval, widest above the middle; sepals 5, triangular, persistent on fruit
Stamens	typically 20, pink or purple
Stigmas	1, on a short style
Ovaries	1, sunk into base of fruit
Fruit	berry-like, 7–14mm, globose or egg-shaped, ripening scarlet to maroon
Seeds	1, rarely 2, stony

SIMILAR TREES

1 Midland Hawthorn (*Crataegus laevigata*) and **2** *Crataegus calycina*, both native to woodlands in northwestern and central Europe, have finely toothed leaf-lobes and stipules. Midland Hawthorn also has two stigmas and two seeds per fruit.

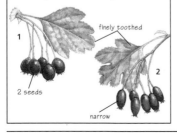

1

finely toothed

2 seeds

2

narrow

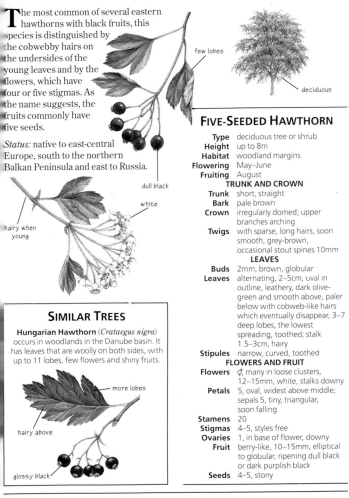

The most common of several eastern hawthorns with black fruits, this species is distinguished by the cobwebby hairs on the undersides of the young leaves and by the flowers, which have four or five stigmas. As the name suggests, the fruits commonly have five seeds.

Status: native to east-central Europe, south to the northern Balkan Peninsula and east to Russia.

few lobes

deciduous

dull black

white

hairy when young

FIVE-SEEDED HAWTHORN

Type	deciduous tree or shrub
Height	up to 8m
Habitat	woodland margins
Flowering	May–June
Fruiting	August

TRUNK AND CROWN

Trunk	short, straight
Bark	pale brown
Crown	irregularly domed; upper branches arching
Twigs	with sparse, long hairs, soon smooth, grey-brown, occasional stout spines 10mm

LEAVES

Buds	2mm, brown, globular
Leaves	alternating, 2–5cm, oval in outline, leathery, dark olive-green and smooth above, paler below with cobweb-like hairs which eventually disappear, 3–7 deep lobes, the lowest spreading, toothed; stalk 1.5–3cm, hairy
Stipules	narrow, curved, toothed

FLOWERS AND FRUIT

Flowers	⚥, many in loose clusters, 12–15mm, white, stalks downy
Petals	5, oval, widest above middle; sepals 5, tiny, triangular, soon falling
Stamens	20
Stigmas	4–5, styles free
Ovaries	1, in base of flower, downy
Fruit	berry-like, 10–15mm, elliptical to globular, ripening dull black or dark purplish black
Seeds	4–5, stony

SIMILAR TREES

Hungarian Hawthorn (*Crataegus nigra*) occurs in woodlands in the Danube basin. It has leaves that are woolly on both sides, with up to 11 lobes, few flowers and shiny fruits.

more lobes

hairy above

glossy black

Azarole *Crataegus azarolus*

Azarole owes its present fairly widespread distribution to its edible fruits, which taste somewhat of apple. They are sufficiently large and fleshy to be worth gathering, and the tree was taken from its eastern Mediterranean home to other areas, notably France and Italy, as a fruit tree.

Status: native to Crete; cultivated and naturalized in southern Europe.

most not toothed

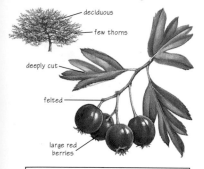
deciduous
few thorns
deeply cut
felted
large red berries

AZAROLE

Type	deciduous tree or shrub
Height	up to 8m
Habitat	humid scrubland
Flowering	March–April
Fruiting	June–September
TRUNK AND CROWN	
Trunk	short, slender
Bark	pale grey-brown
Crown	rounded, bushy; branches spreading
Twigs	downy, becoming smooth; few, stout spines up to 10mm
LEAVES	
Buds	3–4mm, rounded, red-brown
Leaves	alternate, 3–5cm, oval to triangular in outline, base wedge-shaped and extending onto stalk, 3–5 deep lobes, sometimes with a few teeth, downy on both sides; stalk 3–8mm
Stipules	curved, coarsely toothed
FLOWERS AND FRUIT	
Flowers	♂, 3–18 in compact clusters, 12–18mm, white, stalks woolly
Petals	5, oval, widest above middle; sepals 5, short-pointed, persistent on fruit
Stamens	15–20
Stigmas	1–2, rarely 3, styles thick
Ovaries	1, in base of fruit
Fruit	berry-like, 20–25mm, roughly globular with longitudinal, rounded ridges, ripening yellow or orange-red
Seeds	1–3, stony

SIMILAR TREES

Oriental Hawthorn (*Crataegus laciniata*), from the Balkan Peninsula and parts of eastern Europe, has leaf-lobes with few teeth, compact flower clusters, four or five stigmas and globular fruits.

hairy above
smaller
narrow, toothed

Crataegus crus-galli **Cockspur Hawthorn**

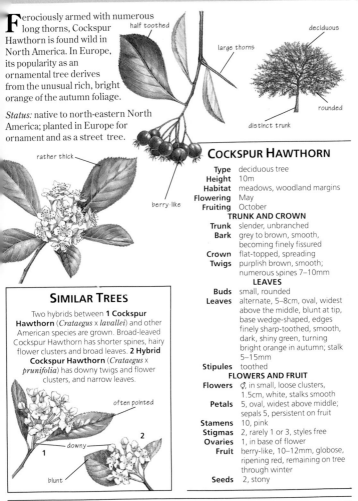

Ferociously armed with numerous long thorns, Cockspur Hawthorn is found wild in North America. In Europe, its popularity as an ornamental tree derives from the unusual rich, bright orange of the autumn foliage.

Status: native to north-eastern North America; planted in Europe for ornament and as a street tree.

half toothed

large thorns

deciduous

rounded

distinct trunk

rather thick

berry-like

SIMILAR TREES

Two hybrids between **1 Cockspur Hawthorn** (*Crataegus* x *lavallei*) and other American species are grown. Broad-leaved Cockspur Hawthorn has shorter spines, hairy flower clusters and broad leaves. **2 Hybrid Cockspur Hawthorn** (*Crataegus* x *prunifolia*) has downy twigs and flower clusters, and narrow leaves.

often pointed

downy

blunt

1

2

COCKSPUR HAWTHORN

Type	deciduous tree
Height	10m
Habitat	meadows, woodland margins
Flowering	May
Fruiting	October
TRUNK AND CROWN	
Trunk	slender, unbranched
Bark	grey to brown, smooth, becoming finely fissured
Crown	flat-topped, spreading
Twigs	purplish brown, smooth; numerous spines 7–10mm
LEAVES	
Buds	small, rounded
Leaves	alternate, 5–8cm, oval, widest above the middle, blunt at tip, base wedge-shaped, edges finely sharp-toothed, smooth, dark, shiny green, turning bright orange in autumn; stalk 5–15mm
Stipules	toothed
FLOWERS AND FRUIT	
Flowers	♂, in small, loose clusters, 1.5cm, white, stalks smooth
Petals	5, oval, widest above middle; sepals 5, persistent on fruit
Stamens	10, pink
Stigmas	2, rarely 1 or 3, styles free
Ovaries	1, in base of flower
Fruit	berry-like, 10–12mm, globose, ripening red, remaining on tree through winter
Seeds	2, stony

Peach *Prunus persica*

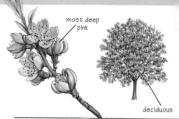

most deep
pink

deciduous

Prized for its succulent, downy fruits, the Peach was brought from China and is now widely grown in southern Europe. In harsher northern climes, fruit production is less reliable. This tree is also planted for ornament and in places has established itself in the wild. Nectarine is a smooth-fruited variety of Peach, cultivated on a commercial scale.

Status: native to China; cultivated in fields and gardens; naturalized in some parts of southern Europe.

large, furry

nectarine is
smooth

finely
toothed

SIMILAR TREES

Apricot (*Prunus armeniaca*) has pale pink flowers and smaller fruits.

most paler

broad

smaller

PEACH

Type	deciduous tree
Height	6m
Habitat	gardens, orchards, parks, woods, thickets
Flowering	March–May
Fruiting	June–July

TRUNK AND CROWN

Trunk	straight, slender
Bark	grey-brown, finely cracked
Crown	rounded, bushy
Twigs	smooth, reddish, angular

LEAVES

Buds	6mm, oval, greenish brown with white hairs
Leaves	alternate, 5–15cm, narrowly oval-oblong to elliptical, long-pointed, edges with small, sharp teeth, smooth; stalk 1.5cm, glandular
Stipules	narrow, papery, falling early

FLOWERS AND FRUIT

Flowers	⚥, single or paired, appearing before the leaves, deep pink, rarely pale pink or white, flower-tube bell-shaped
Petals	5, 10–20mm, equal, broadly oval, widest above middle, tapered at base; sepals 5, 6–8mm
Stamens	20–30, red when young
Stigmas	1, 2-lobed, style long and slender
Ovaries	1, downy
Fruit	berry-like, 4–8cm, globular, ripening greenish or yellow tinged with red, sweet-tasting
Seeds	1, in a grooved stone

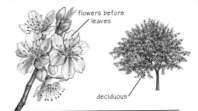

flowers before leaves

deciduous

One of the first trees to flower in spring, Almond can turn hillsides white with blossom. The fruits have only a thin fleshy layer covering the large, pitted stone containing the familiar edible seed.

Status: probably native to south-western and central Asia; anciently cultivated in southern Europe as a fruit tree and sometimes naturalized.

long, toothed

green, furry

ALMOND

Type	deciduous tree
Height	8m
Habitat	orchards, parks, hillsides
Flowering	February–April
Fruiting	May–June

TRUNK AND CROWN

Trunk	straight, slender
Bark	black, cracking into small squares
Crown	rounded; branches angled upwards, later spreading, tangled in wild trees, straight in cultivated trees
Twigs	smooth, spiny in wild trees

LEAVES

Buds	brown, scales fringed with hairs
Leaves	alternate, 4–13cm, narrowly oval-oblong, long-pointed, edges with small, blunt teeth, smooth; stalk 2cm, glandular
Stipules	narrow, papery, falling early

FLOWERS AND FRUIT

Flowers	☿, paired, appearing before the leaves, pink fading to white, flower-tube bell-shaped
Petals	5, 15–25mm, broadly oval and widest above middle, tapered at base; sepals 5, 7–8mm, woolly, reddish
Stamens	15–25, yellow
Stigmas	1, slender, long
Ovaries	1, hairy
Fruit	leathery, 3.5–6cm, egg-shaped, ripening grey-green
Seeds	1, in a large, pitted stone, which is ridged around the edge

SIMILAR TREES

Cherry Plum (*Prunus cerasifera*) has white flowers and smooth, fleshy fruits, for which it is widely grown. A variety with pink flowers and red leaves (cv. 'Pissardii') is a common street tree.

most white

some dark-leaved

juicy fruit

Blackthorn *Prunus spinosa*

deciduous

flowers before leaves

spiny

White flowers of Blackthorn contrast starkly with its blackish, thorny shoots, brightening the hedgerows before its leaves appear. Typically a shrub spreading by suckers to form dense thickets, it can reach tree size. Small blue-black fruits (sloes) have a whitish, waxy covering and are very sour.

Status: native; widespread in Europe except the extreme north.

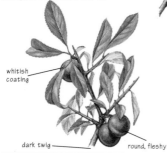

whitish coating

dark twig

round, fleshy

BLACKTHORN

Type	deciduous shrub or tree
Height	usually up to 4m
Habitat	scrub, light woodland, hedgerows; most soils
Flowering	March–April
Fruiting	September–October

TRUNK AND CROWN

Trunk	often several, suckering
Bark	blackish, rough
Crown	irregular, dense
Twigs	spiny, initially shortly hairy, dull blackish or dark brown

LEAVES

Buds	egg-shaped, hairy
Leaves	on alternate sides of stem, 2–4.5cm, oval, tip blunt or pointed, edge with fine rounded or pointed teeth, base wedge-shaped, hairless above, shortly hairy on veins below, dull green; stalk 2–10mm
Stipules	present

FLOWERS AND FRUIT

Flowers	♂, before leaves, 10–15mm, single or some paired; stalk c5mm, hairless
Petals	5, 5–8mm, broadest towards tip, blunt, white; sepals 5
Stamens	c20
Stigmas	single; anthers reddish
Ovaries	1
Fruit	1, berry-like, 10–15mm, globular, bluish black with whitish waxy covering, sour
Seeds	single, in globular, smooth or slightly rough, 'stone', 7.5–10mm

SIMILAR TREES

1 Wild Plum (*Prunus domestica*), part of a variable species which includes cultivated plums, damsons and greengages, has a brown bark and larger fruit. Native mainly to southern Italy and the Balkans, **2** *Prunus cocomilia* differs in the non-spiny twigs, hairless leaves and yellow fruit.

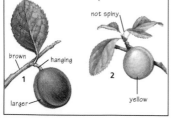

brown

hanging

1

larger

not spiny

2

yellow

Long branches of this attractive tree are smothered with white flowers just before the toothed leaves appear, and later weighed down with fruit. Edible sweet cherries are derived from this species. The double white cv. 'Plena' is one of the last ornamental cherries to flower.

Status: native except in the extreme north and east; planted for ornament and fruit.

deciduous

flowers as leaves open

raised rows

drooping

toothed · usually ripens red

WILD CHERRY

Type	deciduous tree
Height	10–30m
Habitat	woods, hedges, especially on lime-rich, clay soils
Flowering	April–May
Fruiting	July

TRUNK AND CROWN

Trunk	single, well-defined
Bark	reddish brown with horizontal peeling strips, bands of lenticels and blackish fissures
Crown	conical, becoming rounded
Twigs	pale reddish brown, hairless

LEAVES

Buds	pointed, glossy reddish brown
Leaves	on alternate sides of stem, drooping, 8–15cm, oval, broader above, tip slender, with rounded, forward-pointing, blunt teeth and tapered base, dull green, smooth above, paler, slightly hairy below, stalk 2–5cm, glands near top

FLOWERS AND FRUIT

Flowers	☿, before leaves; in stalkless clusters of 2–6; each flower 25–35mm, white, base swollen, narrowed above; stalk 2–5cm, sepals 5
Petals	5, 9–15mm; sepals 5
Stamens	c20
Stigma	1
Ovaries	1
Fruit	berry-like, in bunches, 9–12mm, globular, glossy dark red, yellow or blackish
Seeds	1, in globular, smooth, 'stone'

SIMILAR TREES

Usually shrubs, two other cherries reach tree size. **1 Dwarf Cherry** (*Prunus cerasus*) has spreading, glossy leaves and a broader, bell-shaped base to the flower. **2 Saint Lucie Cherry** (*Prunus mahaleb*) has smaller, very glossy, minutely toothed leaves and branched heads of small, bitter, black fruits.

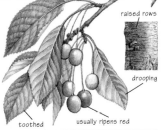

branched head

small, black

small, glossy

glossy

spreading

1   2

Bird Cherry *Prunus padus*

An attractive tree, easily recognized amongst native deciduous cherries by its long spikes of fragrant white flowers in late spring. The small, glossy black fruit has a bittersweet or astringent taste, but is edible to birds.

Status: native to much of Europe; planted for ornament in parks, gardens and streets.

deciduous

berry-like

ripens black

finely toothed

flowers with leaves

hanging, elongated heads

SIMILAR TREES

Two introduced North American species have smaller flowers. **1 Rum Cherry** (*Prunus serotina*) has glossy, dark green leaves with wavy, toothed edges, the teeth curving forwards. **2 Choke Cherry** (*Prunus virginiana*) has dull leaves with fewer veins and very sharp, spreading teeth, and bears dark red fruits.

dull

2

1

glossy

small

BIRD CHERRY

Type	deciduous tree or shrub
Height	3–17m
Habitat	common on lime-rich soils, often in woods or by water
Flowering	May
Fruiting	July–August
TRUNK AND CROWN	
Trunk	distinct, upright
Bark	dark greyish brown, smooth, peeling in horizontal strips
Crown	conical, becoming rounded; branches angled upwards, or lower branches level
Twigs	brown or grey
LEAVES	
Buds	egg-shaped, glossy brown
Leaves	5–10cm, oval or oblong with slender tip, edge finely toothed, base rounded, dull green above, paler and sometimes hairy below, stalk 1–2cm, grooved, red-brown
FLOWERS AND FRUIT	
Flowers	♂, strongly scented, 15–40 in drooping cluster 7–15cm long on leafy shoot, each flower 14–20mm, white
Petals	5, 6–9mm, irregularly toothed; sepals 5, short, blunt
Stamens	numerous
Stigmas	1
Ovaries	1
Fruit	berry-like in long heads, each 6–8mm, almost globular, glossy black, bitter
Seeds	1, in globular, grooved 'stone'

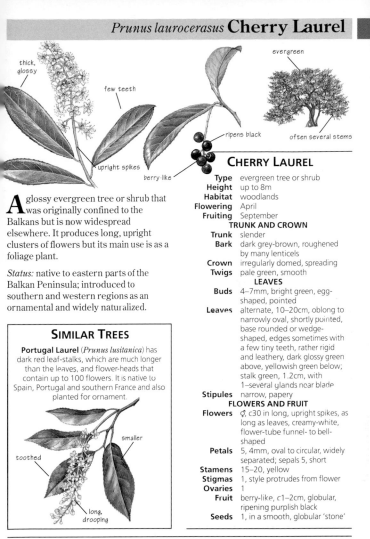

A glossy evergreen tree or shrub that was originally confined to the Balkans but is now widespread elsewhere. It produces long, upright clusters of flowers but its main use is as a foliage plant.

Status: native to eastern parts of the Balkan Peninsula; introduced to southern and western regions as an ornamental and widely naturalized.

SIMILAR TREES

Portugal Laurel (*Prunus lusitanica*) has dark red leaf-stalks, which are much longer than the leaves, and flower-heads that contain up to 100 flowers. It is native to Spain, Portugal and southern France and also planted for ornament.

CHERRY LAUREL

Type	evergreen tree or shrub
Height	up to 8m
Habitat	woodlands
Flowering	April
Fruiting	September
TRUNK AND CROWN	
Trunk	slender
Bark	dark grey-brown, roughened by many lenticels
Crown	irregularly domed, spreading
Twigs	pale green, smooth
LEAVES	
Buds	4–7mm, bright green, egg-shaped, pointed
Leaves	alternate, 10–20cm, oblong to narrowly oval, shortly pointed, base rounded or wedge-shaped, edges sometimes with a few tiny teeth, rather rigid and leathery, dark glossy green above, yellowish green below; stalk green, 1.2cm, with 1–several glands near blade
Stipules	narrow, papery
FLOWERS AND FRUIT	
Flowers	♂, c30 in long, upright spikes, as long as leaves, creamy-white, flower-tube funnel- to bell-shaped
Petals	5, 4mm, oval to circular, widely separated; sepals 5, short
Stamens	15–20, yellow
Stigmas	1, style protrudes from flower
Ovaries	1
Fruit	berry-like, c1–2cm, globular, ripening purplish black
Seeds	1, in a smooth, globular 'stone'

Japanese Cherry *Prunus serrulata*

Horizontal or wide-spreading branches give this tree a characteristically low-domed shape. It is widely planted, especially in streets and avenues, which it brightens in spring with prolific displays of blossom. There are many hybrids and cultivars, with a range of leaf and petal colours, and single or double flowers.

Status: origin obscure but probably native to China; widespread throughout Europe as an ornamental tree.

often broad

often double

white or pink

deciduous

many grafted

long tip

fine teeth

bristle-tipped

SIMILAR TREES

Two common ornamental Japanese species are **1 Sargent's Cherry** (*Prunus sargentii*), which has deep pink flowers, and **2 Yoshino Cherry** (*Prunus* x *yedoensis*), a hybrid with glossy leaves.

pointed teeth

notched

pale

1

2

JAPANESE CHERRY

Type	deciduous tree
Height	up to 15m
Habitat	streets, parks and gardens
Flowering	April–May
Fruiting	June

TRUNK AND CROWN

Trunk	short, abruptly branching to form crown
Bark	purplish-brown, with bands of lenticels
Crown	spreading; branches horizontal or angled upwards
Twigs	smooth

LEAVES

Buds	large, dark brown
Leaves	alternate, 8–20cm, broadly oval and widest above middle, tip tapering abruptly, teeth sharp with spreading, hair-like points; stalk 2–4cm, with 1–4 reddish glands near blade
Stipules	narrow, papery

FLOWERS AND FRUIT

Flowers	☿, 2–4, in clusters appearing before leaves, white or pink, flower-tube narrowly bell-shaped
Petals	5, 15–40mm, oval, notched at tip; sepals 5, long, narrow
Stamens	c25–30
Stigmas	1, style long and slender
Ovaries	1
Fruit	berry-like, 7mm, globular, ripening purplish red, seldom produced
Seeds	1, in globular stone

S pring Cherry normally flowers in the early months of the year, but the cultivar 'Autumnalis', the Autumn Cherry, flowers from October to April. Various other cultivars, including weeping and double-flowered forms, are also planted as ornamentals, but it is the Autumn Cherry which is most often seen.

Status: native to Japan; widespread as a street tree and garden ornamental.

SPRING CHERRY

Type	deciduous tree
Height	up to 20m
Habitat	parks, gardens, streets
Flowering	March–April
Fruiting	June

TRUNK AND CROWN

Trunk	thick, straight
Bark	grey-brown
Crown	dense, rounded; branches slender
Twigs	crimson, downy

LEAVES

Buds	3–5mm, egg-shaped, dark
Leaves	alternate, c6cm, oval to oblong, drawn out to a long point, base wedge-shaped, sharply toothed, smooth above, downy on veins beneath; stalk 7–12mm, downy, crimson
Stipules	narrow, papery

FLOWERS AND FRUIT

Flowers	⚲, 2–5 on short stalks, in clusters appearing before leaves, very pale or rose pink, flower-tube urn-shaped
Petals	5, 8–12mm, oval, widest above middle, notched at tips; sepals 5, 3mm, triangular
Stamens	c20
Stigmas	1, style slender, longer than stamens, hairy towards base
Ovaries	1
Fruit	berry-like, 7–9mm, globose or ellipsoid, ripening purplish black
Seeds	1, in globular stone

SIMILAR TREES

Tibetan Cherry (*Prunus serrula*) has glossy red-brown, peeling bark, white flowers and bright red fruits. It is a common tree in parks.

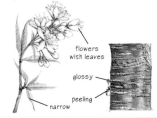

Carob *Ceratonia siliqua*

CAROB

Type	evergreen tree
Height	up to 10m
Habitat	dry soils
Flowering	August–October
Fruiting	September onwards
TRUNK AND CROWN	
Trunk	short, often branched from base
Bark	grey, rough
Crown	dense, low dome
Twigs	stout, minutely downy
LEAVES	
Buds	small, golden-hairy
Leaves	alternate, 2–5 pairs of leaflets, each 3–5cm, narrowly oval to almost circular, tips notched, smooth, leathery, dark and shiny above, paler below; stalk brown or green
Stipules	tiny, soon falling
FLOWERS AND FRUIT	
Flowers	♂ and ♀ on same tree or on different trees, many, in short spikes in angles of leaves, green
Petals	0; sepals 5, tiny, soon falling
Stamens	5, radiating from a central disc
Stigmas	1, very shortly lobed, style thick, green
Ovaries	1, flask-shaped
Fruit	pod, 10–20cm, drooping, flattened, ripening violet-brown
Seeds	many, not released

Leathery-leaved and surviving well in dry conditions, Carob is a characteristic tree of the Mediterranean landscape. The flowers are unusual among members of the pea family, completely lacking petals. A native tree, Carob is also widely cultivated for its pods. Found on the tree at most times of year, these are large and contain seeds and a sugary pulp. They are a rich source of food, used mainly for animal feeds.

Status: native to the Mediterranean region; naturalized in some countries; widely grown as a fodder crop.

Similar trees: none.

Gleditsia triacanthos **Honey Locust**

spines

deciduous

twisted pod

paired leaflets

greenish white

clustered

A tall tree formidably armed with clusters of spines on the trunk and main branches. On smaller branches and twigs, the spines are usually grouped in threes. There are spineless varieties, generally preferred for planting as street trees.

Status: native to the Mississippi basin; introduced to southern and central Europe and sometimes naturalised.

SIMILAR TREES

Siberian Pea-tree (*Caragana arborescens*) is a native of Northern Asia often planted for ornament, and naturalized in France. It has leaves with 8–12 leaflets and clusters of yellow flowers.

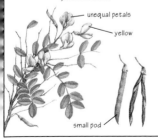

unequal petals

yellow

small pod

HONEY LOCUST

Type	deciduous tree
Height	up to 45m
Habitat	mainly parks and streets, also rivers and woods
Flowering	June
Fruiting	July–September

TRUNK AND CROWN

Trunk	long, with large clusters of spines
Bark	brown, vertically fissured
Crown	tall and spreading
Twigs	smooth, ribbed

LEAVES

Buds	1–2mm, pyramidal, reddish
Leaves	alternate, 10–20cm, either once divided, when leaves have 7–18 pairs of leaflets, each 20–35mm, or twice divided, when leaflets are themselves divided into 8–14 segments, each 8–20mm, leaf tip ending with a spine; stalk short
Stipules	minute

FLOWERS AND FRUIT

Flowers	♂, ♀ or ⚥, many, in clusters in angles of leaves, each c3mm, greenish white
Petals	3–5, oval, equal; sepals 3–5, joined below
Stamens	6–10
Stigmas	1, lobed, style short and thick
Ovaries	1, narrow, upright
Fruit	pod, 30–45cm long, 2–3cm wide, flattened, curved and often twisted
Seeds	numerous, not released

125

Judas Tree *Cercis siliquastrum*

An unusual tree that bears its bright pink flowers directly on the trunk and main branches as well as on the twigs. Almost circular leaves with characteristic radiating veins follow the flowers. Attractive reddish purple pods are formed later in the year.

Status: native throughout Mediterranean regions; often planted and sometimes naturalized in other areas.

often on trunk

pods

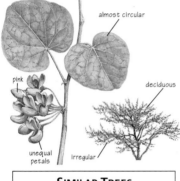

almost circular

pink

deciduous

unequal petals

Irregular

JUDAS TREE

Type	deciduous tree or shrub
Height	up to 10m
Habitat	mainly on dry, rocky soils
Flowering	April–May
Fruiting	July
TRUNK AND CROWN	
Trunk	slender, often several
Bark	dark, blackish, cracked
Crown	rounded
Twigs	reddish brown, warty
LEAVES	
Buds	5–8mm, reddish brown or crimson, egg-shaped, pointed
Leaves	alternate, 7–12cm, almost circular, rounded or notched at tips, base heart-shaped, smooth, bluish green when young, becoming dark green above, veins radiating; stalk shorter than blade
Stipules	small, soon falling
FLOWERS AND FRUIT	
Flowers	♂, in loose clusters, before or with leaves, on twigs, trunk and branches, pink, 1.5–2cm
Petals	5, unequal, lower pair joined, side pair overlapping, upper erect; sepals 5, equal, joined below to form a tube
Stamens	10, free
Stigmas	1, style curved
Ovaries	1, narrow
Fruit	pod, 6–10cm, flattened, with a very narrow wing on one side, smooth, ripening reddish purple, eventually brown
Seeds	many, released when pod splits

SIMILAR TREES

Coral Tree (*Erythrina crista-galli*) is a Brazilian species forming a small, thick-trunked tree or shrub and grown in mild areas for its scarlet flowers.

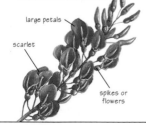

large petals

scarlet

spikes or flowers

A densely foliaged tree with pink, brush-like flowers borne on the upper branches. Individual flowers are small, but have very long, showy stamens and are crowded into dense heads.

Status: native to Asia; widely planted as an ornamental and street tree in southern Europe, and as an annual in northern Europe.

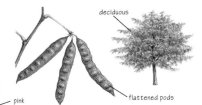

deciduous

flattened pods

pink

long stamens

small leaflets

divided twice

PINK SIRIS

Type	deciduous tree
Height	up to 13m
Habitat	woods, stream sides
Flowering	July–August
Fruiting	October

TRUNK AND CROWN

Trunk	slender
Bark	smooth
Crown	dense, slightly flattened dome; branches spreading
Twigs	brown, warty lenticels

LEAVES

Buds	short, black, hairy
Leaves	alternate, 20–30cm, divided into 10–25 paired segments, each segment with 35–50 paired leaflets, each 1–1.5cm, narrowly oval, curved, green above, edges and underside shortly hairy; stalk with cup-shaped gland on upper side
Stipules	absent

FLOWERS AND FRUIT

Flowers	♂, ♀ and sometimes ⚥, in branched clusters, each branch with 20 flowers
Petals	5, joined into a narrow tube, 7–9mm, pink; sepals forming a 5-lobed tube, 3mm
Stamens	many, 3.5–4cm, pink, extending well beyond petals
Stigmas	1
Ovaries	1
Fruit	pod, 8–15cm, flat with tapering tip, slightly pinched in between seeds, ripening brown
Seeds	10–15, orbicular

SIMILAR TREES

Plume Albizia (*Albizia lophantha*), from south-western Australia, is also planted in Mediterranean regions. It has densely hairy twigs and cylindrical heads of yellow flowers.

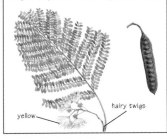

yellow

hairy twigs

Silver Wattle *Acacia dealbata*

A pale, silvery green tree, with finely divided, feathery leaves. It is the mimosa of floristry. The pretty, globular flower-heads are very numerous and can turn the whole crown yellow.

Status: native to south-eastern Australia and Tasmania; planted on a large scale in southern Europe as a timber tree and soil stabilizer; now widely naturalized and spreading.

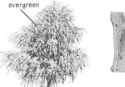
evergreen

smooth, greenish

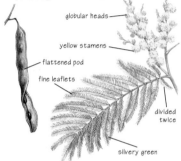

globular heads

yellow stamens

flattened pod

fine leaflets

divided twice

silvery green

SILVER WATTLE

Type	evergreen tree
Height	up to 30m
Habitat	hillsides, forests and plantations
Flowering	January–March
Fruiting	May

TRUNK AND CROWN

Trunk	slender
Bark	smooth, greyish green, becoming black
Crown	irregular, rather open
Twigs	densely hairy, hairs short, white

LEAVES

Buds	minute
Leaves	alternate, divided into 8–20 pairs of segments, each segment with 30–50 pairs of leaflets, each 3–5mm, very narrow, densely white-hairy when young; stalk with cup-shaped glands wherever segments branch off

FLOWERS AND FRUIT

Flowers	♀, in branched, spreading clusters of globular heads, each head 5–6mm, containing 30–40 bright yellow flowers, stalks of flower-heads with dense hairs
Petals	5, equal, short; sepals 5, hairy
Stamens	many, protruding well beyond petals, yellow
Stigmas	1, style very long, slender
Ovaries	1
Fruit	pod, 4–10cm, flattened, of equal width for most of its length, ripening waxy brown
Seeds	many, released when pod splits

SIMILAR TREES

Green Wattle (*Acacia mearnsii*) has bright green deciduous leaves with spiny stipules. Native to the Caribbean, it is grown in south-western Europe for ornament and for the perfume industry.

bright green

constricted

Aslender tree with drooping foliage and distinctly blue-green leaves. The bright yellow flower-heads are relatively large among *Acacia* species found in Europe.

Status: native to western Australia; widely planted in many Mediterranean countries as a soil stabilizer and ornamental.

evergreen

globular heads

yellow stamens

long pod

not divided

1 vein

constricted

GOLDEN WREATH

Type	evergreen tree or shrub
Height	up to 10m
Habitat	mainly in dry, coastal areas
Flowering	March–May
Fruiting	July

TRUNK AND CROWN

Trunk	often forked from base and suckering
Bark	smooth, grey, becoming grey-brown and cracked
Crown	broad, irregular
Twigs	smooth, ribbed, drooping, bluish green

LEAVES

Buds	tiny, egg-shaped to rounded
Leaves	alternate, variable, usually 6–20cm, spear-shaped, straight or curved, drooping, dull or shiny, bluish green, with a single vein; stalkless
Stipules	absent

FLOWERS AND FRUIT

Flowers	♀, in drooping clusters of 2–8 globular heads, each head 1–1.5cm in diameter and containing 25–70 bright yellow flowers
Petals	5, 1.5mm, equal; sepals 5
Stamens	many, yellow
Stigmas	1; style long, slender
Ovaries	1
Fruit	pod, 6–12cm, narrow, flattened, pinched in between each seed, ripening brown
Seeds	many, attached by short, whitish stalk encircling seed, released when pod splits

SIMILAR TREES

1 Blackwood (*Acacia melanoxylon*) and **2 Swamp Wattle** (*Acacia retinodes*), both native to southern Australia, are also planted and naturalized in southern Europe. Swamp Wattle has seeds with scarlet stalks. Blackwood has leaves with two to six veins, and twisted pods.

several veins

often twisted

1

2

narrower

Common Laburnum *Laburnum anagyroides*

An erect tree with arching branches and cascades of flowers hanging from the twigs. Split pods hang on the tree for some time after the seeds are shed. All parts are poisonous, especially the seeds.

Status: native to mountainous areas of southern and central Europe; widely planted for ornament; naturalized elsewhere.

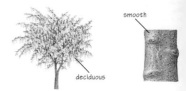
smooth

deciduous

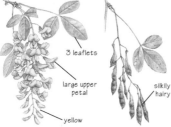
3 leaflets

large upper petal

silkily hairy

yellow

COMMON LABURNUM

Type	deciduous tree or shrub
Height	up to 7m
Habitat	mountain woods and scrub
Flowering	May–June
Fruiting	July–September

TRUNK AND CROWN

Trunk	slender
Bark	smooth, greenish to brown
Crown	irregular, open; branches angled upwards or arching
Twigs	grey-green, downy with long, silky, close-pressed hairs

LEAVES

Buds	5–6mm, egg-shaped, with white, silky hairs
Leaves	alternate, 3 leaflets, each 3–8cm, blunt but with a tiny, sharp tip, grey-green, young leaves hairy below; stalk 2–6cm

FLOWERS AND FRUIT

Flowers	♂, many, in long, drooping clusters from angles of leaves and tips of shoots, each 2cm, golden yellow
Petals	5, unequal, lower pair joined, side pair overlapping, upper erect; sepals joined into a 2-lipped tube, with short teeth
Stamens	10, fused together into a tube
Stigmas	1, style curved upwards
Ovaries	1, narrow, curved, silky-hairy
Fruit	pod, 4–6cm, hairy, ripening smooth, dull brown, persisting on tree after splitting
Seeds	numerous, black, round, released after pod splits

SIMILAR TREES

1 Scotch Laburnum (*Laburnum alpinum*), native to the same areas as Common Laburnum, is a shrub or small tree with glossy leaves and longer flower clusters.

2 Voss's Laburnum (*Laburnum x watereri*) is a hybrid between the above two species, which has largely replaced Common Laburnum as an ornamental in many areas.

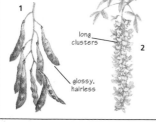
long clusters

glossy, hairless

1

2

Suckering readily, False-acacia may produce many young stems. Mature trees develop ridged and furrowed bark. It has attractive yellowish green leaves and fragrant white flowers, which are sometimes confined to the upper branches.

Status: a woodland species native to eastern and central North America; widespread as an ornamental; naturalized in southern and western Europe.

deciduous

smooth

ridged or deeply furrowed

paired leaflets

unequal petals

white

FALSE-ACACIA

Type	deciduous tree
Height	up to 25m
Habitat	streets, parks, woods
Flowering	June
Fruiting	September–October

TRUNK AND CROWN

Trunk	short, often suckering
Bark	smooth, dark brown, becoming grey with spiralled ridges
Crown	broad, open; branches twisted
Twigs	green with dark reddish lines

LEAVES

Buds	sunk in base of leaf-stalk, flanked by 2 spines
Leaves	alternate, 15–20cm, 7–21 leaflets, mostly paired leaflet at tip, each 2.5–4.5cm, oval or elliptic, yellowish green, leaves and leaflets stalked
Stipules	woody and spiny; tiny stipules at base of each leaflet

FLOWERS AND FRUIT

Flowers	☿, many, in long, drooping clusters of 10–20cm, white with yellow spot, fragrant
Petals	5, unequal, lower pair joined, side pair overlapping, upper erect; sepals joined into a tube with 2 shallow lips
Stamens	10, 9 joined in a tube, 1 free
Stigmas	1, style curved, hairy at tip
Ovaries	1, long, narrow, hairy
Fruit	pod, 5–10cm, smooth, ripening brown, slow to release seeds
Seeds	4–8, brown with black streaks, kidney-shaped

SIMILAR TREES

Pink flowered and stickily hairy **1 Clammy Locust** (*Robinia viscosa*) is also planted for ornament. **2 Pagoda-tree** (*Sophora japonica*) is a mountain species from Asia. It is tall, with twisted branches; the white flowers appear only on old trees.

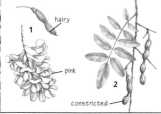

hairy

1

pink

2

constricted

131

Sweet Orange *Citrus sinensis*

A small evergreen tree bearing delightfully scented flowers and familiar, juicy fruits. Oranges take up to a year or more to ripen; there may be one or even two crops of fruit still on the tree when it flowers. Various cultivars with different ripening times ensure oranges are available more or less all year round.

Status: native to China and eastern Asia; a common orchard tree in Mediterranean regions.

not toothed

orange

evergreen

juicy, globular

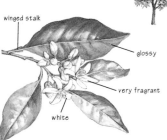

winged stalk

glossy

very fragrant

white

SIMILAR TREES

Several relatives, each with distinctive fruits, are commonly cultivated. **1 Lemon** (*Citrus limon*) has leaves with a spine at the base of the stalk. **2 Grapefruit** (*Citrus paradisi*) has large, broadly winged leaves as well as large fruits.

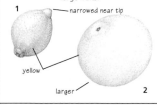

narrowed near tip

yellow

larger

1

2

SWEET ORANGE

Type	evergreen tree
Height	up to 10m
Habitat	orchard tree, often near sea
Flowering	mainly May, also other times of year
Fruiting	up to 1 year or more after flowering
TRUNK AND CROWN	
Trunk	short, slender
Bark	blackish brown
Crown	rounded, bushy
Twigs	angled, spiny when young, becoming cylindrical, unarmed
LEAVES	
Buds	very small, domed, green
Leaves	alternate, 5–8cm oval, pointed, base rounded, glossy, smooth and leathery but thin, dotted with shiny oil glands; stalk with a narrow, leafy wing
Stipules	absent
FLOWERS AND FRUIT	
Flowers	☿, single or few in short, loose spikes in leaf angles, pure white, fragrant
Petals	5, narrowly oval; sepals 4–5, short, pointed, joined below
Stamens	20–60, grouped in bundles
Stigmas	1, club-shaped on thick style
Ovaries	1, green, 10–13-chambered
Fruit	berry-like, with nearly smooth, leathery rind enclosing sweet juicy pulp, ripening orange
Seeds	6–many, creamy, pointed, not released

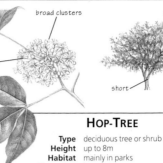

broad clusters

deciduous

white

short

encircling wing

3 leaflets

HOP-TREE

Type	deciduous tree or shrub
Height	up to 8m
Habitat	mainly in parks
Flowering	June–July
Fruiting	July–October

TRUNK AND CROWN

Trunk	short, often branching
Bark	brown, strong-smelling
Crown	rounded
Twigs	smooth, dark, shiny brown

LEAVES

Buds	small, very hairy, hidden by base of leaf stalk
Leaves	alternate, 3 leaflets, each 6–12cm, oval, tapered at both ends, edge unbroken or with faint teeth, smooth, shiny; stalkless
Stipules	absent

FLOWERS AND FRUIT

Flowers	♂, ♀ and ♀̥, mixed in clusters at tips of shoots, greenish white
Petals	4–5, 4mm, narrowly oval, blunt, hairy on inner surface; sepals 4–5, c1.5mm, pointed, hairy
Stamens	4, woolly below, rudimentary in ♀ flowers
Stigmas	1, 2-lobed on short, thick style
Ovaries	1, 2-chambered, rudimentary in ♂ flowers
Fruit	nut-like, with a circular, notched, straw-coloured wing 1.5–2.5cm across and net-veined
Seeds	1, not released

S trong and unpleasant-smelling when crushed, the leaves of this tree are divided into three spreading leaflets. The bark and young fruits are similarly aromatic. The ripe, straw-coloured fruit has a broad, papery wing.

Status: native to eastern North America; planted for ornament and naturalized in central Europe.

SIMILAR TREES

Amur Cork-tree (*Phellodendron amurense*), from China, has leaves with 5–11 leaflets and black, berry-like fruits. It is grown in parks and gardens.

ripens blackish

5–11 leaflets

berry-like

Tree-of-Heaven *Ailanthus altissima*

A stately tree with young leaves emerging bright red before turning green. Unfortunately, the foliage is rank-smelling. The fruits hang in large bunches, each fruit with a twisted, propeller-like wing. In Europe, the tree reproduces most easily by means of suckers.

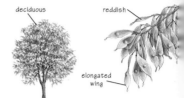

deciduous

reddish

elongated wing

Status: native to China; very common as a street and park tree, and naturalized in much of Europe except for the far north.

greenish

strong-smelling

smooth

paired leaflets

whitish lines

SIMILAR TREES

A second Chinese species, **Downy Tree-of-Heaven** (*Ailanthus vilmoriniana*), is more rarely grown. The leaves have a bright red stalk, and darker leaflets that are hairy below, with unbroken edges.

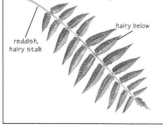

hairy below

reddish, hairy stalk

TREE-OF-HEAVEN

Type	deciduous tree
Height	20–30m
Habitat	light, dry and unstable soils
Flowering	May–July
Fruiting	August–September

TRUNK AND CROWN

Trunk	straight, often suckering
Bark	grey, often with silvery lines
Crown	irregular; branches stout
Twigs	thick, smooth, brown, with large leaf-scars and lenticels

LEAVES

Buds	2mm, scarlet, egg-shaped
Leaves	alternate, 45–60cm, deep red when emerging, later glossy green, unpleasant-smelling; 13–25 paired leaflets, each 7–12cm, narrowly oval, pointed, smooth but for fringe of hairs, with 2–4 teeth towards base; stalked

FLOWERS AND FRUIT

Flowers	usually ♂ and ♀, on different trees, sometimes ⚥; many in branched clusters 10–20cm long, each 7–8mm, greenish white, strong-smelling
Petals	5, pointed; sepals 5, green
Stamens	10 in ♂ flowers, 2–3 in ♀ flowers
Stigmas	2–5, joined
Ovaries	1, 5–6-chambered
Fruit	nut-like, with papery wing 3–4cm long, reddish, ripening straw-coloured
Seeds	1, not released

A slender, open tree with delicately coloured and scented flowers. United stamens form an upright tube that is darker than the spreading petals. Bead-like fruits remain on the tree for a long time after the leaves have fallen.

Status: a mountain species native to eastern Asia; naturalized in the Balkan Peninsula; widely planted in southern Europe for ornament and shade.

deciduous

yellow

globular

PERSIAN LILAC

Type	deciduous tree or shrub
Height	up to 15m
Habitat	dry mountain areas, planted elsewhere
Flowering	June
Fruiting	July–October
TRUNK AND CROWN	
Trunk	short, often slender
Bark	greyish brown, furrowed
Crown	open and spreading
Twigs	sparsely hairy with star-shaped hairs, becoming smooth
LEAVES	
Buds	small, globular, densely white-hairy
Leaves	alternate, up to 90cm, divided into segments, each segment divided into leaflets, each 2.5–5cm, narrowly oval, pointed, base wedge-shaped, sharply-toothed, glossy green; stalked
Stipules	absent
FLOWERS AND FRUIT	
Flowers	♂, many, in branched, open clusters 10–20cm long, in leaf angles, lilac, fragrant
Petals	5, 18mm, narrow, spreading or curved back; sepals 5, green, short, joined below
Stamens	10, joined into an erect tube
Stigmas	1, club-shaped with a thick style, hidden in stamen tube
Ovaries	1, 5–8-chambered
Fruit	6–18mm, globular, ripening creamy-yellow
Seeds	1, not released

purplish

doubly divided

furrowed

branched heads

many leaflets

SIMILAR TREES

Chinese Cedar (*Cedrela sinensis*) has shaggy bark and drooping white flowers. Native to eastern Asia, it is grown for its fragrant timber.

paired leaflet

drooping, white

Stag's-horn Sumach *Rhus typhina*

Velvet-hairy twigs, and leaves with drooping leaflets immediately distinguish this small, suckering tree. It produces bright autumn colours and female plants have dark crimson fruiting heads.

Status: native to eastern North America; widespread as an ornamental and naturalized in parts of northern and central Europe.

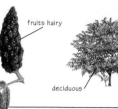

fruits hairy

deciduous

♂ flowers

autumn colour

clustered

♀ flowers

toothed

paired leaflets

hairy

STAG'S-HORN SUMACH

Type	deciduous tree or shrub
Height	10m
Habitat	thickets
Flowering	May–July
Fruiting	September–October
TRUNK AND CROWN	
Trunk	slender, often several and suckering
Bark	brown, with yellow warts
Crown	flattened, open dome; branches forking regularly
Twigs	curved, velvety when young
LEAVES	
Buds	minute, lacking scales
Leaves	alternate, oval in outline, drooping, 11–29 stalkless leaflets, paired with one at the tip, each 5–12cm, very narrowly oval, pointed, coarsely toothed, softly hairy, rich orange and red in autumn; stalk hairy
FLOWERS AND FRUIT	
Flowers	♂, more usually ♂ and ♀ on different trees in branched clusters 10–20cm; ♂ greenish, clusters open; ♀ dull red, clusters downy, spike-like
Petals	5, narrow, spreading; sepals 5, short, hairy
Stamens	5 in ♂ and ♂ flowers
Stigmas	3, on a single short style
Ovaries	1, in ♀ and ♂ flowers
Fruit	nut-like, c4mm, covered with crimson hairs, remaining on tree through winter
Seeds	1, not released

SIMILAR TREES

1 Sumach (*Rhus coriaria*) is a semi-evergreen shrub or small tree with narrowly winged, hairy leaflets and purplish fruits. It occurs in rocky places in southern Europe.
2 Varnish-tree (*Rhus verniciflua*), from China, is sometimes planted. It has loose, branched fruiting heads.

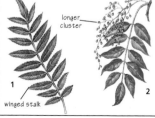

longer cluster

1

winged stalk

2

Pistacia terebinthus **Turpentine Tree**

A common tree in dry, chalky scrubland. It has leathery leaves with 2–6 pairs of leaflets and a single leaflet at the tip. Dull flowers are followed by bright, coral red young fruits.

Status: native to Mediterranean regions and south-western Asia.

deciduous

clustered flowers

paired leaflets

leaflet at tip

many fruits

TURPENTINE TREE

Type	deciduous tree or shrub
Height	up to 10m
Habitat	scrub, light woodland, on dry chalky slopes
Flowering	March–April
Fruiting	September–October

TRUNK AND CROWN

Trunk	short, slightly sinuous, forking
Bark	grey, finely cracked into oblong plates
Crown	open, irregular; branches few, twisted
Twigs	reddish, becoming brown, stout, sticky with resin

LEAVES

Buds	3–9mm, dark-red, egg-shaped
Leaves	alternate, 3–9, stalked leaflets, each 2–8.5cm, oval, tipped with a small spine, leathery, smooth and shiny, dark green; stalks smooth, round in cross-section
Stipules	absent

FLOWERS AND FRUIT

Flowers	♂ and ♀ on different trees, many in long-branched clusters, greenish brown, appearing with the leaves
Petals	absent
Stamens	3–5 in ♂ flowers
Stigmas	3, on a single style
Ovaries	1 in ♀ flowers
Fruit	nut-like, 5–7mm, egg-shaped, tipped with slender point, coral-red, ripening brown
Seeds	1, not released

SIMILAR TREES

An Asian species cultivated in Mediterranean regions for its edible nuts, **1 Pistachio** (*Pistacia vera*) has leaves with hairy stalks and usually only 3 leaflets. **2 Mastic Tree** (*Pistacia lentiscus*), a native of dry parts of the Mediterranean, is usually an evergreen shrub; the leaves have 4 leaflets and end in a short spine.

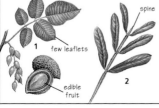
spine

few leaflets

1

2

edible fruit

Pepper Tree *Schinus molle*

narrow leaflets

long cluster

evergreen

pink,
berry-like

An evergreen tree with a crown of weeping foliage. The leaves are aromatic, smelling distinctly of pepper. It is most attractive in autumn, when the long clusters of pink fruits appear. Only flourishing in warm climates, it is widely planted in Mediterranean regions.

Status: native to Central and South America, grown as an ornamental in southern Europe and naturalized in places.

PEPPER TREE

Type	evergreen tree
Height	12m
Habitat	warm, dry areas
Flowering	June–August
Fruiting	July–December
TRUNK AND CROWN	
Trunk	stout, straight, cylindrical
Bark	grey-brown
Crown	tall, domed; branches slender
Twigs	bluish, drooping
LEAVES	
Buds	scaly, tiny
Leaves	alternate, tipped with a leaflet or with a short spine, 7–13 pairs of leaflets, each 2–6cm, very narrow, spine-tipped, often toothed, hairy, becoming smooth, aromatic; stalk flattened
Stipules	absent
FLOWERS AND FRUIT	
Flowers	♂ or ♂ and ♀ on different trees, many in loose, hanging clusters 25cm long, creamy-white
Petals	5, c2mm, oval, widest above middle, blunt; sepals 5
Stamens	10 in ♂ and ♀ flowers
Stigmas	3, on a single style
Ovaries	1, in ♀ and ♂ flowers
Fruit	berry-like, 6–7mm, globular, ripening shiny pink, remaining on tree throughout winter
Seeds	1, not released

SIMILAR TREES

A less frequent South American species, **Brazilian Pepper** (*Schinus terebinthifolia*), has erect branches, broader leaflets and bright red fruits.

winged

red

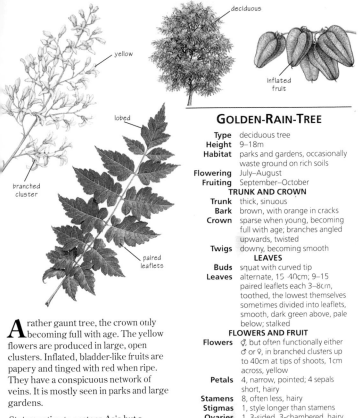

deciduous

yellow

inflated
fruit

lobed

branched
cluster

paired
leaflets

GOLDEN-RAIN-TREE

Type	deciduous tree
Height	9–18m
Habitat	parks and gardens, occasionally waste ground on rich soils
Flowering	July–August
Fruiting	September–October

TRUNK AND CROWN

Trunk	thick, sinuous
Bark	brown, with orange in cracks
Crown	sparse when young, becoming full with age; branches angled upwards, twisted
Twigs	downy, becoming smooth

LEAVES

Buds	squat with curved tip
Leaves	alternate, 15–40cm; 9–15 paired leaflets each 3–8cm, toothed, the lowest themselves sometimes divided into leaflets, smooth, dark green above, pale below; stalked

FLOWERS AND FRUIT

Flowers	♂, but often functionally either ♂ or ♀, in branched clusters up to 40cm at tips of shoots, 1cm across, yellow
Petals	4, narrow, pointed; 4 sepals short, hairy
Stamens	8, often less, hairy
Stigmas	1, style longer than stamens
Ovaries	1, 3-sided, 3-chambered, hairy
Fruit	pod-like, 5.5cm, conical and papery, red-tinged and veined, splitting into 3 when ripe
Seeds	3, black, released

A rather gaunt tree, the crown only becoming full with age. The yellow flowers are produced in large, open clusters. Inflated, bladder-like fruits are papery and tinged with red when ripe. They have a conspicuous network of veins. It is mostly seen in parks and large gardens.

Status: native to eastern Asia but a common ornamental tree, especially in southern Europe; occasionally naturalized in eastern and northern regions.

Similar trees: none.

Horse-chestnut *Aesculus hippocastanum*

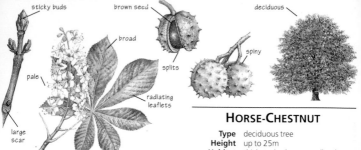

sticky buds · brown seed · deciduous · broad · splits · spiny · pale · radiating leaflets · large scar

A massive, spreading tree with large leaves divided like the fingers of a hand. Showy, upright clusters of flowers are visible from some distance away. Shiny seeds, called conkers, are enclosed in a thick, prickly case. Winter twigs have distinctive horseshoe-shaped leaf scars and very large, sticky buds.

Status: originally a mountain species native to the Balkan Peninsula; widely planted in much of Europe for timber, ornament and shade; often naturalized.

SIMILAR TREES

The widely planted **Red Horse-chestnut** (*Aesculus x carnea*) is a hybrid between Horse-chestnut and an American species. It has red flowers and non-spiny fruits.

not spiny · pink

HORSE-CHESTNUT

Type	deciduous tree
Height	up to 25m
Habitat	thickets, hedges, woodland
Flowering	May–June
Fruiting	September

TRUNK AND CROWN

Trunk	stout, broad-based, fluted
Bark	dark red- or grey-brown, scaly
Crown	huge, spreading dome; branches arching, tips upturned
Twigs	red-brown with pale lenticels; leaf-scars horseshoe-shaped

LEAVES

Buds	up to 3.5cm, brown, sticky
Leaves	paired on stem; 5–7 radiating, stalkless leaflets, the largest up to 25cm, pointed, tapering at base, toothed, woolly below, becoming smooth; long-stalked

FLOWERS AND FRUIT

Flowers	♀ or ♂, in showy, erect, pyramidal spikes of 15–30cm at tips of shoots
Petals	5, or 4, c10mm, frilly, unequal, the lowest largest, white with yellow to pink spot at base; sepals 5, unequal, short, joined in a tube
Stamens	6–7, protruding, down-curved
Stigmas	1, on a long, curved style
Ovaries	1, 3-chambered
Fruit	spiny, 6cm, globular, ripening brown and splitting into 3
Seeds	1, sometimes 2–3, smooth, dark glossy brown with a round, pale scar, released when fruit splits

Aesculus indica Indian Horse-chestnut

Very similar to Horse-chestnut, this Indian species differs in having stalked leaflets and fruits lacking prominent spines. The smaller spikes of flowers are white or pink, spotted with red and yellow. Winter buds are green, not brown like those of its more common relative.

Status: native to the Himalayas; planted in parks and gardens for ornament.

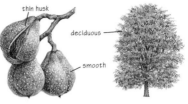

thin husk

deciduous

smooth

pinkish

narrow

radiating leaflets

SIMILAR TREES

Yellow Buckeye (*Aesculus flava*), from south-eastern North America, has narrow yellow or sometimes pink flowers; it is frequently planted in parks.

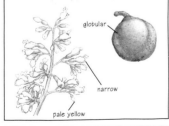

globular

narrow

pale yellow

INDIAN HORSE-CHESTNUT

Type	deciduous tree
Height	19–30m
Habitat	moist soils
Flowering	June
Fruiting	October

TRUNK AND CROWN

Trunk	stout, straight, rather short
Bark	greenish to reddish grey, smooth, cracking into rectangular plates
Crown	tall, rounded; spreading branches arching upwards
Twigs	grey-brown, with prominent horseshoe-shaped leaf scars

LEAVES

Buds	c10mm, green, sticky
Leaves	paired on stems; 5–9, but usually 7, radiating, short-stalked leaflets up to 8cm, narrowly oval, widest above middle, base tapered at both ends, finely toothed

FLOWERS AND FRUIT

Flowers	♂, in erect, pyramidal spikes of usually 10–15cm
Petals	5 or 4, white or pink, the lowest largest, the upper spotted with red or yellow; 5 sepals small, joined in a tube
Stamens	5–8, long and protruding
Stigmas	1, on a long, protruding style
Ovaries	1, 3-chambered
Fruit	pear-shaped, ripening greenish brown with thin, rough-skinned husk splitting into 3 when ripe
Seeds	2–3, wrinkled, glossy brown, released when fruit splits

Sycamore *Acer pseudoplatanus*

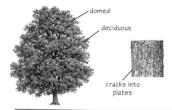

domed

deciduous

cracks into plates

Originally confined to mountain regions, Sycamore has been introduced to many parts of Europe and is now widely naturalized. The winged seeds help it to spread easily and rapidly. It makes a large, spreading tree, often wider than it is tall.

Status: native to mountains of central and southern Europe, and western Asia; naturalized as far north as Sweden.

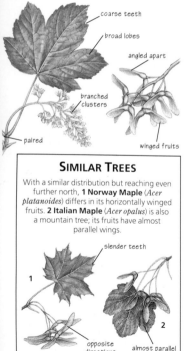

coarse teeth

broad lobes

angled apart

branched clusters

paired

winged fruits

SIMILAR TREES

With a similar distribution but reaching even further north, **1 Norway Maple** (*Acer platanoides*) differs in its horizontally winged fruits. **2 Italian Maple** (*Acer opalus*) is also a mountain tree; its fruits have almost parallel wings.

slender teeth

1

2

opposite directions

almost parallel

SYCAMORE

Type	deciduous tree
Height	up to 35m
Habitat	woods, hedges, mountainous areas; often planted
Flowering	April–May
Fruiting	June–September

TRUNK AND CROWN

Trunk	stout, often developing buttresses
Bark	smooth, grey, becoming pinkish brown, fissured and cracking into small irregular plates
Crown	domed, spreading, dense
Twigs	short, grey-green, smooth

LEAVES

Buds	0.8–1cm, oval, reddish green
Leaves	opposite, 10–15cm, with 5 deep and broad spreading lobes, each pointed and coarsely toothed, dark green above, pale blue-green beneath; stalk up to 20cm, usually reddish

FLOWERS AND FRUIT

Flowers	♂ and ♀ in separate clusters, many in branched, hanging clusters 6–12 cm long, with the leaves, greenish yellow, each c6mm
Petals	5; sepals 5
Stamens	8 in ♂; sterile in ♀
Stigmas	2, on short style
Ovaries	1, 2-chambered, hairy
Fruit	paired, smooth, each with a grey-brown wing c2.5cm long; diverging at right-angles
Seeds	1 per fruit, not released

upright cluster

3-5 lobes

spreading
horizontally

toothed

paired

broad

deciduous

often tinged
red

ridged

A small, colourful tree with young
leaves that are pink in spring and
turn deep yellow in autumn. It is most
common in northern Europe, where it
often grows in hedges. The twigs become
winged with thick, corky flanges, and the
leaves have either 3 or 5 lobes.

Status: native more or less throughout
Europe and western Asia; planted for
autumn colour.

SIMILAR TREES

Two species from southern and central
Europe are distinguished by their parallel-
winged fruits. **1 Montpellier Maple** (*Acer
monspessulanum*) has leaves with toothless
lobes. The rarer **2 Tartar Maple** (*Acer
tataricum*) has undivided leaves
and striped bark.

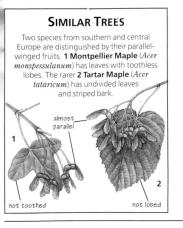

almost
parallel

1

2

not toothed

not lobed

FIELD MAPLE

Type	deciduous tree or shrub
Height	up to 26m
Habitat	hedgerows, open woods, usually on chalk or limestone soils
Flowering	April–June
Fruiting	May–September
Trunk	sinuous, usually distinct

TRUNK AND CROWN

Bark	grey or light brown, finely ridged and fissured
Crown	broadly domed; branches angled upwards at tips
Twigs	dark brown and finely hairy, becoming paler and ribbed

LEAVES

Buds	3mm, red-brown, hairy at tip
Leaves	opposite, 4–7cm, thick, deeply divided into 3 or 5 rounded lobes, opening pinkish, later dull green above, downy below, turning yellow in autumn; stalk c5cm

FLOWERS AND FRUIT

Flowers	♂ and ♀, few in separate, upright, branched clusters, appearing with the leaves, each c6mm, yellow-green; stalkless
Stamens	8 in ♂; sterile in ♀
Stigmas	2, on single, short style
Ovaries	1, 2-chambered
Fruit	paired, each with a pale green wing, often tinged with crimson and hairy, spreading horizontally
Seeds	1 per fruit, not released

Box-elder *Acer negundo*

A fast-growing North American tree that is readily distinguished from other maples by its leaves, which are mostly divided into 5 leaflets. The flowers open before the leaves, the crimson anthers of male trees being particularly noticeable. The fruits mature early and persist on the tree for a long time. The cultivar 'Variegatum' is planted for its yellow and green variegated leaves.

Status: native to eastern North America; planted for ornament and shelter; naturalized mainly in central regions.

hanging clusters

red ♂

greenish ♀

3 or 5 leaflets

paired

angled apart

deciduous

SIMILAR TREES

The decorative **Paper-bark Maple** (*Acer griseum*), from China, has reddish bark, which peels in broad, papery strips.

papery strips

3 leaflets

BOX-ELDER

Type	deciduous tree
Height	up to 20m
Habitat	parks and gardens, street tree
Flowering	March–April
Fruiting	June–September
TRUNK AND CROWN	
Trunk	short, often sprouting numerous burrs
Bark	smooth, grey, becoming darker and shallowly fissured
Crown	irregularly domed, spreading
Twigs	green, straight, smooth
LEAVES	
Buds	small, with 2 silky white scales
Leaves	opposite, with 2 or 4 paired leaflets and a leaflet at tip, each oval, long-pointed, shallowly toothed; stalk 6–8cm
Stipules	absent
FLOWERS AND FRUIT	
Flowers	♂ and ♀ on different trees, appearing before leaves
[*M*]	in short, hanging clusters of 12–16, red
[*F*]	6–12 in loose hanging clusters 5cm long, greenish
Petals	absent; sepals 5
Stamens	4–6 in ♂, red
Stigmas	2, spreading, styles very short
Ovaries	1, 2-chambered
Fruit	paired, c2cm, smooth, each with a brown wing and diverging at a narrow angle
Seeds	1 per fruit, not released

sharp teeth

deep lobes

silvery below

narrow angle

deciduous

paired

small clusters

Valued in North America as a source of maple syrup, which is made from the sap, this tree is planted in Europe mainly for ornament. The leaves are silvery beneath and attractive in summer, before turning pale yellow or red later.

Status: North American, native from Quebec to Florida; widely cultivated.

SILVER MAPLE

Type	deciduous tree
Height	up to 36m
Habitat	roadsides, parks, gardens
Flowering	March
Fruiting	May–June

TRUNK AND CROWN

Trunk	short, stout, often with burrs
Bark	smooth, grey-brown, later flaking and becoming shaggy
Crown	tall, spreading above; branches numerous, slender, arching
Twigs	brown or purplish

LEAVES

Buds	c1cm, oval, angular, red
Leaves	opposite, 9–16 cm, deeply 5-lobed, lobes deeply and irregularly toothed, silvery-hairy beneath, pale yellow or occasionally brilliant red in autumn; stalk 8–13cm, pink
Stipules	absent

FLOWERS AND FRUIT

Flowers	♂ and ♀ in separate clusters of 4–5, appearing before the leaves, greenish or red
	♂ short-stalked
	♀ long-stalked
Petals	absent; sepals 5
Stamens	3–7 in ♂s
Stigmas	2, on short style
Ovaries	1, 2-chambered
Fruit	paired, 1 often fails to develop, 5–6 cm, stalked, with elliptical, twisted wing diverging at a narrow angle
Seeds	1 per fruit, not released

SIMILAR TREES

A more important source of maple syrup, and the brightest autumn-coloured species, is **1 Sugar Maple** (*Acer saccharophorum*). **2 Red Maple** (*Acer rubrum*) has dense red flower clusters, red fruits and red autumn leaves. Both are North American trees that are commonly planted in Europe.

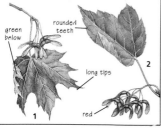

green below

rounded teeth

long tips

1

2

red

Père David's Maple *Acer davidii*

deciduous

paired

scarcely lobed

drooping cluster

usually red

striped bark

fruits spread widely

One of a group of decorative trees known as 'snake-bark' maples. The young olive-green bark is patterned with a network of white lines, resembling the skin of a reptile. The lines fade with age and the bark turns uniform dark brown. Several cultivars, all differing somewhat in overall shape, are planted.

Status: native to China; cultivated for ornament.

SIMILAR TREES

Native to Japan, **1 Snake-bark Maple** (*Acer rufinerve*) has downy grey twigs and leaves with three triangular lobes. **2 Hers's Maple** (*Acer hersii*), from China, has marbled bark and long spikes of flowers.

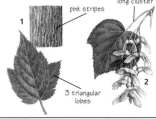

pink stripes

long cluster

1

2

3 triangular lobes

PÈRE DAVID'S MAPLE

Type	deciduous tree
Height	up to 16m
Habitat	parks and gardens
Flowering	May
Fruiting	July–August

TRUNK AND CROWN

Trunk	short, stout
Bark	smooth, greenish, with white stripes when young, becoming brown and fissured
Crown	narrow; branches angled upwards
Twigs	smooth, purple or red when young, white striped

LEAVES

Buds	c1cm, narrowly conical, dark red with paler markings
Leaves	opposite, up to 15 x 10 cm, broadly oval, heart-shaped at the base, with a short slender tip, edges finely toothed, shiny green above, whitish green beneath; stalk 6cm, red

FLOWERS AND FRUIT

Flowers	♂ and ♀ in separate clusters, many in arching clusters 7–10 cm long, appearing with leaves, greenish yellow
Petals	absent; sepals 5
Stamens	4–10 in ♂
Stigmas	2, spreading
Ovaries	1, 2-chambered
Fruit	paired, each with a wing 2.5–3.7cm long, spreading nearly horizontally
Seeds	1 per fruit, not released

Acer palmatum **Smooth Japanese-maple**

Various maples are cultivated for ornament and this species is particularly attractive, with many different forms. In the typical tree the leaves have narrow, pointed lobes and turn red or purple in autumn. In some cultivars they are finely divided and deep purple throughout the year. Others have bright red winter shoots.

Status: native to China, Japan and Korea, and a common ornamental, especially in small gardens.

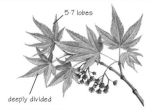

5-7 lobes

deeply divided

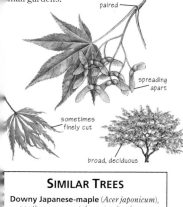

paired

spreading apart

sometimes finely cut

broad, deciduous

SMOOTH JAPANESE-MAPLE

Type	deciduous tree or shrub
Height	up to 16m
Habitat	gardens and parks
Flowering	April–May
Fruiting	June–September

TRUNK AND CROWN

Trunk	usually very short, sinuously twisted and soon dividing
Bark	smooth and rich brown striped with pale yellow, becoming grey
Crown	domed and spreading
Twigs	slender, smooth, reddish above, green beneath

LEAVES

Buds	oval, 2–3mm, often red-tinged
Leaves	opposite, 7–9cm, deeply divided into 5–7 spreading, oval, pointed and sharply toothed lobes, bright green, turning yellow, red or crimson in autumn; stalks 3–5cm
Stipules	absent

FLOWERS AND FRUIT

Flowers	♂, in upright clusters of 12–15; each 6–8mm across, dark purple; stalks slender, c4cm long
Petals	absent; sepals 5
Stamens	4–10
Stigmas	2 on short style
Ovaries	1, 2-chambered
Fruit	paired, each with a pale green wing tinged with red, c1cm long and diverging at a wide angle
Seeds	1 per fruit, not released

SIMILAR TREES

Downy Japanese-maple (*Acer japonicum*), another ornamental species, has leaves with 7–11 short lobes. It too has fine-leaved cultivars.

7-11 lobes

shallowly divided

Holly *Ilex aquifolium*

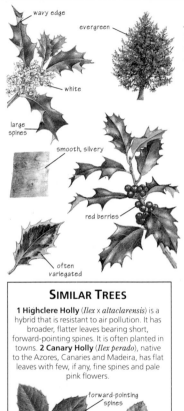

wavy edge

evergreen

white

large spines

smooth, silvery

red berries

often variegated

A stiff and prickly-leaved evergreen tree, often a shrub. When growing in deep shady woods it is often sterile. In more open sites it bears white flowers and, on female trees, bright red berries.

Status: native to western and southern Europe and western Asia.

HOLLY

Type	evergreen tree or shrub
Height	2–25m
Habitat	woods, scrub, on moist soils
Flowering	May–August
Fruiting	September–March
TRUNK AND CROWN	
Trunk	straight, cylindrical
Bark	silvery grey, smooth, warty or fissured when old
Crown	narrow, conical to cylindrical; branches curved upwards
Twigs	slightly hairy and bright green when young, becoming smooth and darker
LEAVES	
Buds	2–3mm, egg-shaped
Leaves	alternate, oval to roughly oblong, 5–12cm, edges wavy and spiny, leathery and waxy, dark, shiny green above, pale and matt below; stalk 1cm, thick and grooved
Stipules	very small and inconspicuous
FLOWERS AND FRUIT	
Flowers	♂ and ♀ on different trees, in clusters in angles of leaves on old wood, white
Petals	4, c4mm, joined at base; sepals 4, joined
Stamens	4 in ♂ flowers, rudimentary in ♀ flowers
Stigmas	1 in ♀
Ovaries	1, green, barrel-shaped, rudimentary in ♂ flowers
Fruit	berry-like, 8–10mm, globular, ripening scarlet, on ♀ trees only
Seeds	several, not released

SIMILAR TREES

1 Highclere Holly (*Ilex x altaclarensis*) is a hybrid that is resistant to air pollution. It has broader, flatter leaves bearing short, forward-pointing spines. It is often planted in towns. **2 Canary Holly** (*Ilex perado*), native to the Azores, Canaries and Madeira, has flat leaves with few, if any, fine spines and pale pink flowers.

forward-pointing spines

2

1

few, fine or no spines

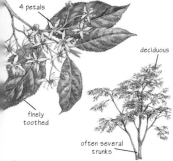

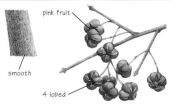

A slender tree, often with several trunks, and small, inconspicuous flowers. In contrast the 4-lobed fruits are very obvious, ripening deep pink and splitting to reveal the fleshy, orange covering of the seeds.

Status: native to all but the extreme north and south of Europe; several cultivars are used as ornamentals.

SIMILAR TREES

A second European species, **1 Broad-leaved Spindle** (*Euonymus latifolius*), has flowers with 5 broad, pink petals. **2 Japanese Spindle** (*Euonymus japonicus*), from eastern Asia, has thick, blunt leaves and broad, yellowish petals.

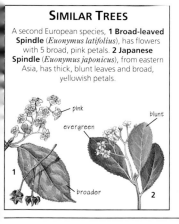

SPINDLE

Type	deciduous tree or shrub
Height	2–6m
Habitat	woodland and scrub on chalky soils
Flowering	May–June
Fruiting	September–October

TRUNK AND CROWN

Trunk	slender, often several
Bark	fawn to grey-green, smooth, with fine vertical lines
Crown	bushy; numerous branches arching upwards
Twigs	green, 4-angled

LEAVES

Buds	5–6mm, greenish brown, slightly curved
Leaves	paired on stem, up to 10cm, narrowly oval to elliptical, pointed, base wedge-shaped, edges finely toothed, red in autumn; short-stalked
Stipules	absent

FLOWERS AND FRUIT

Flowers	♂, in clusters of 3–8 in angles of leaves, 8–10mm across, yellow with a green central disc
Petals	4, narrow, widely separated; sepals 4, 1–2mm, green
Stamens	4, alternating with petals
Stigmas	1, style short, straight
Ovaries	1, bright green
Fruit	10–15mm across, 4-lobed, pink and fleshy, splitting to release seeds
Seeds	4, each with a fleshy, bright orange covering

149

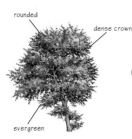

rounded

dense crown

evergreen

clustered flowers

glossy

small fruit

notched tip

A neat, dense evergreen, often no more than a shrub. Slow-growing and small-leaved, it forms a dense bush when clipped. Tiny flowers form inconspicuous clusters. Fruits are tipped with distinctive, spreading and woody styles. The many cultivars are popular hedging and topiary plants.

Status: native and scattered through parts of western Europe with chalky soils.

SIMILAR TREES

The larger-leaved **Balearic Box** (*Buxus balearica*) is a stiff tree with pinkish bark, confined to parts of Spain, the Balearic Islands and Sardinia.

larger leaves

BOX

Type	evergreen tree or shrub
Height	2–5m, rarely as much as 11m
Habitat	calcareous soils
Flowering	April
Fruiting	September

TRUNK AND CROWN

Trunk	cylindrical, often leaning
Bark	brown, ageing grey
Crown	dense, rounded
Twigs	4-angled, white-woolly, becoming smooth

LEAVES

Buds	5–7mm, narrow, bright green
Leaves	paired on stem, 15–30mm, oval, oblong or elliptical, tip notched, edges turned under, thick and leathery, glossy green above, pale below; stalk short

FLOWERS AND FRUIT

Flowers	♂ and ♀, in clusters 5mm across in angles of leaves, each cluster with one stalked ♀ and several stalkless ♂ flowers
Petals	absent; ♂ flowers with 4 small sepals; ♀ flowers with only a whorl of small bracts
Stamens	4 in ♂ flowers
Stigmas	3 in ♀ flowers, each 2-lobed on a thick, spreading style
Ovaries	1, 3-chambered, blue-green
Fruit	nut-like, c7mm, oblong to egg-shaped, tipped with the horn-like styles, ripening brown, splitting into 3 parts
Seeds	6, 5–6mm, glossy black, released when fruit splits

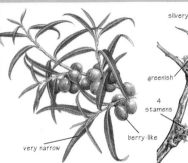

A small, silvery, thorny tree. All parts of the plant, particularly the leaves and twigs, are covered with intricately shaped but minute silver scales. Growing in coastal sites, it is often only a shrub in more exposed habitats.

Status: native to much of Europe, mainly coastal regions of the north-west, but also occurring inland; widely planted on sand dunes and often naturalized.

SIMILAR TREES

1 Oleaster (*Elaeagnus angustifolia*), from western Asia, and the North American **2 Silver Berry** (*Elaeagnus commutata*) are widely naturalized ornamentals. Both have fragrant flowers c1cm long. Oleaster has juicy berries; Silver Berry, dry berries.

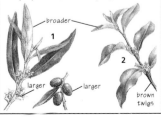

SEA-BUCKTHORN

Type	deciduous tree or shrub
Height	up to 11m but often shorter
Habitat	dunes and sea-shores
Flowering	March–April
Fruiting	September–November

TRUNK AND CROWN

Trunk	much-branched near the base, suckering
Bark	pale-brown, ridged
Crown	open, rounded
Twigs	thorny, covered with minute silvery scales

LEAVES

Buds	3mm, squat with thick scales
Leaves	alternate or spiralled on stem, 1–6cm, very narrow, pointed, silvery green; stalks very short
Stipules	absent

FLOWERS AND FRUIT

Flowers	♂ and ♀ on different trees, in short spikes appearing before leaves on previous year's growth; ♂ 4mm, stalkless, ♀ 1.5mm, stalked, greenish with rusty scales
Petals	absent; sepals 2, joined, short in ♂ flowers, long in ♀
Stamens	4 in ♂ flowers
Stigmas	1, thread-like on a long cylindrical style
Ovaries	1, sunk into base of ♀ flowers
Fruit	berry-like, 6–8mm, almost globular, ripening orange
Seeds	1, not released

151

Common Jujube *Ziziphus jujuba*

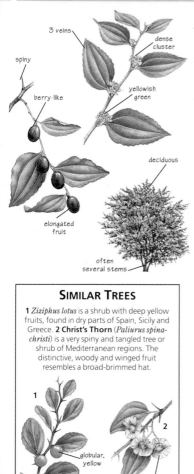

3 veins

dense cluster

spiny

yellowish green

berry-like

deciduous

elongated fruit

often several stems

A small tree or tangled shrub, armed with very sharp, curved and straight spines. The long, slender twigs are markedly zigzag. Sweet and juicy, the fruits are edible.

Status: native to Asia; widely grown in southern Europe for the edible fruits and often naturalized.

COMMON JUJUBE

Type	deciduous tree or shrub
Height	up to 8m
Habitat	hedgerows near houses, orchards
Flowering	April–May
Fruiting	September
TRUNK AND CROWN	
Trunk	slender, sinuous, often several
Bark	dark grey-brown
Crown	dense, rounded
Twigs	zigzag, smooth, green, non-flowering twigs often spiny
LEAVES	
Buds	pointed, hairy
Leaves	alternate, 2–5.5cm, oval, blunt, with 3 conspicuous veins, bright, shiny green above, downy on veins below, edges with tiny, gland-tipped teeth
Stipules	transformed into sharp, brown spines, 1 long and straight, 1 short and curved
FLOWERS AND FRUIT	
Flowers	♂, in small, dense, stalked clusters in angles of leaves, yellowish green
Petals	5, 1.5mm, hooded, tapering at base; sepals 5, 2mm
Stamens	5, alternating with, and often concealed by, petals
Stigmas	2, minute, styles joined at base
Ovaries	1, sunk into 5-lobed disc in base of flower
Fruit	berry-like, 1.5–3cm, egg-shaped, ripening red to black, sweet-tasting
Seeds	1, 6–7mm, stony, not released

SIMILAR TREES

1 *Ziziphus lotus* is a shrub with deep yellow fruits, found in dry parts of Spain, Sicily and Greece. **2 Christ's Thorn** (*Paliurus spina-christi*) is a very spiny and tangled tree or shrub of Mediterranean regions. The distinctive, woody and winged fruit resembles a broad-brimmed hat.

1

globular, yellow

2

winged fruit

152

deciduous

paired leaves

finely, toothed

4 petals

paired buds

berry-like, black

short side shoots

spiny

A regularly branched tree, its new twigs always growing out at right angles. The shoots are of two kinds, long and short; only short shoots bear flowers and fruits.

Status: native to much of Europe but confined to chalky soils and absent from the Mediterranean region.

BUCKTHORN

Type	deciduous tree or shrub
Height	4–6m
Habitat	hedges and woodland on chalky soils
Flowering	May–June
Fruiting	September–October

TRUNK AND CROWN

Trunk	short, often several or forking near the ground
Bark	black, flaking to reveal orange patches
Crown	regular; branches spreading at right angles to trunk
Twigs	grey, some ending in spines, many short side shoots

LEAVES

Buds	4mm, brown, pointed
Leaves	paired on twigs, crowded on short side shoots, 3–7cm, oval or elliptical, blunt or even notched at tip, edges finely toothed, 2–4 pairs of curving veins; stalk short
Stipules	soft, soon falling

FLOWERS AND FRUIT

Flowers	♂ and ♀ on different trees, in clusters on short side shoots, 4mm across, greenish white, fragrant
Petals	4, rarely 5, triangular; sepals 4
Stamens	4, rudimentary in ♀ flowers
Stigmas	4 in ♀ flowers, on single style
Ovaries	1 in ♀ flowers, globose
Fruit	berry-like, 6–8mm, globose but slightly flattened, ripening black
Seeds	2–4, stony, yellow

SIMILAR TREES

1 Mediterranean Buckthorn (*Rhamnus alaternus*) is an evergreen shrub lacking spines, with yellow sepals. **2 Alder Buckthorn** (*Frangula alnus*) has leaves with unbroken edges, ♂ flowers with 5 sepals and fruits ripening from yellow, through red to black. It grows in wet woods through most of Europe.

evergreen

leaves not paired

no teeth

1

few teeth

red, then black

2

Tamarisk *Tamarix gallica*

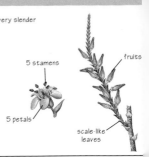

deciduous

very slender

slender

usually pink

5 stamens

5 petals

fruits

scale-like leaves

Resistant to the drying effects of salt winds, this feathery tree or shrub is often seen near coasts, and thrives on sand-dunes. The pink flower-spikes normally appear in summer but may occur up to December in mild areas.

Status: native to western Europe as far north as France; often planted and naturalized elsewhere.

SIMILAR TREES

Two other species widespread in western Europe can be distinguished by their flowers.
1 African Tamarisk (*Tamarix africana*) has larger, white flowers with petals 2–3mm long. It grows mainly in salt-marshes and along rivers. **2 Canarian Tamarisk** (*Tamarix canariensis*) has pinkish petals, only 1.5mm or less, and is found on coastal sands.

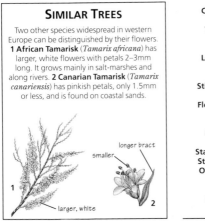

1

larger, white

smaller

longer bract

2

TAMARISK

Type	deciduous shrub or small tree
Height	up to 10m
Habitat	riversides, coastal areas, marshes
Flowering	April–September
Fruiting	May–October

TRUNK AND CROWN

Trunk	usually curved or twisted, slender
Bark	dull brown to dark purple, rough and fibrous
Crown	much-branched with long slender branches
Twigs	willowy, very slender, reddish

LEAVES

Buds	minute, green
Leaves	alternate, c2mm, scale-like and clasping the stem, blue-green; stalkless
Stipules	absent

FLOWERS AND FRUIT

Flowers	♂, in spike-like clusters to 3cm long on young shoots, each c2mm, pink or white
Petals	5, 1.5–2mm, elliptical; sepals 5, 0.75–1.25mm
Stamens	5
Stigmas	3–4, styles very short
Ovaries	1, bottle-shaped
Fruit	hard brown capsule, splitting to release seeds
Seeds	numerous, oval, brown, each with a long tuft of hairs

Tamarix parviflora **Small-flowered Tamarisk**

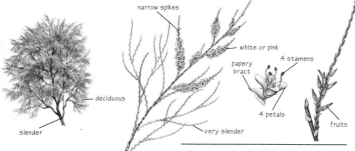

narrow spikes

deciduous

slender

very slender

white or pink

papery bract

4 stamens

4 petals

fruits

A predominantly eastern Mediterranean species that is more often seen as a shrub than a tree. The very slender twigs and tiny, scale-like, clasping leaves give a delicate, wispy effect. The flower spikes are also very slim, being less than 5mm wide. The pink or white petals usually number 4, but sometimes there are 5.

Status: native to the Balkan Peninsula and Aegean region, planted elsewhere for ornament.

SIMILAR TREES

Two very similar species are **1** *Tamarix tetrandra* and **2** *Tamarix dalmatica*, also from south-eastern Europe. Both have longer, broader flower spikes and larger petals. *Tamarix tetrandra* has black bark.

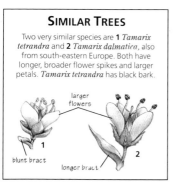

larger flowers

blunt bract   **1**

2   longer bract

SMALL-FLOWERED TAMARISK

Type	deciduous shrub or small tree
Height	2–3m
Habitat	hedges and river banks
Flowering	March–June
Fruiting	April–June
TRUNK AND CROWN	
Trunk	slender, often several or branching low-down
Bark	brown to purple
Crown	low, rounded
Twigs	very slender, drooping, red-brown, black in winter
LEAVES	
Buds	minute, egg-shaped
Leaves	alternate, 3–5mm, scale-like and half clasping stem with tips spreading, sharply pointed, edges papery-edged; stalkless
Stipules	absent
FLOWERS AND FRUIT	
Flowers	⚥, in dense, spike-like clusters 3–5mm wide, white or pink
Petals	4, less than 2mm, upright, persistent; sepals 2–2.5mm, minutely toothed
Stamens	4
Stigmas	3, styles very short
Ovaries	1, bottle-shaped
Fruit	hard capsule, splitting to release seeds
Seeds	numerous, each with a long tuft of hairs

Large-leaved Lime *Tilia platyphyllos*

heart-shaped

narrow ridges

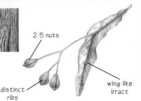

2-5 nuts

deciduous

distinct ribs

wing-like bract

whitish, fragrant

hanging clusters

often sprouts

This is the first of the limes to begin flowering. A tall tree, it has upwardly angled branches and large leaves. The fragrant flowers hang in clusters beneath a narrow, wing-like bract, attracting large numbers of bees.

Status: native from central Europe to Russia and western Asia; introduced elsewhere and often planted.

SIMILAR TREES

Common Lime (*Tilia* x *vulgaris*), a hybrid between Large and Small-leaved Limes, is widely planted. In many areas it is more common than the parent species. The leaves have tufts of white hairs beneath and drooping yellowish flowers.

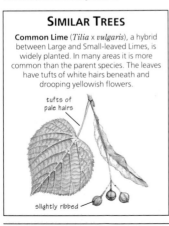

tufts of pale hairs

slightly ribbed

LARGE-LEAVED LIME

Type	deciduous tree
Height	up to 40m
Habitat	woods, often on limestone
Flowering	June–July
Fruiting	July–October

TRUNK AND CROWN

Trunk	occasionally with outgrowths of bushy stems from base
Bark	smooth, dark grey, developing narrow cracks and ridges
Crown	tall and narrowly domed; branches angled upwards
Twigs	dark reddish green, softly hairy

LEAVES

Buds	oval, dark red
Leaves	alternate, up to 12cm, heart-shaped, sharply pointed, sharply toothed, dark green, hairy above, paler, more densely hairy below; stalk 1.5–5cm
Stipules	small, acting as bud scales, falling early

FLOWERS AND FRUIT

Flowers	☿, yellowish white, fragrant, in clusters of 2–5 hanging beneath a whitish green, wing-like bract 5–12 cm
Petals	5, 5–8mm, spreading; sepals 5
Stamens	numerous
Stigmas	1, 5-lobed
Ovaries	1, 5-chambered
Fruit	cluster of hard, globular nuts, each 8–10mm, 3- to 5-ribbed, densely hairy; whole cluster and bract shed together
Seeds	1, not released

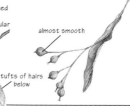

finely toothed

almost circular

almost smooth

tufts of hairs below

deciduous

branches arch downwards

clusters angled upwards

Growing on lime-rich soils, this tree has downward-arching branches and heart-shaped leaves. It is often planted as a street tree but aphids attack the leaves, dripping half-digested sap onto the pavements below, leaving them sticky and unpleasant. Fungi also attack and disfigure the leaves. Other, resistant, trees are now preferred. Bees are attracted by the nectar-rich flowers.

Status: native to most of Europe and northern Asia; frequently planted.

SIMILAR TREES

Caucasian Lime (*Tilia x euchlora*) is a natural hybrid from the Crimea. It has rich yellow flowers and leaves with tufts of reddish brown hairs in the vein angles beneath.

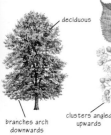

glossy, dark above

larger

slightly ribbed

SMALL-LEAVED LIME

Type	deciduous tree
Height	up to 32m
Habitat	woods, often on limestone
Flowering	June–July
Fruiting	July–September

TRUNK AND CROWN

Trunk	burred
Bark	smooth, grey, becoming dark, fissured, cracked into plates
Crown	irregularly domed; branches downwardly arching
Twigs	smooth, reddish above, greenish brown beneath

LEAVES

Buds	dark red, smooth and shiny
Leaves	alternate, 3–9cm, almost circular, finely pointed, notched at base, sharply toothed, dark shining green above, paler beneath, smooth except for reddish brown tuft of hair in vein angles 1.5–4cm
Stipules	small, scale-like, soon falling

FLOWERS AND FRUIT

Flowers	♀, greenish yellow, fragrant, in clusters of 4–15 held above leaf-like bract up to 8cm long
Petals	5, 7–8mm, narrowly oval; sepals 5–6, 3mm, elliptical
Stamens	c40
Stigmas	1, 5-lobed
Ovaries	1, 5-chambered
Fruit	cluster of hard, globular nuts, each c6mm, ribbed; whole cluster and bract shed together
Seeds	1, not released

Silver-lime *Tila tomentosa*

deciduous

unequal teeth

white-woolly below

large bract

warty, downy

hanging clusters

A handsome tree with contrasting leaf surfaces, green above and silver below. Upwardly angled branches give a full, rounded crown. It is resistant to drought and frequently used as a street tree. The ground around these trees is often littered with drowsy and dying bees, drugged by the narcotic nectar from the flowers.

Status: native from Hungary and the Balkans to western Asia; planted elsewhere for ornament.

SIMILAR TREES

Of unknown origin, and sometimes regarded as merely an odd form of Silver-lime, **Weeping Silver-lime** (*Tilia petiolaris*) has branches that are angled upwards before drooping conspicuously towards the tips.

weeping twigs

long stalk

usually sterile

SILVER-LIME

Type	deciduous tree
Height	up to 30m
Habitat	woods; often planted
Flowering	July–August
Fruiting	July–September
TRUNK AND CROWN	
Trunk	stout, well-defined
Bark	dark grey-green or grey, networked with shallow ridges
Crown	broadly domed, compact; branches upwardly angled
Twigs	whitish hairy when young, becoming green, smooth
LEAVES	
Buds	6–8mm, oval, green-brown
Leaves	alternate, 8–10cm, heart-shaped, finely pointed, lop-sided at base, sharply toothed, dark green above, white-woolly beneath, the hairs star-shaped; stalk c5cm
Stipules	small, acting as bud scales, falling early
FLOWERS AND FRUIT	
Flowers	☿, dull white or pale yellow, fragrant, in clusters of 6–10 hanging beneath a yellowish green, leaf-like bract
Petals	5, 5–8mm; sepals 5
Stamens	numerous
Stigmas	1, 5-lobed
Ovaries	1, 5-chambered
Fruit	cluster of nuts, each 6–12 mm long, 5-sided, warty and downy; cluster and bract shed together
Seeds	1, not released

Davidia involucrata **Handkerchief-tree**

heart-shaped

toothed

woolly below

white

large bracts

large, single fruit
ripens purplish brown

cracks into plates

deciduous

A spectacular tree when in full bloom, becoming completely covered with conspicuous, white flower-heads. The tree's real flowers are small and grouped into a globular, purplish head. This is enveloped by two large, triangular, handkerchief-like bracts – hence the common name. When the bracts unfold, they give the impression of a single large flower with white petals and a purple centre. Though the flower-heads are similar in structure to those of the dogwoods, Handkerchief-tree is usually placed within its own family. The most commonly planted form is var. *vilmoriniana*, which is distinguished by narrow, smooth and shiny leaves.

Status: native to China; cultivated as an ornamental in parks and gardens.

Similar trees: none.

HANDKERCHIEF-TREE

Type	deciduous tree
Height	up to 18m
Habitat	parks and gardens
Flowering	May
Fruiting	October
TRUNK AND CROWN	
Trunk	straight, well-defined
Bark	grey-brown to purplish, cracking
Crown	tall, domed; branches wide-spreading
Twigs	brown, with lines of warty lenticels
LEAVES	
Buds	9mm, dark, shiny red, pointed
Leaves	alternate, 3.5cm, broadly oval, pointed, base heart-shaped, edges sharply toothed, dull green above, white-woolly below, fragrant when unfolding; stalkless
FLOWERS AND FRUIT	
Flowers	♂ and ♀ in separate clusters, or ♀; flower cluster c2cm across, purplish, flanked by 2 very large, showy white bracts
Perianth	0 in ♂ flowers, many in ♀ and ♂ flowers
Stamens	usually 5–6
Stigmas	1, lobed, style curved
Ovaries	1, 6–10-chambered, sunk into base of flower
Fruit	single, berry-like, 4cm, egg-shaped, ridged, ripening purplish brown
Seeds	6–10, not released

159

Black-gum *Nyssa sylvatica*

berry-like · ripens blackish · glossy

clustered ♂ flowers · not toothed · deciduous · turns red or orange · few ♂ flowers

BLACK-GUM

Type	deciduous tree
Height	up to 30m
Habitat	parks and gardens; wet soils
Flowering	June
Fruiting	October

TRUNK AND CROWN

Trunk	tapering
Bark	grey or brown, deeply ridged and fissured
Crown	cylindrical, flat-topped
Twigs	grey-brown, smooth

LEAVES

Buds	small, red-brown, downy tips
Leaves	alternate, 4.5cm, oval, widest above middle, tapered at both ends, edge unbroken, slightly leathery, glossy green above, pale and matt below, stalkless

FLOWERS AND FRUIT

Flowers	♂ and ♀ on different trees; ♂ in rounded clusters 1cm across; ♀ single or paired
Petals	5, free in ♂, in ♀ joined into a bell-shaped tube; sepals 5, tiny, tooth-like
Stamens	8, longer than petals in ♂ flowers
Stigmas	1 in ♀ flowers, on a long, curved style
Ovaries	1 in ♀ flowers, sunk into base of flower
Fruit	berry-like, 12mm, oval, widest above middle, ripening blue-black
Seeds	1, stony

G rowing in swampy areas, Black-gum forms a very tall tree, up to 100m, where it is native in eastern North America. In Europe, however, it is generally much smaller, reaching only 30m at the most. Producing inconspicuous flowers and rather dull fruits, it is planted for its brilliant autumn leaf colours, which are dominated by bright reds and orange. Black-gum only thrives in mild areas, so is little planted in northern regions. However, it is quite common from southern England southwards.

Status: native to the swamps of eastern North America; grown in Europe mainly for ornament.

Similar trees: relatives of the Black-gum are only rarely cultivated, in private gardens.

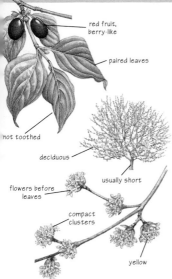

red fruit, berry-like

paired leaves

not toothed

deciduous

usually short

flowers before leaves

compact clusters

yellow

A very attractive tree in late winter, when bright yellow flowers appear. Dull green leaves which follow have strongly marked veins. The succulent fruits are often used in conserves.

Status: native to central and south-eastern Europe; widely cultivated and naturalized elsewhere.

CORNELIAN CHERRY

Type	deciduous tree or shrub
Height	up to 8m
Habitat	scrub, thickets and woodland, especially on chalk
Flowering	February–March
Fruiting	August–September

TRUNK AND CROWN

Trunk	short, often several
Bark	grey-brown, scaly
Crown	open; branches spreading or downswept
Twigs	greenish yellow, minutely downy

LEAVES

Buds	7mm, paired, pointed, yellowish, lacking scales but with short, close-pressed hairs
Leaves	paired on stem, 4–10cm, elliptical to oval, drawn out to a pointed tip, base rounded, downy, dull green, 3–5 pairs of curved veins; stalk 6mm

FLOWERS AND FRUIT

Flowers	☿, yellow, before leaves in paired, thick-stalked clusters of 10–25, 4 yellowish bracts at base of cluster soon falling
Petals	4, 2–2.5mm, hooded; sepals very small
Stamens	4, alternating with petals
Stigmas	1–several, in base of flower-tube
Ovaries	1, sunk in base of flower
Fruit	berry-like, 12–20mm, roughly cylindrical, drooping, ripening bright red
Seeds	1, stony, not released

SIMILAR TREES

1 Dogwood (*Cornus sanguinea*) is a common summer-flowering shrub with clusters of small white flowers and black berries. **2 Nuttall's Dogwood** (*Cornus nuttallii*) is a widely planted American species. The tight flower clusters are surrounded by 4–7 large pink or white bracts, the whole assembly resembling a single, large, flower.

large bracts

white flowers

blackish fruit

161

Orange-bark Myrtle *Myrtus apiculata*

many stamens

evergreen

4 petals

white

not toothed

oval, dark green

ripens black

orange and white bark

S eldom more than a large shrub outside its South American home, this spicily aromatic plant has gland-dotted leaves, which release their scent when crushed. Attractive, cinnamon-coloured bark peels away from the base of the trunk, revealing the grey or creamy inner bark.

Status: native to Chile; planted for ornament.

SIMILAR TREES

1 Myrtle (*Myrtus communis*), from southern Europe, is very similar but always shrubby, and lacks colourful bark. **2 Crape Myrtle** (*Lagerstroemeria indica*), a deciduous shrub or small tree from China is grown in gardens and streets. Clusters of red, pink or white flowers, each up to 4cm across, have crinkled petals.

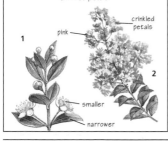

crinkled petals

pink

1

2

smaller

narrower

ORANGE-BARK MAPLE

Type	evergreen tree or shrub
Height	up to 13m
Habitat	parks, gardens
Flowering	August–October
Fruiting	October–November

TRUNK AND CROWN

Trunk	slender, often several
Bark	orange to cinnamon, peeling to leave areas of white; old trees with broad, tapering white streaks
Crown	loosely conical
Twigs	dark pink above, green to pale brown beneath, hairy

LEAVES

Buds	minute, globular, deep red, shiny
Leaves	opposite, 2.5 x 1.5cm, oval, finely and sharply pointed, dark green above, paler beneath and minutely hairy; almost stalkless
Stipules	absent

FLOWERS AND FRUIT

Flowers	♂, 2cm across, white; stalks c1.5cm, pink
Petals	4, round, c1.3cm; sepals 4, bowl-shaped, persisting on fruit
Stamens	many, arranged in several rings
Stigmas	1, style long, straight
Ovaries	1
Fruit	berry, initially red, ripening to black
Seeds	3–6, not released

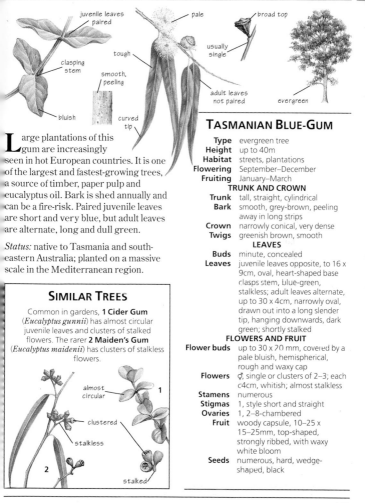

Eucalyptus globulus **Tasmanian Blue-gum**

juvenile leaves paired

clasping stem

smooth, peeling

bluish

curved tip

tough

pale

usually single

broad top

adult leaves not paired

evergreen

Large plantations of this gum are increasingly seen in hot European countries. It is one of the largest and fastest-growing trees, a source of timber, paper pulp and eucalyptus oil. Bark is shed annually and can be a fire-risk. Paired juvenile leaves are short and very blue, but adult leaves are alternate, long and dull green.

Status: native to Tasmania and south-eastern Australia; planted on a massive scale in the Mediterranean region.

SIMILAR TREES

Common in gardens, **1 Cider Gum** (*Eucalyptus gunnii*) has almost circular juvenile leaves and clusters of stalked flowers. The rarer **2 Maiden's Gum** (*Eucalyptus maidenii*) has clusters of stalkless flowers.

almost circular

clustered

stalkless

stalked

TASMANIAN BLUE-GUM

Type	evergreen tree
Height	up to 40m
Habitat	streets, plantations
Flowering	September–December
Fruiting	January–March

TRUNK AND CROWN

Trunk	tall, straight, cylindrical
Bark	smooth, grey-brown, peeling away in long strips
Crown	narrowly conical, very dense
Twigs	greenish brown, smooth

LEAVES

Buds	minute, concealed
Leaves	juvenile leaves opposite, to 16 x 9cm, oval, heart-shaped base clasps stem, blue-green, stalkless; adult leaves alternate, up to 30 x 4cm, narrowly oval, drawn out into a long slender tip, hanging downwards, dark green; shortly stalked

FLOWERS AND FRUIT

Flower buds	up to 30 x 20 mm, covered by a pale bluish, hemispherical, rough and waxy cap
Flowers	⚥, single or clusters of 2–3; each c4cm, whitish; almost stalkless
Stamens	numerous
Stigmas	1, style short and straight
Ovaries	1, 2–8-chambered
Fruit	woody capsule, 10–25 x 15–25mm, top-shaped, strongly ribbed, with waxy white bloom
Seeds	numerous, hard, wedge-shaped, black

Red Mahogany *Eucalyptus resinifer*

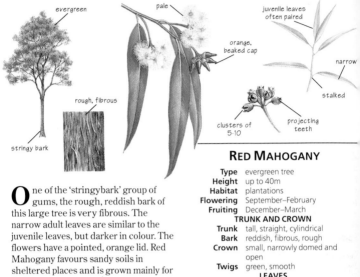

evergreen

pale

juvenile leaves often paired

orange, beaked cap

narrow

rough, fibrous

stalked

stringy bark

clusters of 5–10

projecting teeth

O ne of the 'stringybark' group of gums, the rough, reddish bark of this large tree is very fibrous. The narrow adult leaves are similar to the juvenile leaves, but darker in colour. The flowers have a pointed, orange lid. Red Mahogany favours sandy soils in sheltered places and is grown mainly for timber.

Status: native to Queensland and New South Wales; planted from Portugal to Italy, mainly in coastal areas.

SIMILAR TREES

Swamp Mahogany (*Eucalyptus robustus*) has pink-lidded fruits and prefers wet ground. It has larger fruits with a rim raised above the short teeth.

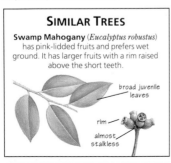

broad juvenile leaves

rim

almost stalkless

RED MAHOGANY

Type	evergreen tree
Height	up to 40m
Habitat	plantations
Flowering	September–February
Fruiting	December–March
TRUNK AND CROWN	
Trunk	tall, straight, cylindrical
Bark	reddish, fibrous, rough
Crown	small, narrowly domed and open
Twigs	green, smooth
LEAVES	
Buds	minute, concealed
Leaves	juvenile leaves opposite, to 6 x 2cm, lance-shaped, pale green, stalked; adult leaves alternate, up to 16 x 3cm, lance-shaped to narrowly oval, dark, glossy green above; stalked
Stipules	absent
FLOWERS AND FRUIT	
Flower buds	up to 17mm, with an orange, conical or beak-like cap
Flowers	☿, in clusters of 5–10, white; stalks of clusters up to 2cm, flattened
Stamens	numerous
Stigmas	1; style short
Ovaries	1, 2–8-chambered
Fruit	woody capsule, 5–18 x 5–18mm, hemispherical, stalked, opening by 3–4 teeth
Seeds	numerous

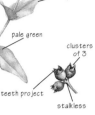

juvenile leaves paired

pale green

clusters of 3

teeth project

stalkless

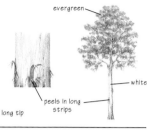

evergreen

white

peels in long strips

long tip

A large, pallid tree with thin outer bark, which shreds and hangs from the trunk and branches in long ribbons, revealing the white inner bark. Both juvenile and adult leaves are pale green. Red flowers have rounded, woody lids. Ribbon Gum provides timber but is mainly used for shade and shelter in towns.

Status: native to southern and eastern Australia and Tasmania; planted in Spain, Portugal and Italy.

SIMILAR TREES

Snow Gum (*Eucalyptus niphophila*) has peeling grey outer bark over white inner bark, and leaves which age from orange-brown to grey-green. It grows at high altitudes in the wild and is planted as a cold-tolerant ornamental.

young leaves often orange

smaller

cup-shaped

pale

RIBBON GUM

Type	evergreen tree
Height	up to 50m
Habitat	plantations
Flowering	December–June
Fruiting	January–July
TRUNK AND CROWN	
Trunk	tapering from base
Bark	smooth, white, falling away in long ribbon-like strips
Crown	drooping branches festooned with ribbons of bark
Twigs	greenish brown, smooth
LEAVES	
Buds	minute, concealed
Leaves	variable, pale green, juvenile leaves opposite, up to 10 x 3cm, oval, stalkless, surrounding the stem at their base; adult leaves alternate, up to 18 x 2cm, narrowly oval, drawn out into a long slender tip; stalked
FLOWERS AND FRUIT	
Flower buds	7mm, covered by a scarlet, hemispherical to conical cap
Flowers	♂, in shortly stalked clusters of 3, 1.5cm across
Stamens	numerous
Stigmas	1; style short
Ovaries	1, 2–8-chambered
Fruit	woody capsule, 5–8 x 7–9mm, more or less spherical, slightly tapering to the base, opening by 3–4 valves; stalkless
Seeds	numerous

165

Red Gum *Eucalyptus camaldulensis*

smooth

falls in plates

projecting teeth

dull green

red

conical cap

evergreen

juvenile leaves bluish

Cultivated for its timber, this tree is widely planted on a world scale. Large and spreading, it shows considerable natural variation. The white bark is mottled with pink and grey and is shed in plates. It has red flowers with conical, woody lids, and fruit with projecting teeth.

Status: native to much of Australia; planted in the Mediterranean region, especially Spain.

SIMILAR TREES

Lemon-scented Spotted Gum (*Eucalyptus citriodora*), from Queensland, is a slender tree with strongly lemon-scented leaves. The flowers have domed lids and the fruits have inward-pointing teeth. It is grown as an ornamental in Spain, Portugal and Italy.

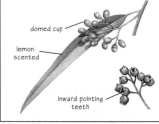

domed cup

lemon-scented

inward-pointing teeth

RED GUM

Type	evergreen tree
Height	up to 20m
Habitat	plantations
Flowering	December–February
Fruiting	May
TRUNK AND CROWN	
Trunk	short, stout, soon forking
Bark	smooth, white, pink and grey, falling away on plates
Crown	open; irregularly branched
Twigs	green, strongly ribbed
LEAVES	
Buds	minute, concealed
Leaves	young leaves opposite, up to 9 x 4cm, oval, bluish green; adult leaves alternate, up to 25 x 2cm, narrowly oval, drawn out into a long slender tip, dull green; shortly stalked
Stipules	absent
FLOWERS AND FRUIT	
Flower buds	up to 10 x 5mm, cap brownish, conical or beak-like
Flowers	♂, in clusters of 5–10, white; stalk of cluster up to 2.5cm, slender
Stamens	numerous
Stigmas	1; style short
Ovaries	1, 2–8-chambered
Fruit	woody capsule, 7–8 x 5–6mm, hemispherical with a broad raised rim, opening by 4 teeth
Seeds	numerous

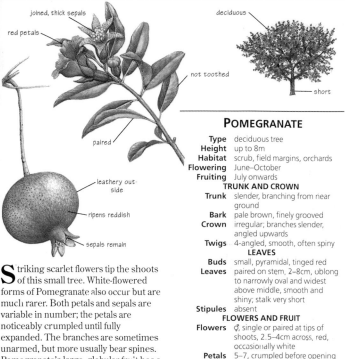

joined, thick sepals

red petals

deciduous

not toothed

short

paired

leathery out-side

ripens reddish

sepals remain

POMEGRANATE

Type	deciduous tree
Height	up to 8m
Habitat	scrub, field margins, orchards
Flowering	June–October
Fruiting	July onwards

TRUNK AND CROWN

Trunk	slender, branching from near ground
Bark	pale brown, finely grooved
Crown	irregular; branches slender, angled upwards
Twigs	4-angled, smooth, often spiny

LEAVES

Buds	small, pyramidal, tinged red
Leaves	paired on stem, 2–8cm, oblong to narrowly oval and widest above middle, smooth and shiny; stalk very short
Stipules	absent

FLOWERS AND FRUIT

Flowers	☿, single or paired at tips of shoots, 2.5–4cm across, red, occasionally white
Petals	5–7, crumpled before opening fully; sepals 5–7 hooded, leathery, red, joined into a long tube, persisting on fruit
Stamens	numerous, in whorls in throat of flower
Stigmas	1, globular on a long style
Ovaries	1, sunk into base of flower
Fruit	berry-like, 5–8cm, globular, leathery skin surrounding translucent purple or yellowish pulp, ripening reddish or yellow
Seeds	numerous, embedded in pulp, not released

Striking scarlet flowers tip the shoots of this small tree. White-flowered forms of Pomegranate also occur but are much rarer. Both petals and sepals are variable in number; the petals are noticeably crumpled until fully expanded. The branches are sometimes unarmed, but more usually bear spines. Pomegranate's large, globular fruit has a leathery, rather hard rind and a tubular crown formed by the persistent sepals; the pulp contains numerous seeds. Although at first acid-tasting, the fruit usually becomes sweet.

Status: introduced from western Asia in ancient times for its fruit; cultivated and widely naturalized in Mediterranean regions.

Similar trees: none.

Date-plum *Diospyros lotus*

not toothed

sepals remain

cracks into plates

globular, fleshy

deciduous

glossy

4 petals

Persimmons, the group to which this tree belongs, produce edible fruit, but that of Date-plum is small, only *c*1.5cm across, and rather insipid. It may be either yellow or blue-black when ripe. The tree is cultivated in the south as a fruit tree but in the north only as an ornamental.

Status: native to Asia; cultivated and sometimes naturalized in Europe.

SIMILAR TREES

1 Common Persimmon (*Diospyros virginiana*), from eastern and central North America, has tart fruit. **2 Chinese Persimmon** (*Diospyros kaki*), from Asia, has much larger fruit, up to 7.5cm, which is very sour until overripe.

large

2

broad

1

DATE-PLUM

Type	deciduous tree
Height	up to 14m
Habitat	gardens, parks, orchards
Flowering	July
Fruiting	July–October

TRUNK AND CROWN

Trunk	well-defined
Bark	grey, tinged pink, cracking into small plates
Crown	tall and narrowly domed
Twigs	downy when young

LEAVES

Buds	4–5mm, sharp-pointed
Leaves	alternate, elliptical to oblong with wavy edges, base rounded, somewhat leathery, dark green above, bluish below, hairy on both sides but becoming almost smooth; stalk hairy

FLOWERS AND FRUIT

Flowers	♂ and ♀ on different trees, stalkless, reddish or greenish white, petals forming an urn-shaped tube with 4 fringed, curved-back lobes, sepals forming a 4-lobed cup
♂	in clusters of 2–3, each c5mm
♀	single, each 8–10mm
Stamens	4 in ♂; reduced and sterile in ♀
Stigmas	4 in ♀
Ovaries	1, several chambers
Fruit	1.5cm, globular, fleshy and ripening yellow or nearly black with a glistening bloom
Seeds	3–4, large, not released

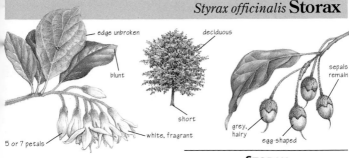

edge unbroken

blunt

deciduous

short

5 or 7 petals

white, fragrant

sepals remain

grey, hairy

egg-shaped

A small tree in which all the parts, including the drooping white flowers and grey fruits, are covered with star-shaped hairs. It is one of the very few plants native to the climatically similar Mediterranean region and California. Storax yields an aromatic gum, also called storax, collected from cuts made in the trunk and branches, and used for incense.

Status: native from Italy eastwards; naturalized in parts of France.

STORAX

Type	deciduous shrub or small tree
Height	2–7m
Habitat	thickets, woods, stream-sides
Flowering	April–May
Fruiting	July–September

TRUNK AND CROWN

Trunk	short, slender
Bark	brown, shredding slightly
Crown	irrgularly branched
Twigs	white-woolly

LEAVES

Buds	small, ellipsoid, white-woolly
Leaves	alternate, 3–7cm, oval, blunt-tipped, base rounded, edge unbroken, green above, white-hairy, especially beneath; stalked
Stipules	absent

FLOWERS AND FRUIT

Flowers	♂, in short, drooping clusters of 3–6, each 2cm long, bell-shaped, white, fragrant
Petals	5 or 7, overlapping at the edges above, joined into a short tube at the base; sepals joined for most of their length, cup-shaped, hairy
Stamens	10, fused to base of the petal-tube
Stigmas	1, style long, slender
Ovaries	1, 3-chambered
Fruit	egg-shaped, dry, leathery, grey and densely hairy, cupped by persistent white-woolly sepals
Seeds	1 or 2, large, hard

SIMILAR TREES

1 Snowbell-tree (*Styrax japonica*), from the Far East, reaches 11m and flowers prolifically.
2 Snowdrop-tree (*Halesia monticola*) is a North American species with flowers opening mostly before the leaves, and 4-winged fruits up to 5cm long.

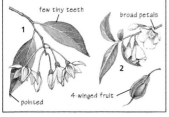

few tiny teeth

broad petals

pointed

4-winged fruit

Manna Ash *Fraxinus ornus*

stalked leaflets

4 petals, fragrant

smooth, grey

paired leaflets

flowers with leaves

bunched fruit, winged

deciduous

U nlike most European ashes, this species has scented flowers with petals, forming large showy heads after the leaves appear. In winter it can be distinguished by its very smooth bark and pale brown buds. It is a commercial source of manna, not the biblical food but an edible sugary gum, which seeps from cuts in the trunk and dries into flakes on contact with air.

Status: native to central Europe and the Mediterranean region; planted for ornament.

SIMILAR TREES

Two North American species are planted, mainly for timber. **1 Red Ash** (*Fraxinus pennsylvanica*) has sharp-toothed leaves, hairy below. **2 White Ash** (*Fraxinus americana*) has bluntly toothed, smooth leaves.

1

sharp teeth

hairy below

2

blunt teeth

before leaves

smooth

MANNA ASH

Type	deciduous tree
Height	up to 24m, often smaller
Habitat	open woods, thickets, rocky places; often planted
Flowering	April–June
Fruiting	May–September

TRUNK AND CROWN

Trunk	cylindrical
Bark	smooth, dark grey, or black
Crown	hemispherical, fairly dense
Twigs	grey to yellowish, smooth

LEAVES

Buds	pyramidal, blunt, grey or brown
Leaves	opposite, up to 30cm, with 4–8 paired, stalked leaflets and a leaflet at the tip, each 3–10cm long, oblong-oval, abruptly and sharply pointed, shallowly toothed, unequal at base, pale and hairy on the veins beneath; stalks up to 1.5cm

FLOWERS AND FRUIT

Flowers	⚥, many in pyramidal clusters to 20cm long, white, fragrant
Petals	4, 5–6mm, narrow, strap-shaped; sepals 4, joined near base
Stamens	2, on long stalks
Stigmas	2
Ovaries	1, 2-chambered
Fruit	1.5–2.5cm, on wiry stalks 3–10mm long, with slender wing 1.5–2.5cm, sometimes notched at tip, green becoming brown
Seeds	1 per fruit, not released

leaflets stalkless

paired leaflets

no petals

before leaves

black bud

becomes fissured

deciduous

toothed

winged

ASH

A common tree, readily distinguished by its divided leaves in pairs on the stem and by its distinctive, winged fruits. In winter it is recognized by the prominent, paired, black buds. Growing mainly on lime-rich soils, it is sometimes planted for its tough timber. The cultivar 'Pendula' is a weeping form, often grafted onto the trunk of the common form and grown as an ornamental.

Status: native throughout Europe, western Asia and North Africa.

Type	deciduous tree
Height	up to 40m
Habitat	hedgerows, open woods, roadsides, often on limestone
Flowering	April–May
Fruiting	July–November

TRUNK AND CROWN

Trunk	suckering; many pollarded
Bark	smooth, grey, becoming rough and shallowly fissured
Crown	domed; branches well-spaced
Twigs	flattened at nodes, greenish grey, smooth

LEAVES

Buds	pyramidal, hard, black
Leaves	opposite, up to 35cm, with usually 6–12 paired leaflets and a leaflet at tip, each 3–12cm, oblong-oval, with long slender tip, shallowly toothed, dark green above, hairy at the base and on the midrib beneath; stalked

FLOWERS AND FRUIT

Flowers	☿, or ♂ and ♀ in separate rounded clusters before leaves, purplish, dark red, then yellow
Petals	absent; sepals absent
Stamens	2
Stigmas	2
Ovaries	1, 2-chambered
Fruit	2.5–5cm, with twisted wing notched and spiny at tip, green ripening dull brown, in hanging clusters
Seeds	1 per fruit, not released

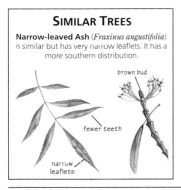

SIMILAR TREES

Narrow-leaved Ash (*Fraxinus angustifolia*) is similar but has very narrow leaflets. It has a more southern distribution.

brown bud

fewer teeth

narrow leaflets

Olive *Olea europaea*

not toothed

paired

scaly below

4 petals

elongated clusters

grey, fissured

evergreen

berry-like

ripens purplish

often twisted

Long-lived, this evergreen tree has a distinctive silvery grey bark. Old trees have gnarled trunks pitted with holes. Ripe fruits are black; green olives are simply unripe fruits. Widely cultivated since classical times, olives crop heavily and are the basis for the important olive and olive-oil industries. Wild Olives (var. *sylvestris*) are bushy, spiny trees of dry woodlands, with smaller leaves and fruits.

Status: native throughout the Mediterranean region.

SIMILAR TREES

Phillyrea (*Phillyrea latifolia*) is a dense, rounded tree with shallowly toothed leaves and round, purplish black fruits. It grows in evergreen woods and is planted for ornament.

toothed

rounded

short clusters

OLIVE

Type	evergreen tree or shrub
Height	up to 15m
Habitat	dry rocky places, woods and scrub; planted in large groves
Flowering	May–June
Fruiting	September–November

TRUNK AND CROWN

Trunk	thick, becoming gnarled and twisted, developing holes
Bark	silvery grey, shallowly fissured
Crown	broad; irregularly, branching
Twigs	slender, greyish, covered with small, scurfy scales

LEAVES

Buds	very small, greyish
Leaves	opposite, 2–10cm, lance-shaped, with a sharp tip, leathery, dark grey-green and smooth above, greyish or brownish white and hairy beneath; almost stalkless

FLOWERS AND FRUIT

Flowers	mostly ♂, many in branched or unbranched clusters from angles of leaves, each c1cm across, yellowish white
Petals	4, joined for most of their length, spreading at the top; sepals 4, short, joined
Stamens	2
Stigmas	1, style short
Ovaries	1, 2-chambered
Fruit	berry-like, 1–3.5cm, oval, somewhat fleshy with a tough outer skin, green ripening blackish purple
Seeds	1, stony, brown

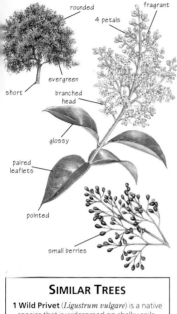

H ighly glossed leaves and clusters of fragrant white flowers produced late in the year, when few other trees are flowering, make this an attractive ornamental tree. It is often seen in towns and cities.

Status: native to China; planted for ornament, mainly in southern Europe.

GLOSSY PRIVET

Type	evergreen tree
Height	up to 15m
Habitat	gardens, especially as a hedge, streets, parks
Flowering	August–September
Fruiting	October–November, often not produced

TRUNK AND CROWN

Trunk	short, often several
Bark	grey with brown streaks, smooth or finely cracked
Crown	domed
Twigs	grey with white lenticels

LEAVES

Buds	globular to egg-shaped, tiny
Leaves	opposite, 8–12cm, oval, tip drawn out to a long point, edge unbroken, thick and leathery, reddish when young, later very glossy dark green above, pale and matt below; stalked

FLOWERS AND FRUIT

Flowers	♂, many in branched, conical clusters 12–20cm long, at shoot-tip; each white, fragrant
Petals	4, joined in a long tube with spreading lobes; sepals 4, forming bell-shaped, short-toothed tube
Stamens	2, attached to petal-tube
Stigmas	1, style short
Ovaries	1, 2-chambered
Fruit	rather egg-shaped berry, c1cm long, ripening black with conspicuous white bloom
Seeds	1, not released

SIMILAR TREES

1 Wild Privet (*Ligustrum vulgare*) is a native species that is widespread on chalky soils. Always a shrub, it is semi-evergreen, sometimes losing its leaves late in the year.
2 Garden Privet (*Ligustrum ovalifolium*) is the commonly seen hedge plant. Also semi-evergreen, it tolerates poor soil but sheds leaves in polluted air and cold weather. It originates in Japan.

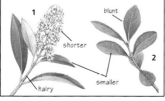

Strawberry-tree *Arbutus unedo*

forward-pointing teeth

scaling in strips

evergreen

tiny bumps

globular berry

very short

bell-shaped
5 jointed petals
branched cluster

ripens red

Taking a full year to mature, the fruits on this tree ripen as the next year's flowers open. The fruits barely resemble strawberries, being round and covered with soft pimples; they are edible though insipid. Attractive bell-shaped flowers hang in large clusters.

Status: native to Mediterranean region and Atlantic Europe north to Ireland; planted for ornament.

SIMILAR TREES

1 Eastern Strawberry-tree (*Arbutus andrachne*), from the Aegean region, has orange-red bark, and flowers in spring. Fruits are nearly smooth. This and Strawberry-tree are the parents of **2 Hybrid Strawberry-tree** (*Arbutus* x *andrachnoides*), which has bright bark, and flowers in spring or autumn.

often not toothed

flowers in spring

1

2

nearly smooth

small teeth

STRAWBERRY-TREE

Type	evergreen tree or shrub
Height	tree up to 10m, or shrub
Habitat	dry rocky slopes, bushy places
Flowering	October–November
Fruiting	October of following year

TRUNK AND CROWN

Trunk	very short, soon forking
Bark	dull reddish brown, rough, scaling away in thin strips
Crown	dense, rounded
Twigs	red above and hairy when young, green beneath

LEAVES

Buds	1–2mm, conical, purplish red
Leaves	alternate, 4–10 x 1.5–5cm, oblong-oval, leathery, with forward-pointing teeth towards tip, dark glossy green above, paler beneath; stalks 5–10mm, pinkish red, hairy

FLOWERS AND FRUIT

Flowers	♂, many in drooping, branched clusters 4–5cm long, pinkish white, each urn-shaped, 0.5–1cm
Petals	5, joined for most of length, tips bent back; sepals 5, c1.5mm, forming circular lobes
Stamens	10
Stigmas	1
Ovaries	1, 5-chambered
Fruit	fleshy, globular berry, 1.5–2cm across, covered with pimples, yellow, ripening to orange and finally bright red
Seeds	numerous, tiny, pear-shaped, brown, not released

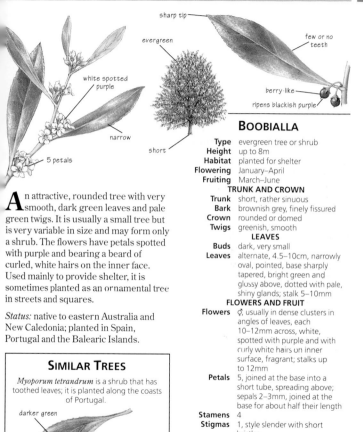

sharp tip

evergreen

few or no teeth

white spotted purple

berry-like

ripens blackish purple

narrow

short

5 petals

BOOBIALLA

Type	evergreen tree or shrub
Height	up to 8m
Habitat	planted for shelter
Flowering	January–April
Fruiting	March–June

TRUNK AND CROWN

Trunk	short, rather sinuous
Bark	brownish grey, finely fissured
Crown	rounded or domed
Twigs	greenish, smooth

LEAVES

Buds	dark, very small
Leaves	alternate, 4.5–10cm, narrowly oval, pointed, base sharply tapered, bright green and glossy above, dotted with pale, shiny glands; stalk 5–10mm

FLOWERS AND FRUIT

Flowers	☿, usually in dense clusters in angles of leaves, each 10–12mm across, white, spotted with purple and curly white hairs on inner surface, fragrant; stalks up to 12mm
Petals	5, joined at the base into a short tube, spreading above; sepals 2–3mm, joined at the base for about half their length
Stamens	4
Stigmas	1, style slender with short bristles
Ovaries	1
Fruit	berry-like but only slightly fleshy, 7–9mm, oval, ripening blackish purple
Seeds	1, stony

An attractive, rounded tree with very smooth, dark green leaves and pale green twigs. It is usually a small tree but is very variable in size and may form only a shrub. The flowers have petals spotted with purple and bearing a beard of curled, white hairs on the inner face. Used mainly to provide shelter, it is sometimes planted as an ornamental tree in streets and squares.

Status: native to eastern Australia and New Caledonia; planted in Spain, Portugal and the Balearic Islands.

SIMILAR TREES

Myoporum tetrandrum is a shrub that has toothed leaves; it is planted along the coasts of Portugal.

darker green

sharply toothed

blunt tip

Foxglove-tree *Paulownia tomentosa*

deciduous

blue flowers

tubular

softly hairy below

smooth, blistered

broad fruit

heart-shaped, undivided

splits open

large leaves

The branches of this deciduous tree are clothed with very large leaves. They are heart-shaped with unbroken edges but in young trees may have up to 3 short, tapering lobes on each side. The tubular flowers, violet to bluish on the outside and flushed yellow within, form large and very showy heads before the leaves appear.

Status: native to China; common as an ornamental and, in southern Europe, a street tree.

FOXGLOVE-TREE

Type	deciduous tree
Height	up to 15m
Habitat	roadsides, parks and gardens
Flowering	April–May
Fruiting	July

TRUNK AND CROWN

Trunk	slightly sinuous
Bark	greyish, smooth, marked with orange blisters
Crown	domed; branches stout, spreading
Twigs	pale pink-brown

LEAVES

Buds	minute, purplish, hairy
Leaves	opposite, to 30cm long, oval to heart-shaped with 3 to 5 lobes, tip long and slender, pale green above, softly hairy below; stalk 10–15cm, pink-yellow, densely hairy

FLOWERS AND FRUIT

Flowers	♂, in large upright clusters 20–30 cm long, opening before the leaves, each 5–6 cm long, violet-blue, yellow within
Petals	bell-shaped tube with 5 spreading lobes; sepals 5, joined below
Stamens	4, inside petal-tube
Stigmas	2-lobed, style long
Ovaries	1, 2-chambered
Fruit	3–5cm long, oval, beaked, green, ripening brown and splitting to release seeds, sticky; stalk 1.5cm, stout, hairy
Seeds	numerous, winged, released when fruit splits

SIMILAR TREES

Jacaranda (*Jacaranda mimosifolia*), an especially attractive ornamental tree from Argentina, has leaves twice-divided into small leaflets, and clusters of drooping, blue, trumpet-like flowers.

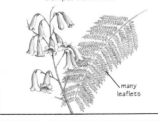

many leaflets

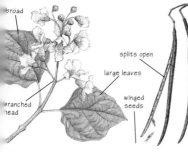

broad

splits open

large leaves

branched head

winged seeds

white, spotted

long, pod-like

deciduous

Conspicuous in winter, when the very long, slender pods hang in numbers from the bare branches, this showy tree is a common sight in parks and gardens. The leaves are light, matt green and heart-shaped. The large flowers have spreading, frilled lobes and are borne in branched, conical heads.

Status: native to south-eastern North America; widely planted in all but northern parts of Europe.

INDIAN BEAN-TREE

Type	deciduous tree
Height	up to 15m, occasionally taller
Habitat	streets, parks and gardens
Flowering	June–August
Fruiting	July–October but persisting on tree all winter

TRUNK AND CROWN

Trunk	short, stout
Bark	dull pink- or grey-brown, fissured or scaling
Crown	domed; branches wide-arching
Twigs	stout, grey-brown, smooth, with prominent oval leaf scars

LEAVES

Buds	minute, orange-brown
Leaves	opposite or in 3s, up to 25 x 22cm, heart-shaped with slender tip, pale green, smooth above, hairy beneath; stalk 10–18cm

FLOWERS AND FRUIT

Flowers	♂, in branched, pyramidal heads, each to 5cm across, bell-shaped, white, spotted with yellow and purple, fragrant
Petals	5, unequal, upper 2 smaller, crinkly-edged, joined for most of their length; sepals 5, joined
Stamens	2, curved
Stigmas	2-lobed, style long, slender
Ovaries	1, 2-chambered
Fruit	pod-like, slender, 15–40cm, hanging, dark brown,
Seeds	many, 2.5cm, white, flat, with a tuft of long hairs at each end and papery wing, released in spring

SIMILAR TREES

1 Hybrid Catalpa (*Catalpa x erubescens*) has 5-sided leaves, up to 60cm, and large heads of white flowers. **2 Yellow Catalpa** (*Catalpa ovata*), from China, has roughly 5-sided leaves and smaller, yellow flowers. Both are planted for ornament.

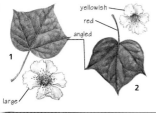

yellowish

red

angled

1

2

large

Elder *Sambucus nigra*

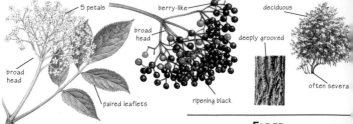

L arge, plate-like heads of white flowers decorate this common tree in summer. They are followed by heavy clusters of berries, which droop as the fruit ripens. The flowers have a sweet, slightly cloying scent, in contrast to the leaves, which smell unpleasant when bruised. Both flowers and fruit are used to make wines; the fruit is also used in pies and preserves, and Elder is often planted near houses for this reason.

Status: native throughout Europe, western Asia, North Africa; often cultivated in southern Europe.

SIMILAR TREES

Red-berried Elder (*Sambucus racemosa*), also native to Europe, is a shrub to only 4m, with egg-shaped clusters of flowers and scarlet fruit.

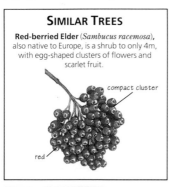

compact cluster

red

ELDER

Type	deciduous tree, often shrubby
Height	up to 10m
Habitat	damp woods, hedgerows, on rich, disturbed soils
Flowering	June–July
Fruiting	August–September

TRUNK AND CROWN

Trunk	often crooked, vigorous straight shoots grow from base
Bark	deeply grooved, brownish grey, becoming thick and corky
Crown	irregularly rounded; branches arching downwards
Twigs	thick, fawn, warty, filled with white pith

LEAVES

Buds	lacking scales, tight-furled young leaves purplish
Leaves	paired on stem; 2–4 pairs of leaflets, leaflet at tip, 3–12cm, oval to elliptical, pointed, sharply toothed, sparsely hairy below, dull green; stalkless
Stipules	very small or absent

FLOWERS AND FRUIT

Flowers	♂, many in large, circular, branched heads, each 5mm, white, rarely pink
Petals	5, equal, spreading; sepals 5, small joined into a tube
Stamens	5, yellowish white
Stigmas	3–5, very short
Ovaries	1
Fruit	berry-like, globular, 6–8mm, ripening black
Seeds	3, leathery, not released

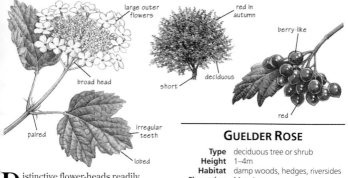

large outer flowers

broad head

paired

irregular teeth

lobed

red in autumn

short   deciduous

berry-like

red

Distinctive flower-heads readily identify this attractive small tree. The small, fertile inner flowers are surrounded by much larger, showy, but sterile blossoms.

Status: native to most of Europe except for much of the Mediterranean region.

SIMILAR TREES

From similar areas, **1 Wayfaring-tree** (*Viburnum lantana*) has oval, lobeless leaves white-felted below, lacks sterile flowers and has fruit eventually ripening black. It favours chalky soils. **2 Laurustinus** (*Viburnum tinus*) is a winter-flowering evergreen with glossy, oval leaves, equal-sized, pink-tinged flowers and metallic blue fruit. Native to southern Europe, it is often planted as an ornamental elsewhere.

flowers equal pink

not toothed

not lobed

GUELDER ROSE

Type	deciduous tree or shrub
Height	1–4m
Habitat	damp woods, hedges, riversides
Flowering	May–June
Fruiting	September–October

TRUNK AND CROWN

Trunk	short, slender
Bark	greyish brown
Crown	spreading; branches few
Twigs	angled, smooth

LEAVES

Buds	5mm, green, edges purple
Leaves	paired on stem, 5–8cm, with 3–5 radiating, pointed, irregularly toothed lobes, sparsely hairy below, becoming smooth, dull red in autumn; stalk 1–2.5cm
Stipules	very narrow, thread-like

FLOWERS AND FRUIT

Flowers	♀, many in broad, circular clusters, stalk of flower-head 1–4cm; funnel- or bell-shaped, inner flowers 6mm, fertile; outer flowers 15–20mm, sterile, both types white
Petals	5, equal; sepals 5, very small
Stamens	5, as long as petals
Stigmas	3, short
Ovaries	1
Fruit	berry-like, c8mm, almost globular, ripening red, drooping and persisting on stems after leaves fall
Seeds	1, stony, not released

Cabbage Palm *Cordyline australis*

branched head

6 petals

sword shaped

leaves at tip

berry

ripens bluish white

branched

This palm-like tree often has several trunks, which fork after flowering. The 2m-long flower-head emerges from the centre of the crown. A hardy tree, often planted as an unusual ornamental.

Status: native to New Zealand; often planted in mild, coastal areas of western and central Europe.

SIMILAR TREES

Two related species, both native to south-eastern North America, are commonly planted in parks and gardens. **1 Spanish Bayonet** (*Yucca aloifolia*) is a much-branched tree up to 10m. **2 Adam's Needle** (*Yucca gloriosa*) has a very short, thick, unbranched trunk topped with a single, dense rosette of leaves. Both species have large, white flowers, tinged with purple.

larger flowers

2

much branched

1

not branched

CABBAGE PALM

Type	evergreen tree
Height	up to 13m
Habitat	dry soils in mild coastal areas
Flowering	June–July
Fruiting	September–October
TRUNK AND CROWN	
Trunk	cylindrical, often forked after flowering, suckering from base
Bark	pale grey-brown
Crown	dense tuft of leaves
LEAVES	
Buds	1, large, hidden by leaves
Leaves	in a single, domed cluster at tip of trunk, mostly upright but lowermost drooping, 30–90cm, sword-shaped, veins all parallel, dark green; stalkless
FLOWERS AND FRUIT	
Flowers	♂, many in very large, upright, branched head from centre of crown, each c10mm, creamy-white, fragrant
Perianth	3 inner and 3 outer segments, all petal-like, joined at base
Stamens	6
Stigmas	1, slender
Ovaries	1
Fruit	berry, 6mm, globose, ripening bluish white
Seeds	several, black, not released

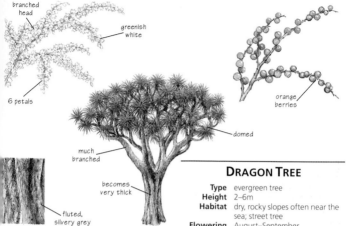

branched head

greenish white

6 petals

orange berries

domed

much branched

becomes very thick

fluted, silvery grey

A very slow-growing tree capable of attaining a great age – one specimen, destroyed in a hurricane in 1867, was said to be over 6000 years old. The tree forms a very thick trunk and short, stubby branches with a dense, umbrella-shaped crown of spiky leaves. It can survive in areas of low rainfall; moisture condensing on the leaves runs down the trunk to the roots. The Dragon Tree is very rare in the wild, but often planted for ornament. A bright red resin obtained from this tree, and known as dragon's blood, has been used medicinally since the Middle Ages.

Status: native to the Canary Islands and Madeira; commonly planted in Mediterranean areas in streets, gardens and parks.

Similar trees: none.

DRAGON TREE

Type	evergreen tree
Height	2–6m
Habitat	dry, rocky slopes often near the sea; street tree
Flowering	August–September
Fruiting	February–April

TRUNK AND CROWN

Trunk	massive, cylindrical, becoming fluted
Bark	silvery
Crown	broad, shallow-domed; branches thick, short, regularly forked

LEAVES

Buds	1, large, hidden by leaves
Leaves	in dense tufts at tips of branches, 30–50cm, sword-shaped, bluish green; stalkless

FLOWERS AND FRUIT

Flowers	⚥, in spreading, much-branched heads from centre of leaf tufts, greenish white
Perianth	3 inner and 3 outer segments, all petal-like and united towards base
Stamens	6
Stigmas	1, style slender
Ovaries	1
Fruit	berry, c1.5cm, globular, ripening deep orange
Seeds	1, not released

European Fan-palm *Chamaerops humilis*

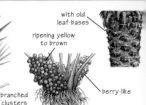

with old
leaf-bases

ripening yellow
to brown

berry-like

evergreen

often very
short

not
branched

radiating
segments

branched
clusters

EUROPEAN FAN-PALM

Type	evergreen tree, often bushy
Height	rarely more than 2m
Habitat	sandy soils near the sea
Flowering	March–June
Fruiting	September–October
TRUNK AND CROWN	
Trunk	short, thick, sometimes absent, covered with white or grey fibres and bases of old leaves
Bark	grey, concealed by fibres
Crown	single, large tuft of leaves
LEAVES	
Buds	1, large, hidden by leaves
Leaves	up to 1m across, stiff, fan-shaped blade deeply divided into spreading segments; segments many, sword-shaped, green, greyish or bluish; stalk very long and spiny
FLOWERS AND FRUIT	
Flowers	♂ and ♀ on separate trees, many crowded in large branched spikes initially sheathed by 2 large bracts and hidden among leaves, yellow
Perianth	6, inner 3 spreading
Stamens	6; in ♂ flowers bases joined into fleshy disc; in ♀ flowers sterile, forming cup-shaped base
Stigmas	3, styles short
Ovaries	1, 3-chambered
Fruit	berry-like, 4.5cm, globular to oblong, ripening yellow or brown
Seeds	3, grooved on one side, not released

Usually forming clumps of several well-developed trunks, this Fan-palm may have only one trunk. Wild trees often produce no trunk at all, the crown of leaves growing directly from the ground. A thick covering of fibres from old leaves protects the stem from fire damage. It is the only common native European palm.

Status: native to coastal areas of the Mediterranean region; often planted for ornament.

SIMILAR TREES

Australian Fan-palm (*Livistona australis*) is native to eastern Australia. It is a tall tree with golden-green leaf-segments, which droop at the tips, and is often planted as a street tree.

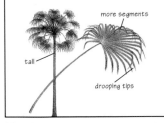

more segments

tall

drooping tips

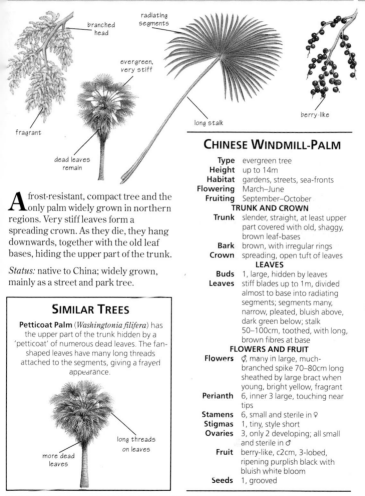

A frost-resistant, compact tree and the only palm widely grown in northern regions. Very stiff leaves form a spreading crown. As they die, they hang downwards, together with the old leaf bases, hiding the upper part of the trunk.

Status: native to China; widely grown, mainly as a street and park tree.

SIMILAR TREES

Petticoat Palm (*Washingtonia filifera*) has the upper part of the trunk hidden by a 'petticoat' of numerous dead leaves. The fan-shaped leaves have many long threads attached to the segments, giving a frayed appearance.

CHINESE WINDMILL-PALM

Type	evergreen tree
Height	up to 14m
Habitat	gardens, streets, sea-fronts
Flowering	March–June
Fruiting	September–October

TRUNK AND CROWN

Trunk	slender, straight, at least upper part covered with old, shaggy, brown leaf-bases
Bark	brown, with irregular rings
Crown	spreading, open tuft of leaves

LEAVES

Buds	1, large, hidden by leaves
Leaves	stiff blades up to 1m, divided almost to base into radiating segments; segments many, narrow, pleated, bluish above, dark green below; stalk 50–100cm, toothed, with long, brown fibres at base

FLOWERS AND FRUIT

Flowers	♂, many in large, much-branched spike 70–80cm long sheathed by large bract when young, bright yellow, fragrant
Perianth	6, inner 3 large, touching near tips
Stamens	6, small and sterile in ♀
Stigmas	1, tiny, style short
Ovaries	3, only 2 developing; all small and sterile in ♂
Fruit	berry-like, c2cm, 3-lobed, ripening purplish black with bluish white bloom
Seeds	1, grooved

Chilean Wine-palm *Jubaea chilensis*

paired leaflets

evergreen

diamond-shaped scars

berry-like

in flat plane

ripening yellow

thick trunk

branched cluster

A very slow-growing tree, producing a dense crown and the thickest trunk of any palm. The leaden-grey bark is distinctive. Native to Chile, where it is cut for its sugary sap, it grows well in mild climates and is a common ornamental palm, especially in southern France.

Status: native to central Chile; widely grown in Mediterranean regions.

SIMILAR TREES

Two other South American palms are also grown as street trees in the Mediterranean region. **1 Royal Palm** (*Roystonea regia*) has a smooth trunk, bulging in the middle, and leaves that are only 3m long. **Queen Palm** (*Arecastrum romanzoffianum*) is a slender tree with a distinctly ringed trunk and leaves 5m long.

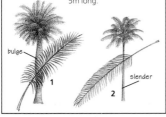

bulge

1

slender

2

CHILEAN WINE-PALM

Type	evergreen tree
Height	up to 30m
Habitat	parks and streets near coasts
Flowering	July–September
Fruiting	November–January

TRUNK AND CROWN

Trunk	straight, up to 2m thick
Bark	grey, smooth, patterned with diamond-shaped leaf-scars
Crown	dense tuft of upright to spreading leaves arranged in almost vertical rows

LEAVES

Buds	1, large, hidden by leaves
Leaves	feathery, up to 4m; numerous paired leaflets up to 70cm, split at tip; stalkless

FLOWERS AND FRUIT

Flowers	♂ and ♀ on the same tree, purplish; many upright, dense, branched clusters 1.5m long in angles of lower leaves and initially sheathed by large woody bracts
Perianth	6; in ♂ 3 outer narrow, joined at base, 3 inner longer, thick, pointed; in ♀ 3 outer broad, 3 inner overlapping
Stamens	c30; in ♀ sterile, joined in a membranous cup
Stigmas	3; minute and sterile in ♂
Ovaries	3-chambered in ♀
Fruit	berry-like, in large, drooping clusters, roughly globose to egg-shaped, ripening yellow
Seeds	1, with 3 vertical lines alternating with 3 black pores

Phoenix canariensis **Canary Island Date-palm**

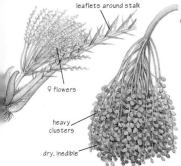

leaflets around stalk

♂ flowers

evergreen

leaf-bases remain

♀ flowers

heavy clusters

dry, inedible

Large and spreading, this is the most common ornamental palm in Europe. The thick trunk is covered with old leaf-bases. These leave diamond-shaped scars when they fall away. The fruits are rather dry and inedible.

Status: native to the Canary Islands; common as an ornamental in streets and parks around the Mediterranean region.

SIMILAR TREES

1 Date-palm (*Phoenix dactylifera*) is a taller, more slender tree with larger, succulent fruits, and is planted for ornament and as a fruit tree in southern Mediterranean areas.
2 *Phoenix theophrasti* is a very small, slender tree with blackish, fibrous fruits, and is restricted to Crete.

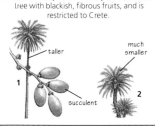

taller

much smaller

succulent

1

2

CANARY ISLAND DATE-PALM

Type	evergreen tree
Height	up to 20m
Habitat	dry places; also streets
Flowering	March–May
Fruiting	September–October

TRUNK AND CROWN

Trunk	stout, straight, patterned with old leaf scars
Bark	brown, with old leaf bases
Crown	large, spreading tuft of up to 200 leaves

LEAVES

Buds	1, large, hidden by leaves
Leaves	feathery, 5–6m; 150–200 pairs of leaflets radiating from stalk at different angles, folded upwards, light green; stalk stout, very spiny

FLOWERS AND FRUIT

Flowers	many in upright, branched clusters up to 2m hanging from angles of lower leaves, ♂ and ♀ on separate trees, creamy yellow
Perianth	6; in ♂ 3 outer fused into a small cup, 3 inner longer, edges touching; in ♀ 3 outer form 3-lobed cup, 3 inner overlapping
Stamens	usually 6, very small in ♀
Stigmas	3, style short, curved
Ovaries	3 in ♀, only 1 developing
Fruit	nut-like, in heavy, hanging clusters, 3cm, egg-shaped, ripening orange
Seeds	1, cylindrical, with a deep longitudinal groove

Index

Index

Index

Index

Societies and Useful Addresses

Botanical Society of the British Isles
66 North Street,
Shrewsbury,
Shropshire, SY1 2JL.
www.rbge.org.uk/BSBI

English Nature
www.english-nature.co.uk

Scottish National Heritage
www.snh.org.uk
enquiries@snh.gov.uk

Countryside Council for Wales
Plas Penrhos,
Penrhos Road,
Bangor,
Gwynedd, LL57 2LQ.
www.ccw.gov.uk

The Woodland Trust England
Autumn Park,
Dysart Road,
Grantham,
Lincolnshire, NG31 6LL.

The Woodland Trust Scotland
Glenruthven Mill,
Abbey Road,
Auchterarder,
Perthshire, PH3 1DP.
www.woodland-trust.org.uk

Royal Society for Nature Conservation
The Kiln,
Waterside,
Mather Road,
Newark,
Nottingham, NG24 1WT.
www.rsnc.org